# The British Economy:
# What will our children think?

**Also by Chris Hawkins**

Capital Investment Appraisal (*with David W. Pearce*)
The Theory of the Firm

**Also by George McKenzie**

International Banking (*with Ingo Walter*)
Measuring Economic Welfare: New Methods
The Economics of the Euro-Currency System
Monetary Theory of International Trade

# The British Economy
## What will our children think?

**Chris Hawkins**
**George McKenzie**

*First published 1982 by*
THE MACMILLAN PRESS LTD
*London and Basingstoke*
*Companies and representatives throughout the world*

ISBN 0 333 33334 9 (hard cover)
ISBN 0 333 33335 7 (paper cover)

*Typeset in Great Britain by*
ILLUSTRATED ARTS
*Sutton, Surrey*

*Printed in Great Britain by*
*Mackays of Chatham Ltd*

**To Susan and Sandy**

# Contents

# Introduction

The British economy is in dire straits. Industrial output has fallen to below its level in 1969; unemployment has soared to over 3 million; industrial profits have collapsed and bankruptcies have reached an all-time high. In the past our economic problems have seemed shortlived and have responded quickly to reflationary measures by governments. Now, our problems are more deep-rooted, seem almost intractable, and are widely expected to continue for a decade at least. Our problems are likely to become our children's problems.

We have prepared this book in the belief that economists must set out to explain the framework of the real economic debate before it is too late. This is not another of those bluffers' guides to economics. Each chapter aims to bring a clear and forthright viewpoint to bear on the British economy.

A well-known academic told us: 'No one should write economics for laymen [i.e. non-economists]. You either have to simplify it till it is no longer true in order to be understood, or you make it so complex to make it true that no one not trained in the subject can follow it.'

The writers might well have agreed if they had not given a course for non-economists through Southampton University's Department of Adult Education. Somewhat to our surprise, and relief, those who took the course said they found it interesting and understandable, that it grappled realistically with major economic issues of interest to most people, and that they found the level more satisfying than that in the average daily paper. For our part we found it challenging to present our subject to non-specialists. In a democracy we progress largely by persuasion, by convincing others with rational argument. Britain's economic problems are serious and touch all our lives, whether through unemployment, inflation, or cuts in expenditure on schools, universities and health. There is at least some reason for believing that if more people understood our economic problems we would be better able to solve them. To understand the problems and the causes may put us at least halfway towards accepting and helping with the cures. Or is that perhaps too much to hope?

At the very least, we believe there is a sizeable minority of people who, although they do not want to study economics as an academic subject or who do not have the time, would none the less like a more detailed look at Britain's economic problems than can be expected from the daily paper. It is for them that this book is written.

The basic format of the book is that in the first half we have chapters by various specialists who look at the performance of the economy as a whole. In Chapter 1 Chris Hawkins outlines the major strands of economic theory needed to understand our problems and our government's policies. Readers may find it helpful to read this chapter first, to pick up the economic theory needed for the chapters that follow. In it Hawkins looks at Keynesian economics, which appeared to work so well till the late 1960s, and at the growth of monetarist theory and policy which have now replaced Keynesianism as the prime policy of so many countries. In Chapter 2 he looks at the progress (or lack of it?) of monetarism when applied to the British economy and asks how best we can go forward from here. The case for incomes policy is made. He also calls for a major reform of the mortgage system. In Chapter 3 David Rowan also analyses the problems of monetarism in the British economy – though from a somewhat different standpoint – and he goes on to look at the major economic forecasters' views on how we will progress to 1984 and beyond.

In Chapter 4 Michael Wickens surveys a range of major theories and tackles the question: 'How much do we really know about how the economy behaves?' He makes the case against undue reliance on the government to solve economic problems.

We conclude the first half of the book with an unusually optimistic view of Britain's progress by Kenneth Hilton. He argues in Chapter 5 that if we look back over a reasonably long time period the economy has not behaved half as badly as many of us might think. Living standards have risen appreciably over the last twenty years or so. Only in the last decade does growth appear to have faltered or ceased.

The second half of the book looks at a number of major special topics – all relevant to the British economy. In Chapter 6 David

Heathfield looks in detail at unemployment, the extent to which it is voluntary or involuntary and how we might improve the present tragic situation; David Heathfield and Ivor Pearce, in Chapter 7, put forward a revolutionary scheme for controlling inflation – create a new kind of money altogether and take its production out of the hands of the government; George McKenzie (in Chapter 8) analyses the banking system in some detail, the ways in which banks create money and the manner in which bank activities tend to offset monetary policy; in Chapter 9 Barry McCormick examines the role of North Sea oil in Britain and the significant effects it has had on our economy for good and sometimes for ill; and in Chapter 10 Alan Hamlin looks at the thorny question of Britain's membership of the European Economic Community (EEC).

Our economic problems have probably never seemed more intractable than now. Probably that is why there seems to be such an upsurge of interest in how the economy works, what its problems are and what cures for them are available. Within the limits of space the aim of this book is to outline what is known about how the economy works and how it sometimes fails to work. We have tried not to conceal what economics does not yet know about the complex and ever-changing systems we are studying. In line with this policy we have made no attempt to try and force a consensus and offer apparent unity.

Indeed, such an effort would defeat one of our objectives: to explain why economists appear to differ in their prognostications. In many areas differences are due to a lack of certain knowledge about how the economy really works: in the absence of knowledge we must speculate and hypothesise. At other times differences of view reflect competing political beliefs. One economist may favour a more free enterprise, market forces solution to a problem – another might favour more state intervention and control. Both viewpoints are represented and we try to give enough information and economic analysis for readers to make their own judgements and choice of policies in line with their own political beliefs.

We would like to thank Dr Stuart Drummond of the Education Faculty at Southampton University for suggesting the lecture series which has led to this book. We also thank the secretaries in the Department of Economics and the Department of Accounting and Management Economics for carefully typing this manuscript under tight deadline conditions: Miss C. Brown, Mrs J. Gerrard, Mrs M.

Grieve, Miss J. Hepworth, Mrs L. Humby, Mrs C. Sherman, Mrs S. Wahnsiedler, Mrs P. Wilson. Finally, we thank John Winckler of Macmillan for acting as the 'interested layman' and for suggesting many modifications which immeasurably improved the presentation of this book.

*Southampton University*                  CHRIS HAWKINS
*May 1982*                          GEORGE MCKENZIE

# 1 From Monetarism to Keynesianism and back to Monetarism again

## by Chris Hawkins

'Put all economists end to end and they still would not reach a conclusion.' This disparaging view of economists is commonplace in the media, in the speeches of politicians and in everyday conversation. That every economist has a different theory is a widely held view. The essence of this viewpoint is that economists know little or nothing about how our economy works, or how to control it to make it work better. Like most generalisations there is an element of truth in this one. There are areas of economics where we do not know *all* the answers, where controversy reigns supreme, where in the absence of certain knowledge we must theorise, hypothesise, even guess. This is not unique to economics. In physics different theories compete to explain the origin of the Universe – physicists examine alternative, competing explanations and try to assess which is the most plausible, which fits the known facts best. In medicine the cures for cancer and arthritis have so far eluded us; yet many and various are the treatments available – each with their own advocates and critics – each offering at least some chance of success or at least alleviation of the symptoms, while none can yet claim anywhere near the complete answer. So, too, in economics. There are areas where we would dearly love to have the complete answer – but we do not. At least, not yet.

The problem with economics is that it affects all our lives, all the time. The press, television, politics – all are full of continuing discussion of economic issues: the standard of living, unemployment, inflation, the value of the pound. These are issues of concern to everyone: so economics is news. That there are unsolved problems in nuclear physics, electronics, and mechanical engineering is not of utmost concern to the layman. That there are now over 3 million unemployed does concern us all. We want a solution; we want it now, not in ten years' time. Economists are supposed to know about these things; why haven't they solved the problem?

Economics is not like chemistry, physics and the other natural sciences. The objects of their study are unchanging in behaviour. If you mix lead with sulphuric acid you get lead sulphate. That was true at the time Jesus was born and is just as true today. And it is true for every pound of lead and every litre of sulphuric acid. Human beings, who form the constituent part of every economy and hence of the study of economics, are not like metals and acids. Every human being is different. One may work more overtime if you pay him more; another may work less – preferring leisure now that he has a higher standard of living even without doing overtime. Even in aggregate, human behaviour may not be stable. It can change over time. Human beings in 1980 are not the same as human beings in 1930. Natural scientists can spend 2000 years improving and perfecting their knowledge of the behaviour of particular substances. Lead is lead is lead and always will be so. Theories become honed, refined, more and more perfect by a process of adaption and improvement as knowledge and testing of an immutable unchanging subject increases and progresses over time. Economics is not like that. The subjects of our study – humans – are changing while we study them. No sooner have we found a cure for, say, unemployment, than behaviour changes, responds to the cure by learning, so that the cure no longer works – rather like a virus developing immunity to a once all-conquering drug.

Prices went up quite closely in line with the money supply for long periods of history. All economists agree about that. This fact led Milton Friedman and others to believe that if we controlled the money supply we might cure inflation: '**However, once we put the controls on, human behaviour appears to have changed and the simple relationship between money and prices appears no longer to be holding. The virus is developing an immunity to the drug.**'

So much for the problems of economics. It is important, however, to realise that huge areas of economics are not controversial. There is much on which there is universal agreement in every area of the subject from the economics of the firm, to international trade, from investment analysis to growth theory. Economists know much about the way the economy is behaving and how it has behaved, and about solving economic problems under particular conditions. It is when economists are pushed into the role of being soothsayers that the real problems arise. To cure inflation we have to predict the way that 55 million people will, in aggregate, respond to various measures we could apply to the economy. Control the money supply and we have to predict how individuals, firms, trade unions, nationalised industries and a host of other complex institutions in our society will respond and how this will affect prices. It is not an easy job, and it never will be. It is important that everyone should realise this and not just blame economists or politicians for our failures. We are never going to be blessed with economic certainty: the perfect economic soothsayer will always elude us.

We can use economics to see how our economy is working, to isolate the problems and select areas where we need to do better. We can also use economics to advise how we should behave in order to improve the workings of our economy. On issues like these we would expect a very real measure of agreement amongst economists. For example, scarcely anyone would doubt that if we *all chose to back an incomes policy and behave in a way that would make it effective*, then the rate of inflation would fall dramatically. Economics can show how this would work, how inflation would be brought down and so on: and go on to describe detailed effects on our competitiveness abroad, ability to export more and the like. Here we are asking what should we do if we want to cure a particular problem.

This is like asking a doctor how to get rid of bronchitis and being told to give up smoking. His diagnosis and cure may be correct and widely accepted by doctors. They can tell us what pills will work: they cannot make us take them.

This is quite different from asking economists what *will* happen if the government *imposes* an incomes policy. Now the economist is being asked to be a soothsayer. It all turns on how we all respond to the government's measure. If we choose to support it and make it work, inflation will come down in the way that economics can show. If, however, we all strike and break the policy, inflation will not come down. This is not like asking a doctor if people smoke less will there be less bronchitis, but is asking if we tax cigarettes more highly will that reduce bronchitis? It all depends, of course, on how people respond to the tax. We now need a medical soothsayer not a doctor. There is no reason why one man cannot be both, nor any reason why he may not be good in one role and bad in the other.

It turns out that much of the controversy about economic issues centres on the soothsayer aspect of economic theory. The great divide between Keynesians and monetarists is much less of a divide on the basic theory than the media's general impression would have us believe. The basis of Keynesianism and the basis of monetarism are not in dispute. **The dispute is over the policies that are deduced from the theory and about the predictions about how people will respond to the policies.**

Towards 1980 many were saying they *believed* that people would behave in such a way that if we controlled the money supply inflation would be cured. All economists know the theory and the way it would work on the assumptions made. Some economists believed that people would not behave in the way assumed in the theory and that, therefore, it would not work. The next two chapters are examples of this viewpoint. Some economists believed that we did not know either whether the theory would work, or would not work in practice. We have not tried modern monetarism before and so can hardly be expected to predict how the economy will respond. An example of this view (which goes even further and argues that we do not yet know enough about the economy to predict with any reasonable certainty the effects of any major policy change) is given by Michael Wickens in Chapter 4. All policy involves predicting how people will respond in future. No one can possibly know for certain the effects of any policy. We can merely have beliefs with differing degrees of certainty. Approaching 1980 those who seemed most certain they had a cure for inflation (and certainly the most vociferous) were the monetarists.

Politicians are easy prey for purveyors of patent economic medicines because politics is about solving problems now, not in five years' time. Or at least it is about trying. Keynesian economics was in disrepute, unemployment was no longer being cured, inflation was rife. Politicians are not allowed the luxury of academics, to say I do not know the answer to this problem. They must appear to know and must do something – now. The monetarists had a tool-kit ready and waiting to be used. If you had a nut they claimed to have a spanner to fit it. The Conservative government bought the toolkit: the monetarist experiment began.

Before we look at this in some detail, nothing much will make sense unless we first of all have a brief look at Keynesian economics, and monetarist economics and at least the basis of how they are supposed to work. We shall try to signpost the areas that are widely agreed and those that are controversial.

## Keynesian economics

John Maynard Keynes wrote his pathbreaking work *The General Theory of Employment, Interest and Money* in the 1930s when Britain – like the rest of the world – was in the grip of the worst recession in history. At the worst over 20 per cent of the workforce were out of work: almost twice as high a percentage as now. Not surprisingly his main concern was how to get an economy out of a slump, not how to cure inflation. He believed that slumps (or recessions) were due to a shortage of total or aggregate demand – that is, the total of the demands by consumers, firms, government and people abroad to buy our output of goods and services (people abroad buy our output in the form of 'exports'). Suppose we start in a situation where total or aggregate demand (the total of goods and services people want to buy) is exactly equal to aggregate supply (the total output of all goods and services). The economy, we say, is in equilibrium: supply equals demand, and there is no reason for anything to change. This is like a boat which is rocking, but which eventually stops rocking and floats dead-level. It is then in equilibrium. It will remain there unless disturbed – e.g. by a wave.

An economy, argued Keynes, could be in equilibrium (i.e. where aggregate demand equalled aggregate supply) at levels of output *below those needed to employ the whole workforce*, i.e. the economy could 'stick' with unemployment. This had major impact because, prior to Keynes, the normal view was that the economy kept adjusting automatically until full employment was reached. Only shocks to the system, outside events, bad harvests and the like, could move the economy to a slump *from which it would automatically self-correct*. The impact of Keynes on economics was as great as that of an engineer who had shown that a pendulum might not settle in the vertical plane, or a yachtsman who had claimed that in smooth water a symmetrical boat when rocked might settle at a pronounced angle of heel. At first he was greeted with scepticism by some and outright disbelief by others.

Put simply, Keynes's argument was as follows. Suppose we begin with the economy at full employment and aggregate supply equal to aggregate demand, i.e. 'a full-employment equilibrium'. Now suppose consumers decide to save more and to spend less on goods and services. Firms who make goods and services for consumers will experience a fall in demand for their output and will reduce it. They will lay off workers. The loss of income of those now out of work will reduce demand still further. Output will be cut again, more lay-offs, further falls in demand. The process will continue in a downward spiral until aggregate demand and supply are again equal – but at less than full employment. The economy will remain stationary with unemployment, in recession, until something happens to cause it to change, e.g. consumers may in time decide to save less, spend more on goods and services, increase demand and thus call forth more output, and more growth.

Prior to Keynes it was thought that if people chose to save more (and hence consume less) then interest rates would fall. This would happen because if people wanted to save more, borrowers would not need to pay so high an interest rate to encourage someone to lend them money – supply and demand. As interest rates fell people would stop wanting to save so much. In addition, because funds could be borrowed cheaply industry would want to borrow more to do more investment (buying plant, machinery, factories). More investment increases total demand. Eventually it was felt that the falling interest rates would lead to the higher savings being offset by higher investment which would once again restore the economy to a full-employment equilibrium where aggregate supply equalled aggregate demand.

What Keynes argued was that interest rates might not fall enough to solve the problem of inadequate demand. They might well fall so much that everyone would expect them to rise. Then extra saving would merely be held as cash waiting for the interest rates to rise. Investment would not be encouraged sufficiently to restore equilibrium partly because interest rates would not fall enough, and partly because there would be so much *uncertainty* in a major slump that businessmen would be loath to increase investment much, even if they could borrow the funds to do so fairly cheaply. Trying to increase investment in a slump by lowering interest rates, when most firms could not even be sure of survival, would be like trying to sell summer clothes to a dying man in winter. Nor would boosting the money supply help, he argued: the extra money would also be held as cash waiting for interest rates to rise.

Thus, according to Keynes, slumps were caused by a failure of aggregate demand, by a failure of interest rates to fall far enough and by a failure of investment to be responsive enough to offset the increased desire to save instead of to consume. Thrift so long regarded as a virtue was now seen as a major cause of unemployment.

'The cure', said Keynes, 'was for the government to borrow the extra money that people wanted to save, and to spend this money on capital works such as schools, roads, hospitals and so on.' Public investment would thus replace the private investment that was not coming forward to use the extra amounts that people wanted to save. 'Demand management', as it became known, was the new key to economic success. We – or rather governments – could spend our way out of slumps. They could do so by spending more than they raised in taxation (i.e. having a 'budget deficit') and by financing the deficit with borrowing from the public. Using a budget deficit to boost demand and the economy, or a budget surplus to 'deflate' or reduce demand, or using a 'neutral' budget (i.e. a balanced budget) to leave the economy where it is, is all part of what is called 'fiscal policy'; it involves adjustments to government expenditure and taxation (and thus the budget deficit or surplus) in order to control aggregate demand.

That the policy was new can be seen from the King's speech to the Commons outlining the new government's policies in 1931 in the midst of the great depression: 'The present condition of the national finances . . . calls for the imposition of additional taxation, and for the effecting of economies in public expenditure.'

With over 20 per cent unemployed the government planned to cut its expenditure and cut that of consumers, too, by higher taxation. By 1936, when Keynes's theory was published, it was seen that the opposite policy should have been pursued. Existing policy had been making the slump worse.

After the Second World War Keynes's theory dominated economics and the policies of almost all major economies were based on it. Throughout the 1950s and 1960s the policies appeared to work well. Unemployment in Britain was rarely above 2 per cent and inflation was minor at well under 5 per cent per annum almost every year. So well did the policy work that the argument turned from not whether we should only manipulate or 'tune' the economy to major changes in aggregate demand but to whether we should try 'fine tuning', i.e. responding to every minor change in aggregate demand as well. Milton Friedman, recently regarded as one of Keynes's severest critics, said, 'we are all Keynesians now'.

Keynesians were aware of the possibility of inflation. Once aggregate demand had been raised enough to give full employment any further increases in demand would be inflationary. Output once at the full-employment level could not be raised in the short run: more demand could not be satisfied. The extra demand would merely raise prices. Governments should take steps to reduce demand if it exceeded the level needed to call forth the full-employment output level. They could cut demand by reducing their expenditure, by raising taxes and so on. Successive attempts to boost demand – when there was too little of it – and to cut demand when there was too much – led to what became known as the 'stop–go' cycle. Governments boosted expenditure and cut taxes in the 'go' phase and did the reverse in the 'stop' part.

It is worth stressing that Keynesian economics worked well for about twenty years until the late 1960s. Output grew at rates we would now envy. Inflation was mainly around 2 to 4 per cent per annum – so small you hardly noticed it: and unemployment at 1½ to 3 per cent of the workforce was, by today's standards (and those of history), insignificant.

It is also worth stressing that the Keynesian model was not an explanation of inflation – except when there was full employment and too much aggregate demand as well. The model was very black and white: either extra demand led to more output and trivial inflation (when there was unemployment) or it led to inflation alone and no significant gains in output once full employment was reached.

The need for an explanation of why inflation might *progressively* increase as we raised demand nearer and nearer to the full-employment level, was filled by A. W. Phillips. He argued that when unemployment was high wage increases would be low. With so much unemployment, labour would be in a relatively weak bargaining position as firms could get far more labour than they needed. By contrast when unemployment was low, wages would rise more rapidly. Firms would be short of labour, loath to fight a strike when demand for their product was high, and labour would be in a strong bargaining position. Phillips collected data over many years to show there was a remarkably stable relationship between unemployment and the rate of change of wages. This relationship became known as the Phillips curve (see Figure 1.1).

The Phillips curve in Figure 1.1 illustrates the relationship that high unemployment leads to low wage increases and low unemployment leads to high wage increases. For example, on the particular curve drawn we can see that 2 per cent unemployment would be associated with 8 per cent wage increases, while 7 per cent unemployment would only be accompanied by 4 per cent wage

**Figure 1.1**

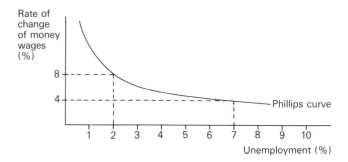

increases. The Phillips curve is developed further by Michael Wickens in Chapter 4; enough here to say that it filled a gap in Keynesian theory. It showed that inflation could occur even when there was unemployment. At a given output level an increase in wages would need to be passed on by the firm to the consumer: prices would be increased to pay for the wage increase or otherwise profits would fall.

*So inflation would increase progressively as we reduced unemployment.* Figure 1.2 shows this relationship having converted the Phillips curve so that we plot the rate of change of prices (rather than wages) on the vertical axis. The rate of change of prices is, of course, the rate of inflation.

**Figure 1.2**

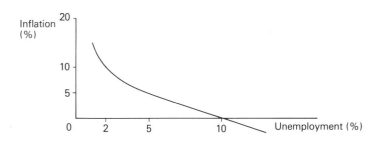

Figure 1.2 shows the Phillips curve for an economy where if the economy is run with only 2 per cent unemployed there will be 10 per cent inflation, 5 per cent unemployed gives 5 per cent inflation and 10 per cent unemployed gives zero inflation, i.e. completely stable

prices. At even higher levels of unemployment prices might actually fall – labour would be so desperate for work (and those in work so scared of losing their jobs because alternatives would be nearly impossible to find) that workers would even accept wage decreases. In 1981 there were numerous examples of workers accepting pay cuts in order to avoid redundancies, e.g. workers employed by Pan American Airways voted for a 10 per cent pay cut to avoid further job losses. Although negative inflation may seem to some to be a remote possibility in the 1980s, there have been prolonged periods in our history when falling prices were a regular feature of our economy.

Originally it was thought that the Phillips curve cut the horizontal axis at full employment as in Figure 1.3 where full employment is defined as only 3 per cent of the workforce out of work.

**Figure 1.3**

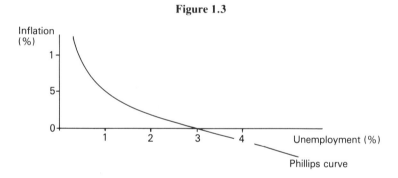

If, as in Figure 1.3, the Phillips curve cuts the horizontal axis at full employment then the government's role is fairly simple. It merely increases aggregate demand (by boosting government expenditure or cutting taxes) until we reach full employment. At this point there would be no inflation. If demand rises, and inflation begins, the government merely takes steps to cut demand, inflation disappears and we all stay fully employed.

It is very tempting today to dismiss this as pure theory, but a look at the data of the 1950s and early 1960s shows that the world really was like this until comparatively recently. We did have full employment, and inflation was so low it was barely noticed. The prices of many goods did not increase over ten or even twenty years.

As we have said, the role of government was simple. They merely needed to boost aggregate demand until full employment was reached. Provided the Phillips curve cut the axis at full employment there would be no inflation. If aggregate demand rose beyond this point either the government should cut it or even if it did not a 'monetary adjustment mechanism' would restore full employment. (Excess demand would drive up prices as output could no longer rise once full employment was reached. But, unless the money supply was increased, we would not have enough money to buy the same output at higher and higher prices. The money shortage would drive up interest rates until interest-sensitive demand – notably investment – fell far enough to restore equilibrium at full employment and zero inflation.)

To begin with, the Phillips-curve analysis really only gave governments one sensible target for the economy: full employment and zero inflation. Subsequently, however, two American economists (Paul Samuelson and Robert Solow) showed that: **'if the government increased the amount of money in the economy (the money supply) by the same percentage as prices were rising then we could choose even in the long run any position on the Phillips curve'**, i.e. we could, for example, choose no inflation and, say, 5 per cent unemployed, or 2 per cent inflation and 3 per cent unemployed, or 5 per cent inflation and 2 per cent unemployed.

All that was needed was for governments to increase the money supply in line with inflation and we could choose between various combinations of unemployment and inflation. You could not choose both. It was a trade-off. More unemployment meant less inflation, less unemployment meant more inflation. In the 1950s and 60s governments and economists openly debated the trade-off: should we have more of one and less of the other, or vice versa?

For fifteen years we ran our economy with almost no unemployment and with only trivial inflation. Unemployment began to seem like something from the past. But in the late 1960s things began to go wrong – not just in Britain but almost everywhere else. The virus appeared to be developing an immunity to the drug. We were changing our behaviour. The stable relationship of the past began to break down. The economics that had worked so well for some considerable time, began to fail. Inflation rates began to rise even when unemployment was high. Where 2 per cent unemployment had only given us 3 per cent inflation in the past it began to give 5 per cent, then 7 per cent then 10 per cent. Either the Phillips-curve relationship had disappeared or the curve had shifted. We appeared to be demanding and getting bigger and bigger wage and price increases at any given level of unemployment, than we had done in the past.

Milton Friedman and Edmund Phelps put forward a highly plausible explanation in the late 1960s which was widely accepted by the early 1970s. When there is no inflation, they argued, people expect no inflation in the coming year. Wage claims are low. With no inflation a 5 per cent money wage increase gives a 5 per cent increase in REAL living standards (i.e. after allowing for inflation – in this case zero inflation). If, however, there is 5 per cent inflation for a while it will be expected to continue. We shall then want a 5 per cent money wage increase **to compensate for expected inflation over the next twelve months**, plus the 5 per cent increase we would have asked for to give us a real increase, i.e. a total of 10 per cent. So if there is no expected inflation the Phillips curve shows wages (and prices if these are going up in line) rising at 5 per cent when there is, say, half a million unemployed: **but if there is 5 per cent inflation expected then there will be a different Phillips curve** showing wages and prices rising by 10 per cent. The more inflation that is expected **the higher and higher will be the Phillips curve as people build in the expected inflation into their wage claims and as these get passed on in price increases**. This is shown in Figure 1.4. Figure 1.4 shows that if no inflation is expected we operate on the lowest Phillips curve drawn. With half a million unemployed we push wages up by 5 per cent. Taking the simplest case where wages and prices go up in line, this gives 5 per cent inflation. After a while we begin to expect it to continue. We build it into our wage claims, i.e. we move to the middle of the three curves drawn. We now push for 10 per cent wage increases (5 per cent for inflation and 5 per cent for a real increase). Firms pass this on and prices rise 10 per cent. Soon we expect 10 per cent inflation to continue. We move to the higher of the three curves, which shows how we behave when we expect 10 per cent inflation. It shows that with half a million unemployed we ask for a 15 per cent wage increase if we expect 10 per cent inflation. This now leads to 15 per cent inflation. Note that inflation does not stay constant. It accelerates, first 5 per cent, then 10 per cent then 15 per cent. What is the cure?

In the Friedman–Phelps view the problems of inflation will get worse and worse if ever unemployment is reduced below the

**Figure 1.4**

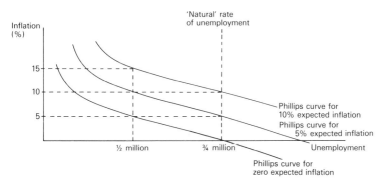

'natural unemployment rate', i.e. that rate which gives actual inflation equal to *expected* inflation. This is the rate of unemployment at which the Phillips curve for zero expected inflation cuts the horizontal axis, e.g. three-quarters of a million unemployed in Figure 1.4.

Only if we increase unemployment to the 'natural' rate will the inflation rate be stable. This is because we then get wage increases exactly equal to the expected rate of inflation. We expect, say, 10 per cent, we get a 10 per cent wage increase, prices go up 10 per cent and our expectations are precisely fulfilled. Or to put it another way, because there was 10 per cent inflation last year we expect 10 per cent this year. We push up our wages by 10 per cent to keep in line and this forces up prices by the 10 per cent we expected. In a very real sense we behave in a way that makes our expectations come true.

Friedman–Phelps go on to point out that to *reduce* inflation it is necessary to increase unemployment to higher than the natural rate. Only then will wages rise by less than the expected rate of inflation. Only then will the rate of inflation fall.

Once inflation starts falling it will go on falling as we reduce our expectations of inflation – so long as the government keeps unemployment above the natural rate. Eventually inflation will fall to zero. After a while we will come to expect zero inflation. Then unemployment can be reduced back to the natural rate. We can then keep unemployment down to the natural rate and yet have no inflation in the long run.

The conclusions of the Friedman–Phelps approach are that:

(a) **It is impossible to reduce unemployment below the natural rate without having continually accelerating inflation**
(b) **at the natural rate of unemployment, inflation will continue indefinitely at whatever rate it now happens to be**
(c) **only by increasing employment above the natural rate can the rate of inflation be brought down: once it has been brought down unemployment can once more be reduced to the natural rate.**

A number of important points follow from this analysis, all of which are consistent with the view that this model has had a profound effect on politicians of both parties who have held power over the last decade.

First, anything which increases our ability to raise wages for a given level of unemployment (e.g. greater union power, improved finance for strikers, more effective picketing and so on) must be expected to shift the Phillips curve upwards and must therefore increase unemployment in the long run by raising the natural level of unemployment. However well-meaning was the intention of increasing our ability to push up money wages, the effect would be to increase unemployment.

Second, the prevalence of incomes policies in Britain is fully consistent with this model. Incomes policies play a dual role. They compel us, or encourage us to volunteer, not to push up wages so much for any given level of unemployment. This lowers the Phillips curve, reduces inflation and reduces the natural rate of unemployment – at least it does so in so far as the incomes policy is successful. In addition, if we believe the incomes policy will work, it reduces our expectations of inflation, which moves us on to a lower Phillips curve.

Third, it is worth stressing that the model is trying to describe what will happen if the government keeps making available enough money for us to be able to buy a given output level at higher and higher prices, i.e. the money supply is increased in line with inflation which 'validates' or makes possible the wage and price increases that occur.

Lastly, the Friedman–Phelps analysis explains the rationale behind some politicians arguing that we either use unemployment to cure inflation now, or (since inflation will increase if we do not) we shall have to use more unemployment to do so later. We might have chosen a nicer way of putting it but, if we accept the Friedman–Phelps analysis, we can hardly argue with the policy. Unless, that is, we argue for not increasing the money supply to validate the wage and price increases (noting that not doing so may also cause unemployment) or we argue for some form of long-run, permanent (?) incomes policy to alter our behaviour to what is consistent with both low inflation and low unemployment.

### Monetarism

There is no simple dividing-line between modern Keynesians (who have developed and expanded Keynes's theory and are usually called neo-Keynesians) and the Monetarists. For example, the model we have just looked at (where the Phillips curve is augmented with inflationary expectations) is used by many monetarists as an explanation of inflation. It is alo accepted by many neo-Keynesians.

To get to the heart of monetarism (and later to see the policy differences they have with neo-Keynesians) we need to take a close look at some elementary theory of money. We are all used to reading in the press the well-known one-line summary of monetarism that, if the government controls the supply of money, inflation will cease! But what is the supply of money, how can it be 'controlled' and how would doing so bring down inflation? These one-line summaries of economics do nothing to really help us understand how the economy works. Like Chinese food they appear to satisfy – at least for a while – but eventually they leave us with an empty feeling, a sense of having consumed something of little lasting value.

**Monetarism has as its basis the Quantity Theory of Money equation,** which is

$$M \times V = P \times T$$

(this was developed in the 1930s by an American economist, Irving Fisher, and elements of it can be found even earlier in the nineteenth-century writings of the Scottish economist, David Hume). Monetarism is not new. It was not invented by Milton Friedman. It was the mainstay of government policy until Keynesian economics took over after the Great Depression of the 1930s called the workings of monetarism into question. What Friedman and others have recently done is to develop, refine and resuscitate the old theories.

The reader will find it most helpful to understand the Quantity Theory of Money equation:

$$M \times V = P \times T$$

**M** is the quantity of money in the economy, i.e. the money supply; **V** is 'the velocity of circulation', the speed or velocity at which the money travels round the economy, or more explicitly the number of times that money is spent on average in a given period of time; **P** is the average price level; and **T** is the number of transactions – the number of goods bought. An example may help.

On Monday Fred buys cigarettes for £1 at his local shop. On Tuesday the tobacconist gives the £1 to his wife. She buys 1 lb. of meat for the dog with it on Wednesday. The butcher spends the £1 on a large Scotch at the pub on Thursday. The pub-owner gives it to the barmaid in her wages on Friday. She spends it on a magazine on Saturday and the paper-seller buys a pound of cheese at his local shop on Sunday.

Now if we do some simple sums we can see how the equation works. The money that is circulating in our example is £1. So $M_1$, the money supply, is £1. In the space of one week (which we are looking at in this case) the pound is spent five times; so we say that **V**, the velocity of circulation of the money, is 5. Each of the goods bought in our example costs £1, so **P** (the average price level) is £1. The number of goods bought is 5 (1 packet of cigarettes, 1 lb of meat, 1 large Scotch, 1 magazine, and 1 lb of cheese) and so 5 is the value of **T**, the number of transactions. Referring back to our equation and putting in these numbers we see

|        | $M \times V =$ | $P \times T$ |
|--------|----------------|--------------|
| or     | $1 \times 5 =$ | $1 \times 5$ |

The original £1 note has been spent five times in one week and so has been able to buy £5 worth of goods (5 goods at an average price of £1 each).

What this says is little more than that total expenditure (total money spending – which is the value of **M** × **V** on the left-hand side of the equation) *must* be equal to the total value of goods bought

($P \times T$ on the right-hand side of the equation).

All economists accept that this is, and must be, true. After very little thought it can be seen to be obviously and necessarily true.

In our example there is only £1 and all prices are the same. It is then quickly and easily seen to be true. It will, of course, be just as true when the money supply is measured in billions of £s and when prices of different goods range from 3p for a box of matches to thousands of £s for an average house. We can simply average all the prices to get $P$ and count the total number of goods bought to get $T$.

So the equation

$$M \times V = P \times T$$

is not controversial: it is the use made of it that has led to controversy. This will be clearer after another example. Let us take an extremely simple economy which only makes and consumes wheat. It makes 1000 tons of wheat and these are sold at £80 per ton. The money supply is 20,000 notes of £1 each, i.e. £20,000, and this circulates or changes hands four times per period.

Putting these numbers into

$$M \times V = P \times T$$

we get $20,000 \times 4 = £80 \times 1000$

There is just enough money to buy all the output at the given market price.

Now we make a few alterations and see what happens. First, we have a forger who starts to print his own money – £5000 worth. He goes out to spend it on wheat. Since this money will circulate (i.e. change hands) four times in the period we are studying it will buy £20,000 worth of wheat. The money supply has gone up to £25,000 and if the velocity of circulation stays at 4 then $M \times V$ (total expenditure) will rise from £80,000 to £100,000. *But there are still only 1000 tons of wheat to buy.* Sellers of wheat will find there is more demand than they can satisfy at the old price of £80 per ton. They will be able to raise prices and still sell all their output. They can raise prices to £100 per ton. The velocity of circulation stays constant and if output does not rise ($T$ the number of transactions) then only by raising prices can we satisfy the equation $M \times V = P \times T$. And it must be satisfied: total expenditure must equal the total value of goods bought.

The numbers in our equation are now:

$$\mathbf{M} \times \mathbf{V} = \quad \mathbf{P} \times \mathbf{T}$$
$$25{,}000 \times 4 \ = £100 \times 1000$$

The result of our forger increasing the money supply has been to drive up prices by 25 per cent (from £80 to £100 per ton). As a result other people's money will buy less goods and the forger can buy goods at their expense. This is analogous to governments printing money to pay for government expenditure: the extra money may drive up prices and the rest of us must consume less to allow the government to buy more.

This example helps us to see why in the Phillips-curve model with inflationary expectations it was noted that the government would need to increase the money supply to finance the higher wages and prices: if these rise by 10 per cent per annum then, if the velocity of circulation stays constant, we need 10 per cent more money to be able to buy the same output at 10 per cent higher prices.

**This example, where extra money works through entirely into higher prices, in the equation M $\times$ V = P $\times$ T, is worth pondering a while because it is the essence of the monetarist view that increasing the money supply causes inflation.**

Now to see that there are other possibilities let us assume that there is unemployment and that wheat producers can raise output by taking on more labour. If they do this and do not raise prices then the forger's extra money in the system could go on extra output of wheat. The numbers in our equation would then be:

$$\mathbf{M} \times \mathbf{V} = \ \mathbf{P} \times \mathbf{T}$$
$$25{,}000 \times \ 4 = 80 \times 1250$$

The 25 per cent increase in the money supply has been offset by a 25 per cent increase in output with no increase in prices.

We can now see why we need the money supply to increase as output increases. If prices are unlikely to fall (i.e. are sticky downwards) then it is necessary to have more money in the system to buy more output. Of course, one could hope for the velocity of circulation to increase instead but even if it did, it would be unlikely always to grow in the long run by exactly the amount that output was growing. *Therefore, in periods of rising output we need a rising money supply.*

Let us, however, use the equation to see exactly what does happen when the velocity of circulation changes. Suppose that when the extra money from our forger enters the system everyone responds by holding on to money for longer before they spend it. So it changes hands only 3.2 times per period instead of 4 times. The numbers in our equation will now be

$$\mathbf{M} \times \ \mathbf{V} = \ \mathbf{P} \times \mathbf{T}$$
$$25{,}000 \times 3.2 = 80 \times 1000$$

Increasing the money supply has not caused inflation (prices are unchanged) and has not affected output. Money is merely changing hands more slowly (i.e. **V** has fallen). The forger is buying goods he could not have bought before he became a money printer. Others therefore are consuming less.

*A change in the money supply which coincides with, or causes, a change in the velocity of circulation may not cause inflation or a change in output.*

**It can now be seen that without more detailed economic analysis all we can argue from the Quantity Theory of Money equation is that increasing the money supply by any chosen percentage may:**

(a) **cause a similar percentage increase in prices with no changes in output or the velocity of circulation**

(b) **cause a similar percentage increase in output, but with no effect on prices or velocity**

or (c) **may be offset by a fall in the velocity of circulation with no changes taking place in prices or output.**

Lastly any combination of some or all of these effects may take place – more money supply could be offset by more output, and higher prices and a fall in the velocity of circulation. The great debate between Keynesians and Monetarists is about the *extent* to which the money supply affects one variable rather than another. Keynesians accept that the money supply will have some effect on prices; monetarists accept it will have some effect on output. The debate is about how much the money supply will affect one rather than the other in both the short and the long run.

Armed with an understanding of the equation $\mathbf{M} \times \mathbf{V} = \mathbf{P} \times \mathbf{T}$ we can now look at monetarism in more detail. To talk about *the* theory of monetarism is just as naïve as to talk about *the* theory of how to play football to win. Just as different football managers pursue and espouse different strategies for winning (though most can be placed in broad categories by the type of strategy they pursue – defensive, attacking and so on) so, too, do monetarists differ in their emphasis on different aspects of the theory. At one extreme a few (very few) would argue that Keynesian economics has no role to play; increasing aggregate demand can only affect prices not output. Most monetarists, however, see a role for a mixture of Keynesian and pure monetarist views.

Keynesians differ in emphasis too. Some see but a minor role for monetary policy, others see a blending of monetary and fiscal policy as the best solution.

Two of the major problems we are concerned with are the causes of cyclical fluctuations in the economy (booms and slumps) and the causes and cures for inflation. We will look at monetarist views on each and contrast them with a more Keynesian view.

## Booms and slumps

In *A Monetary History of the United States 1867–1960* Milton Friedman and Anna Schwartz argued that there was strong correlation between changes in the money supply and the level of economic activity. Booms were associated with expanding money supply, slumps with the reverse. The 1930s slump in America coincided with a big drop in the money supply, partly because several thousand American banks went bankrupt. In the 1930s the USA money supply fell by over a third. In the equation

$$\mathbf{M} \times \mathbf{V} = \mathbf{P} \times \mathbf{T}$$

we can see that a fall in $\mathbf{M}$, if it is not accompanied by an increase in the velocity of circulation ($\mathbf{V}$), must be offset either by a fall in prices or a fall in output. A major cut in the money supply could cause a recession if prices did not adjust fast enough. There would not be enough money to buy the old output levels.

Cyclical fluctuations may be due to money-supply changes, but they will be short-lived, a monetarist would argue. The economy will adjust. Prices and wages will alter and the economy will return to full employment. An almost essential and widely held view of monetarists is that the economy is inherently self-regulating. Leave it alone and it will be all right. Do not cause violent swings in money supply and there will not be violent swings in the economy. Allow the money supply to grow gently in line with the long-run growth of output and the economy will remain at full employment without inflation apart from minor fluctuations which will be short-lived.

Neo-Keynesians accept that the money supply has varied with the level of economic activity, but believe the causation is the other way round. A boom causes an increase in the money supply, a slump reduces it. One explanation, that at least fits the 1945 to early 1970s period, is that governments aimed for stable interest rates. In a boom when more money was needed to finance more activity ($P \times T$ was higher) governments had to expand the money supply or interest rates would have shot up. The reason for this is that firms short of money would offer to pay higher and higher interest rates for the available money; holders of government bonds would sell them to raise money, the price would fall and the interest on them (which is a fixed amount per annum) would yield a higher percentage return since

$$\frac{\text{interest earned}}{\text{price of bond}} = \text{percentage of return}$$

The lower the price of bonds the higher the percentage return or 'rate of interest'.

So the money supply rose in booms and conversely fell in slumps as governments reduced it in line with falling demand to stop interest rates falling.

**The issue is whether changes in the money supply caused the fluctuations in the economy or whether the fluctuations caused the changes in the money supply.**

As we have seen, neo-Keynesians do not believe that the economy is self-regulating except perhaps in the very long run. Depressions may be large and long-lasting unless governments intervene to boost aggregate demand. Mainly fiscal policy is emphasised (varying government expenditure and taxation), but monetary policy can also be effective by lowering interest rates and helping to increase aggregate demand.

**On fluctuations in the level of economic activity (booms and slumps) we can summarise by saying that monetarists see the**

economy as largely self-regulating at around the full-employment level provided the money supply is allowed to grow roughly in line with the long-run growth of output. Neo-Keynesians, by contrast, believe the economy does not always self-adjust to full employment. Recessions may be large and long-lived unless an appropriate mix of fiscal and monetary policy is used to boost aggregate demand.

### Inflation

It is the causes and cures of inflation that have attracted most discussion and controversy in recent years.

Monetarists see excessive growth of the money supply as the main cause of inflation. Most if not all accept the Friedman–Phelps model where expected inflation leads to higher and higher wage claims and more and more inflation so long as

(a) The government prints the extra money needed to validate the wage and price increases (they do this because, if they did not, higher prices would mean an offsetting fall in output and therefore employment): in the equation

$$M \times V = P \times T$$

if neither **M** nor **V** (which monetarists believe is fairly constant) are increased then the left-hand side stays constant. So, therefore, must the right-hand side be constant. It follows that if prices rise by 10 per cent output must fall by 10 per cent. Governments print the extra money to stop wage–price increases from causing falls in output with the resulting increase in unemployment.

(b) Governments manipulate the economy to keep unemployment below the natural rate (remember this causes inflation to accelerate in the Friedman–Phelps model).

It follows from this monetary analysis that the way to cure inflation is to allow unemployment to rise to the natural rate so that wage–price fixing does not increase inflation, i.e. this policy alone stops the rate of inflation from rising. Now all that is needed is a further move to start inflation falling. There are several possibilities. One is to increase unemployment to·above the natural rate. If the Friedman–Phelps analysis is right wages and prices will cease to rise as fast, inflation will come down and with it our expectations of inflation. We then ask for lower wage increases, which pushes prices up more slowly and gradually inflation disappears. When it does, unemployment can be reduced back to the natural rate. Achieving this will be no problem if you believe that the economy self-regulates back to the full-employment level (i.e. defined here as unemployment at the natural rate). Once at the natural rate of unemployment with zero inflation the government must expand the money supply only by roughly the percentage rate of growth of output in the long run. Then there will be little or no inflation, and no expectations of inflation, and so wage claims will be consistent with constant prices. This appears to fit closely the policy being followed in Britain. There are, however, other possibilities. The important thing is to reduce expectations of inflation. That is why the government published medium-term targets for the growth of the money supply – to convince us that inflation would fall at least in the medium term. But expectations could also be affected by a short-term incomes policy. If we did not add our expectations of inflation to our real wage claims the expected inflation would not occur. If we expect 10 per cent inflation we build this into our wage claims and raise firms costs so that prices go up by roughly what we expected. An incomes policy which effectively stopped us all from doing this (if one could be found) would quickly reduce inflation and then, after a while, our expectations of inflation. The appeal of this method is that it does not involve the high unemployment of the present policy.

Although incomes policy is perfectly consistent with monetarism and the Friedman–Phelps expected inflation analysis, most monetarists are noted for being opposed even to short-term incomes policy. They see wages as being determined by supply and demand in the labour market and do not believe it possible to intervene effectively against such powerful market forces. Neo-Keynesians are usually pro-incomes policy. They see wages as being determined in a most imperfect market dominated by giant firms and giant trade unions. The resulting bargaining process frequently yields results wildly different from the market forces rate. Wages rose 20 per cent in 1980 in a major recession – hardly the result one would have expected had it been a perfectly working market based solely on supply and demand. Neo-Keynesians stress the imperfections of the labour market and see union power as able to raise wages even when pure economic forces would lead either to no wage increases or even to a fall in wages. In so far as incomes policies can help put this right, neo-Keynesians would tend to support them.

One further alternative is to introduce trade union reforms to reduce the power of organised labour to push up wages at least in line with our expected rate of inflation, thereby helping our expectations to be fulfilled. Many monetarists support this policy (if it can be implemented without widespread disruption). Unlike incomes policy, they see union reforms as a means of improving the workings of the labour market, as a way of making wages more responsive to the economic facts of life.

Neo-Keynesians mostly do not feel the government can reduce the power of unions enough for the policy to be effective. Co-operation with unions within an incomes policy is seen as the only practical way of stopping the wage–price spiral with which we are all so familiar.

**Other problems with monetarism**

Before leaving monetarism we can use the equation

$$M \times V = P \times T$$

to see some of its other major problems.

Because the equation

$$M \times V = P \times T$$

*must* hold – as we have seen – nobody doubts that if the money supply only goes up by 4 per cent per year, and if its velocity stays constant, then if output stays constant prices must rise by 4 per cent per annum, i.e. exactly in line with the increase in the money supply.

**Transmission mechanisms**

What the doubters query is how the change in the money supply is expected to work through the economy directly to prices, i.e. what is the 'transmission mechanism' which transmits a change in money supply directly through to prices. One such transmission mechanism for making money supply changes affect prices is the Friedman–Phelps model of Phillips curves with inflationary expectations, which we have discussed. Prices and wages are determined only by unemployment, expected inflation and the amount of money governments print to let wages and prices rise in the way described.

Suppose, however, that these factors do not uniquely determine wages and prices, in which case the Friedman–Phelps analysis is not correct. Suppose, for example, that trade-union power and pushfulness determines the rate of increase of wages; and that prices are determined largely by costs of production (not simple supply and demand) and of course wages are the biggest cost of production by far. So if unions push up wages, prices rise roughly in line. Then prices would be determined by union pressure and by governments' raising the money supply. **If the government ceases to raise the money supply to meet the wage claims, the transmission mechanism may not be through to prices but to output and employment.** The reason is that if organised labour goes on pushing up wages, despite a controlled money supply, firms will have to raise prices to cover their costs, but there will not be enough money to buy the same output at the higher prices. So output will fall and unemployment will rise. This view is developed in the next two chapters and is touched on in others. Monetarists do not yet have a transmission mechanism to show how controlling the money supply will act directly on prices, which has been widely accepted outside their own ranks. As we have seen, doubters believe controlling the money supply (**M**) may affect either output alone (**T**), or may affect a mixture of output and prices (**P**).

### Velocity of circulation

A further problem of monetarism is that for their theory to work the velocity of circulation must be roughly constant. If it varies, then prices (and/or output) can change even if the money supply is constant. If money circulates faster it can buy the same output at higher prices.

Doubters claim that the velocity of circulation does vary in the short and in the long run. Unless we can predict how it will vary and by how much we cannot know how much money is needed in the system to finance increasing output without financing inflation.

**If the velocity of circulation varies the claimed direct link between money supply and prices is destroyed.**

### Controlling the money supply

The final problem with monetarism that we shall look at is the problem of how to control the money supply and exactly what it is we should try to control.

Notes and coin are not the only way of buying things. We can buy goods by writing a cheque backed by deposits we have made at a bank in a current or deposit account. (The way banks create money and other problems of banking are dealt with by George McKenzie in Chapter 8.) At the very least we can see that the money supply should include notes and coin in circulation, plus current accounts and deposit accounts in banks. This definition forms the main basis of the so-called '$M_3$' figure for money supply.

Some British people hold deposits of foreign currency at their bank and this is included in $M_3$ though it cannot be spent directly on British goods (unless exchanged for sterling). We sometimes exclude these holdings of foreign money and then we are using the so-called sterling $M_3$ definition of money. This is the money supply which British governments have so far chosen to control.

There are, of course, other definitions of money supply which we could use (to include, for example, money in building society accounts which does represent spending power). But at the moment in Britain it is sterling $M_3$ (sometimes written £$M_3$ for convenience) which is the main instrument of policy. It is worth noting that this includes the deposits in banks of nationalised industries and the whole public sector, as well as those of just private firms and individuals.

Another definition of the money supply, called $M_1$, is often mentioned in the press. This consists mainly of notes and coin plus current accounts in banks of individuals and private firms, i.e. it excludes the holdings of the British public sector and excludes deposit accounts at banks. It is therefore a much narrower definition of money than is sterling $M_3$.

One obvious problem for monetary policy is which money supply to control. Control one, and if people and firms are short of money, they will raise it in a way which avoids the controls. Control money that is lent by banks, and people may borrow more from building societies instead, if they are not in the definition of money which you are controlling.

It is far from easy to find a definition of the money supply which is a roughly constant proportion of total money-spending (i.e. $M \times V$). If $£M_3$ was always one-third of total spending, then if we let $£M_3$ go up by 10 per cent we would know that total spending could only rise by 10 per cent. The problem is we have not yet found any version of the money supply which, except over particular periods, bears a constant relationship to total spending. **Even if we find a money supply that has in the past held this constant relationship to total spending, we need to be sure it will go on doing so in future and will behave after we control it, in the same way as it did before it was controlled.**

**Without this essential constant link between a controlled money supply and total spending there can be no simple relationship between money supply and prices, e.g. of the form that a 10 per cent increase in money supply will be met by a 10 per cent increase in prices.**

Finally, it should be stressed that some economists believe that the money supply cannot be simply controlled; they believe that the money supply is, at least partly, determined by what is going on in the economy and not simply be government fiat. This view is developed in the next chapter.

**INTRODUCTION TO CHAPTER 2**

In the first chapter Chris Hawkins has argued that one of the few basic issues over which economists are in disagreement concerns the speed at which the prices of goods and wages of labour respond to changes in supply and demand. In the next chapter he carries this thesis further by arguing that the failure of economic policy since 1979 has been due to a lack of understanding of how the market mechanism actually works. Current government policy has been based on the assumption that prices will adjust very quickly without undue effect on the levels of output and employment. However, such a process will occur only in a world where all markets involve many buyers and sellers each bidding against each other until the market clears. Today's economy is dominated by large corporations, including government monopolies, and large trade unions. These institutions are capable of isolating themselves against the operation of market forces by the application of their substantial economic and political power. It is thus not surprising to find corporations raising prices and unions seeking higher wages in periods when demand is falling.

It is clear that if the price mechanism does not work smoothly, then control of the money supply will not be an efficient means of reducing people's expectations and hence of reducing the rate of inflation. Hawkins argues that an efficiently working market mechanism is a necessary but not sufficient condition for the monetarist solution to work. The money supply must also be under the control of the authorities. He points out that this has not been the case, arguing that the quantity of money in circulation has been determined by consumer, business and government demands for loans rather than by the supplies made available by the Bank of England. He concludes that the only methods available for controlling expectations and ironically the money supply are either incomes policy or trade union reform. He also urges a major reform of the house mortgage system, a major reduction in the exchange rate of the pound and a major injection of funds into industry.

C. H. and G. M.

# 2 After Monetarism: What Next?

*by Chris Hawkins*

Few governments have come to power in Britain with greater hopes of creating an economic miracle than the Conservative one of 1979. Inflation was to be squeezed out of the system; the gargantuan public sector was to be cut back so that the wealth and job-creating private sector could be expanded; taxes were to be cut to give everyone an incentive to work harder and businessmen an incentive to start new firms; tax cuts were to rekindle the spirit of enterprise on which our economy had been built; and control of the money supply would cure inflation. At last, a start would be made on curing Britain's long-term, deep-seated economic problems – inflation, low productivity and a lack of competitiveness.

That was the dream. The reality has been a collapse of industrial production, a doubling of unemployment, massive bankruptcies, continuing inflation and a series of other economic disasters with which we are all depressingly familiar.

This chapter looks at what the government tried to achieve, how it tried to achieve it, and why it failed. In the process we try to find out what Britain's economic problems really are, and what we will need to do to solve them in future.

## Government objectives

The government's main objectives were to:

1. Cure inflation
2. Cut government expenditure
3. Cut taxation
4. Expand industry

The main argument against inflation was that if we did not cure it now it would simply get worse and be harder to cure later. As we saw in Chapter 1 if inflation continues, we all begin to get used to it and build inflation into our wage claims. We ask for an increase equal to the present or expected rate of inflation plus some more to give us a real increase in wages. This makes inflation next year at least as bad – and usually worse – than inflation this year. So the problem gets worse.

The arguments for cutting government expenditure were partly that the government had a preference for private enterprise, at least in some areas; but mainly it was the cost of financing that was seen as the major problem.

As the public sector becomes a bigger and bigger proportion of national income we have to pay a higher and higher proportion of our incomes to the government in taxation to pay the bills. The higher taxes may act as a disincentive to work and to enterprise. Why work overtime if the government takes away 30 per cent to 40 per cent of the extra money earned in taxes? Why work for promotion and take more responsibility if the extra income is largely taxed away? And why give up a secure job and risk your life-savings to start a business? Until the first Conservative budget in 1979, if you were successful you would pay up to 83p in the £ on your salary and up to 98p in the £ on your dividend. For every £50 you earned in dividends, you would pay £49 in tax. And if the business did badly, you would lose all your savings.

Rather than risk starting a business, building a factory, creating jobs, it seemed safer to many with savings to invest them in rare stamps, wine, paintings, property and the like – anything that might go up in price and give a 'capital gain' which would only be taxed at 30 per cent. And the chance of losing more than a small proportion – if any – of your money was relatively slight: particularly since so many others were pouring their money into the same goods driving their prices relentlessly upwards.

This was the logic behind the objective of cutting taxation. Of course, as employees we work for many reasons; and businessmen start firms for many reasons too (enjoyment from running their own show, something to pass on to their children and so on). Money is not the only motive. But it is one of the major ones, and it is at least possible that cutting taxes, letting us keep more of what we earn, may act as an incentive for many.

A further objection to government expenditure being too large was that if we were not to finance it by high taxation we would have to finance it by government borrowing or by printing money – or to put it another way government expenditure is paid for by taxation plus government borrowing plus printing more money.

Printing too much extra money to pay the bills was seen as the cause of inflation, and borrowing the money brings problems too as we shall see later.

Finally the government wanted to reduce the public sector to make room for the private sector to expand and take up the slack. Industry was to expand, aided by the incentive of tax cuts and by reduced inflation, which would make it more competitive with foreign goods both in the home and in export markets.

### Methods for achieving the objectives

*The money supply*

Being monetarist the government believed if it controlled the money supply inflation would fall into line. Put simply the belief was:

For a given output, prices could only rise 10 per cent if there was only 10 per cent more money to spend.

To control the money supply the government chose to use high interest rates to control T H E  D E M A N D  F O R  M O N E Y. If it was dear to borrow, firms and others would not want to increase their borrowing.

If money (in the form of bank loans) was not demanded, the banking system would not create it. Control the demand and you effectively control the supply.

By analogy if we reduce the demand for cars (say by hire-purchase controls) less will be sold, less will be supplied. So the supply of money was to be *controlled by controlling* the demand for money, by using high interest rates.

*Wages and salaries*

The role of wages (and salaries) in causing inflation was pooh-

poohed. Friedman and other monetarists had said that it was not wage increases that caused inflation. It was governments printing the extra money which enabled firms to pay the higher wages that caused it.

True, in Britain wages and prices go up very much in line. By the end of 1981 both wages and prices had more than doubled since January 1975. However, it was argued, if the government did not provide the extra money then wages and prices could not rise in this way.

In line with this philosophy the following policy emerged:

*In the public sector* the government should withdraw from wage bargaining. It should set cash limits for spending in each public sector, in the nationalised industries and for grants to local authorities. Each ministry and industry and local authority would pay what it could afford within the cash limit.

There would be no incomes policy, no direct government involvement.

*In the private sector* again there would be no incomes policy. Firms would pay what they could afford within the overall amount of money available in the economy. The money supply would limit what they could afford.

As for the other two objectives, the public sector was to be cut by rigorous use of cash limits on all its expenditure; private industry would expand of its own volition once the incentive effect of the tax cuts had worked through, the reduced public sector had made room and lower wage settlements had made it more competitive at home and abroad.


**What has happened so far**

*Inflation and the money supply*

The money supply has not been controlled. The money supply has risen much faster than it did before the government started to control it. Much of the time it has been rising almost twice as fast as the government planned (at a rate of up to 20 per cent p.a. instead of the target of about 10 per cent).

Inflation rose to begin with, has fallen in 1981, but is still higher than when the government came to power.

There is no evidence of the fall in inflation being due to controlling the money supply, since the money supply has not in fact been controlled. Inflation has probably fallen because of the recession, and the lower recent level of wage settlements, due to unemployment, bankruptcies and the fear of losing a job (i.e. the Phillips-curve effect). Taxes have been reduced on incomes, but put up on goods (VAT, etc.). For many there has been no net gain.

*Government expenditure* is *higher* (yes, even allowing for inflation) and its share of national income has *risen* not fallen as planned. Some sectors have been cut, others have expanded.

*Industrial output* has fallen dramatically. *In manufacturing (which excludes oil and the nationalised industries such as gas and electricity) output has fallen more than it did in the 1930s slump.* Bankruptcies have been widespread, factory closures a daily event and unemployment has doubled. One in eight of the workforce have no job and little prospect of finding one. The government is to provide subsidised training schemes for all unemployed young people, and has already done so for large numbers. Men over 60, since the end of 1981 have been offered more benefits if they retire early, i.e. do not register as unemployed. Married women who have not paid the full stamp do not usually register as unemployed, as they cannot claim benefits. Allowing for all such factors the true figure for unemployment is, in 1982, almost certainly around 4 million people.

**What went wrong?**

*Wages*

Trying to control the money supply by using interest rates to control the demand for money did not work. It failed because wages and prices in Britain are determined in such a way that they went on rising despite the controls and they sucked money into the system whether the government wanted it to go there or not.

In the public sector wages rose extremely fast despite cash limits. Agreeing to accept the Clegg Commission's findings on public sector pay made failure a certainty. Even without it, it is doubtful if cash limits would have worked – as we shall see. (The Clegg Commission was set up by the previous Labour government to recommend pay increases for the public sector. During the election campaign the Conservatives agreed to accept its findings.)

In the private sector dear money did not stop wages rising fast either – and prices with them.

So in 1980 average earnings in the whole economy rose by 20 per cent – despite the worst recession since the 1930s. *The ability of organised labour to raise wages, even when the economic arguments against it doing so are overwhelming, is a central problem that Britain must sooner or later face.* It is a problem to which we shall return in detail later.

*The link between wages and the money supply*

The government (and monetarists) appear to have grossly under-estimated the link between rising wages and the demand for money (and hence for supply under this government's policy).

*Rising wages pulled money into the system just as surely as if the government had pushed it in on purpose because:*

(a) the government needed more money to pay higher wages in the public sector,

and (b) industry also needed more money to pay its higher wages.

Industry got the money by continuing to borrow from the banks despite high interest rates. If it had not, it would have gone bankrupt. It also reduced stocks, raided profits, cut investment – all to pay the higher wages and interest charges. The banks lent the money, despite industry's perilous financial state because, as one banker put it, 'you lend them another million because, if you do not, you lose the 10 million you lent them before and which they haven't yet paid back'.

*It was rising wages that forced the money supply to rise – not the other way round.*

*The government halts the rise in interest rates*

The reader may well wonder why the government did not go on raising interest rates until the money supply came under control. Surely they could see from the published data that it had gone out of control? Yes, indeed they could. However, some more problems arose. As a result the government must have felt that it was undesirable economically, as well as politically, to let interest rates go any higher. Once interest rates reached a certain level the government stopped trying to rigorously control the money supply because of three problems.

*The mortgage problem*

Once mortgage rates reached 15 per cent the absurd position was reached that for many people the mortgage on a fairly modest house was costing half their take-home pay. If interest rates had gone to 25 per cent (which would probably have been necessary to meet the government's targets) the mortgage system would have collapsed. While the rent on the average council house was under £12 per week, interest rates of 15 per cent had caused the mortgage repayments on a £20,000 house to soar to £61 per week (before tax relief: maximum tax relief at the standard rate would reduce this to £44 per week).

The problem here is that a pay increase – even in line with inflation – does not compensate for the rise in repayments on a mortgage – **even if interest rates only go up in line with inflation**. This is partly because of our archaic tax system and partly because of the absurd way we calculate mortgage repayments. It is perfectly possible to solve the problem so that a mortgage of £20 per week would buy a house costing £20,000 (see answer to question at end of chapter). However, since the problem had not been solved the government found higher interest rates unacceptable.

*The exchange-rate problem*

The value of the pound is determined by many things, including the fact that we have North Sea oil; but the only major variable that affects the pound, that we can control, is the rate of interest. If interest rates in Britain are high – relative to those in other countries – foreigners use their currency to buy pounds so they can invest them over here at a high interest rate. The more they buy the pound, the more they drive the price up – the exchange rate. High interest rates raise the exchange rate; low interest rates lower it.

Since the mid 1970s the exchange rate has risen by one-third. This makes British exports dearer (so we lose sales, profits and jobs) and makes foreign imports cheaper (so we buy more of them and lose sales, profits and more jobs). Over the same period British wages have risen much faster than those of our competitors (ours have doubled since 1975 while many other countries have raised theirs by 50 per cent or less). Ideally, to keep us competitive in export markets the pound should have gone down and not up.

However, some monetarists saw the high pound as a good thing. For them it provided an alternative transmission mechanism to the Friedman–Phelps model of Phillips curves with expected inflation given in the previous chapter, i.e. the exchange rate was another way that controlling the money supply could act on prices rather than on output. The strands of the argument are complex, but the basic idea is that controlling the money supply drives up the exchange rate. Because pounds are scarce foreigners bid up the price – they offer more of their currency for a given amount of ours. The higher exchange rate cuts the price of imports (as the pound is higher we can buy more for the same money). Cheap imports competing with our home-produced goods help to hold down prices. Seeing that we are uncompetitive, workers volunteer to work harder and to accept lower pay rises: firms become more efficient, and hold down price increases. Controlling the money supply has now worked through to the price level.

That is the theory. If, however, wages and prices do not respond in the way described when faced with cheap imports, what happens? What happens is that cheap imports remain cheap. We buy them instead of British goods. We lose exports too (the high pound makes them dearer for foreigners to buy). Controlling the money supply then transmits through to output - not prices – and causes unemployment as output falls and as firms go bankrupt. This is substantially what happened from 1979 right through to 1981.

The policy was on a hiding-to-nothing because of the way wages are determined in Britain (as we shall see later) and it is interesting to note that one of the main proponents of the theory (Alan Budd of the London Business School, a leading adviser to the Conservative government) has, almost as this is written, stated that the policy has not worked in the way he hoped, at least not in the short run. He retains his belief in the long-run efficacy of the theory.

For our purposes here it is enough to say that high interest rates were driving the pound up. Profits were hit, output was lost, unemployment rose alarmingly. The interest rate could go no higher.

Fortunately for us, the Americans raised their interest rates and so in 1981 the pound began to fall from the dizzy heights of $2.40 to the £. Belatedly this is beginning to help with the third problem.

*Industry's liquidity crisis*

A whole combination of factors have driven industry into a liquidity crisis which has led to many bankruptcies, unemployment and short-time working.

(a) A 2 per cent increase in interest rates costs industry £500 million.
(b) The high pound has lost us exports and flattened profit margins. Many firms have sold abroad at a loss to keep up sales.
(c) Cheap imports have taken sales at home and weakened profit margins.
(d) Industry's costs rise when output volume falls – this has created still further pressure on profits.
(e) Holding stocks is expensive when interest rates are high. Industry has reduced stocks by cutting output. This has increased unemployment, which has reduced demand still further as the unemployed have less to spend. Suppliers have lost sales and reduced their output and the whole industrial sector has been spiralling downwards.
(f) Rapidly rising wages reduced profits further, necessitated large price increases and made industry less competitive.

*By the middle of 1981, industrial output had fallen to below the level of 1969.*
    The howls of protest from industry were highlighted by an almost unheard of attack on a Conservative government by the head of the CBI, when he called for 'a bare-knuckle fight' with the government.
    The interest rate could go no higher.

**Summary so far**

Controlling the money supply (by using interest rates to control the demand for money) has failed so far. It has failed because

1. Attempting to control the money supply did not stop wages and prices rising.
2. The need for money to pay the wages in both the public and private sectors sucked money into the system whether the government wanted it to or not.

3.  The pressure of wage increases was such that to control the demand for money the government would have needed completely unacceptably high interest rates, which would have had disastrous consequences for the exchange rate, for industry (and hence for output and employment) and for people buying their own homes.

**The wages problem**

It is being argued here that excessively rising money wages are the root cause of our problem. Wage increases forced up prices, forced up the demand for money, forced up interest rates and thus the pound, and ultimately caused the collapse of profits, output and employment. It is worth noting that this view has been put forward by virtually every Chancellor of the Exchequer and Prime Minister since the mid-1960s. It has been put in necessarily simplified ways such as 'one man's wage increase is another man's price increase' (Harold Wilson) and in Jim Callaghan's view to the unions that if they had a 5 per cent wage increase they would get 5 per cent inflation, a 10 per cent increase would give 10 per cent inflation and a 20 per cent wage increase would give 20 per cent inflation.

Surely the view that wages may be the main cause of our problems is worth considering at least as much as the view that it is the money supply that causes inflation – especially now that monetarism has so far failed so badly in our country?

One might argue that it is 'greedy' firms pushing up prices to increase their profits who cause inflation and that wages only go up to 'protect our standard of living'. If this is so we would expect wage increases to be closely related to the inflation rate over the last twelve months, i.e. the rate published in the media. How then do we explain that when Labour left office in 1979 the twelve-month inflation rate was below 10 per cent. Yet from September 1979 to September 1980 average earnings soared by 26 per cent. Prices eventually caught up, but there was little doubt about which came first. And when Labour came to office in 1974 the rate of inflation was only about 10 per cent. *Yet within eighteen months wages were raising by 33 per cent per annum in a year when output did not rise.*

It is argued here that the process works in the following way. First, organised labour pushes up wages far faster than output. Firms respond eventually by raising prices roughly in line with wages. Their price increases then lead to further wage increases and the wage–price spiral has begun. It is further argued that firms *should* raise prices in this way, but that we should *not* raise wages in this way, if we are sensible, because we do not gain and in fact we almost certainly lose. We lose growth and we lose jobs. We lose an improved standard of living that we could have had if we did not behave in this way. Let us look at the various strands in the argument.

### Do prices rise in line with wages?

Since January 1975 wages and prices have both doubled, yet output has not risen.

**Table 2.1**

| January 1975 = 100 | | March 1981 |
|---|---|---|
| Wages (average earnings) | 100 | 211 |
| Prices | 100 | 211 |
| Industrial production | 100 | 99 |

### Should they rise in line?

Some writers argue that a 20 per cent wage increase should not lead to a 20 per cent increase (e.g. Peter Donaldson in his *Illustrated Economics*). Their argument is that wages will only be a part of the firm's total costs. Take electricity as an example. Out of every £100 of costs perhaps only £30 are wages to power workers. If their wages go up 20 per cent, the wage bill rises to £36. The industry, so the argument goes, should only put up electricity by £6 per £100 of costs, i.e. 6 per cent when power workers have a 30 per cent pay increase. This is seen in Table 2.2. This argument is, however, grossly misleading. It assumes that only power workers have a wage increase.

What we are concerned with is how much should prices rise in the economy as a whole if wages as a whole rise on average by, say, 20 per cent. It is not enough for firms to raise prices only to cover their own wage increase, because all their other costs will be rising too.

**Table 2.2**

|  | Before wage increase | After wage increase of 20% |
|---|---|---|
|  | £ | £ |
| Wages | 30 | 36 |
| Other costs | 60 | 60 |
| Profit | 10 | 10 |
| Total cost | £100 | £106 |

These other costs will be rising because of wage increases in the industries who supply machinery, raw materials (e.g. coal) and all the other items that go to make up the total cost of producing electricity. The capital cost of the power station will rise if construction workers have a pay rise, or cement manufacturing workers do, and so on endlessly through all the other costs, which are misleadingly shown in Table 2.2 above as staying constant at £60. Take any cost item, whether it is advertising or machinery, and in the end it consists of someone's wages or someone's profits. Even raw-material costs are wages to the workers who extract the raw material and profits to those who provide the capital.

Therefore, to see the effect on prices of an average wage increase throughout the economy we must look at the whole picture – at the total of all wages and all profits. We shall then see what happens to the costs of all firms if all wages are rising on *average* by 20 per cent.

We shall see that it is not enough just to pass on in higher prices, even the increase in total wages. The reason is that these price increases reduce the purchasing power (real value) of profits. If output is constant, **it turns out that prices must be put up by the same percentage as wages if real profits are not to fall.**

To see this we take a simple case. All costs have been broken down into wages and profits. Suppose all firms together make a total output of 100 units which sell at an average price of £1. Let wages be £80 and profits £20. Now let us suppose over a period wages double to £160. Output stays constant at 100 units. If the firms only pass on the wage increases in higher prices and do not increase profits by the same percentage as wages then, as we can see in Position 2 in Table 2.3, real profits are nearly halved.

**Table 2.3**

|  | Original position | Position 2 (only wage increase passed on) | Position 3 (price raised by same % as wages) |
|---|---|---|---|
| Wages | 80 | 160 | 160 |
| Profits | 20 | 20 | 40 |
| Total cost | 100 | 180 | 200 |
| Total output | 100 | 100 | 100 |
| Price | 1 | 1.80p | 2 |
| Real value of profits (i.e. no. of goods that can be bought with profits shown at prices shown) | 20 | 11.1 | 20 |

In Position 2 wages have risen by £80 to £160. The firms have not increased their money profits. Prices rise to £1.80p. The profits of £20 will now only buy 11.1 units of output at £1.80, whereas before they would buy 20 units at the old price of £1. The only way to avoid a fall in real profits is to put up money profits by the same percentage as wages and put up prices by that percentage too – as is shown in Position 3 in the table. Then what happens is that money wages double, so do money profits and the purchasing power of both (their real value) is left unchanged because prices have doubled as well.

Wages make up about two-thirds of the factor cost of goods (costs excluding indirect taxes). Depreciation – the money needed to replace plant and equipment as it ages and wears out – is another major cost. The cost of replacing stocks at higher prices – due to inflation – is another cost, and profits are whatever is left over when all costs are met and the goods sold.

If output does not rise (as in Britain for some years now) then any increase in wages and other costs must be passed on in higher prices or *money* profits will fall. **If *real* profits are not to fall, then prices must be raised by the same percentage as wages and other costs.**

It follows, then, that if wages and other costs rise by 20 per cent, then prices must rise by 20 per cent or real profits will fall.

*Profits*

Some might think this a good thing. Some union leaders have argued publicly that they want a fundamental redistribution of income away from profits towards wages. This sounds fine; but there are two problems.

The first problem is that profits have been annihilated: they have gone; they *have* been redistributed to wages. When the media report that company *XYZ* has made gross profits of £70 million it seems an enormous amount of money. What they do not tell us is that this is probably only 3 per cent rate of return on capital. Companies are big now. They use enormous amounts of capital to buy factories, machines, stocks and work in progress. They need vast profits to make even a derisorily small rate of return on the huge amount of capital they have tied up.

The rate of return on capital in industry is now down to about 3 per cent in Britain – BEFORE TAX (see Figure 2.1). It is therefore inevitable that when wages rise prices rise roughly in line.

**Figure 2.1** *Real profitability**

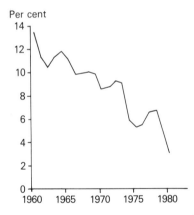

* a *Real profits:* gross trading profits plus rent minus stock appreciation and capital consumption for industrial and commercial companies excluding North Sea activities.

b *Profitability:* real profits as a percentage of capital employed.

We can only consume what we produce and since we are producing the same output as in 1975 (and as in 1969) we cannot have a *real* increase in wages. We have in the past by eroding profit; but now that has all gone.

Now we can only have real increases in wages if we make more output.

It is clear from the data that far from firms raising prices to push up their profits, they have actually experienced falling profits for well over a decade. Profits are now derisorily low: firms have failed to pass on all the cost increases they have faced – that is the only way profits could have fallen. It is no use saying if firms had not put up prices to cover wage increases then inflation would have ceased. They had no alternative. Had they not done so they would all have gone bankrupt.

If not firms, could we blame governments for putting up taxes on goods, e.g. VAT. Surely this raises prices and therefore causes inflation? Or we could argue that rising import prices (especially the quadrupling of oil prices in 1973) are the prime cause of the problem (see Chapter 4). And once import prices or taxes set inflation going then we build expected inflation into our wage claims and set off the well-known wage/price spiral depicted in the Friedman–Phelps analysis in the last chapter. If we accept the basis of that model we can even say that wages and prices are jointly determined and that neither is to blame. That, however, begs the question: it assumes that we behave as we do behave and, given that, any of the things listed above can set off the wage price spiral and lead to inflation. It begs the question, in my view, because it does not ask if we *should* behave in this way – whether it is sensible to do so, whether it is in our best interests or our country's.

Let us take an increase in import prices. Imported goods in the shops will be dearer: and British-made goods will too because we use imported raw materials to make them. So prices go up. We push up wages to compensate. Prices now go up again to cover the higher wage costs. We push up wages again to cover this latest price increase and on and on the process goes. It is easy to claim that the rise in import prices was the initial cause of this inflationary spiral. It would be more sensible to see that it was our own silly behaviour that caused the spiral. We should not have had a wage increase to compensate for higher import prices. Higher import prices are right outside our control. They mean we must give more of our output to foreigners in exchange for their goods. If we must give more output to foreigners we cannot have more for ourselves: in fact we must have less. We should have a wage decrease. It follows that in real terms we *will* have a wage decrease – a reduction in living standards. All we do by pushing up money wages is to raise prices for no real gain. If the wage claims set off the Friedman–Phelps wage–price spiral and if unemployment is increased to cure the inflation, we in fact suffer another real loss. One man's wage increase is not just another man's price increase, it is also another man's job loss.

Nor is it just raising wages to cover higher import prices that is the problem. **We should not raise wages to cover expected inflation either, i.e. if we are sensible we will not behave as the Friedman–Phelps model describes**. The reason for this is simple. Suppose this year we all push up our wages by 10 per cent. Suppose firms then put up prices by 10 per cent but output is constant. No one is better off because although all wages are 10 per cent higher, all prices are too. In real terms we are no better off. We cannot be because there is only the same output to buy and consume. If we stop there, all will be well. There will be no more inflation. If, however, at the end of the year we say 'there's 10 per cent inflation, so I need another 10 per cent wage increase' then there will be another 10 per cent increase in prices and inflation will continue at 10 per cent. If we ask for more than 10 per cent, inflation will accelerate. If we ask for less it will decelerate. If we ask for nothing it will cease.

*It follows therefore that having wage increases to compensate for inflation we expect to occur in the next twelve months, merely causes the expected inflation to happen.* It is not true that we need this kind of wage increase to protect our standard of living: If we did not have the wage increase there would not be the further price increase. Our standard of living would be unchanged. The wage increase merely causes inflation – 10 per cent more on wages and 10 per cent more on prices.

What about higher taxes? If the government puts up VAT it raises prices, and we want a wage increase to compensate. We should not. Taxation is as much a part of our standard of living, whether the tax is on goods or on income, as is take-home pay. The National Insurance stamp provides us all with insurance against redundancy and unemployment just as much as if the government let us keep the money in our take-home pay and we paid for it ourselves. Income-tax, VAT and so on in a similar way pay for schools, roads, hospitals. More tax is not a cut in living standards for which we should seek to compensate ourselves in higher pay. It is spent by the government for us. If they consume more on our behalf, we must consume less. Any money wage increase will, clearly and surely, only raise prices. It cannot be a real wage increase.

Money wage increases can only buy more goods if there are more goods to buy. Money wages backed by a real increase in output will not cause inflation. Money wages not backed by such a real increase in output, must cause inflation, cannot increase living standards and may well increase unemployment as we have seen.

An increase in union pushfulness (for example, when incomes policy is taken off), shifts the Phillips curve upwards. This increases the unemployment needed to stop inflationary wage claims leading to accelerating inflation. The more we ask for, the more we lose our jobs. In addition the inflation caused by the initial kick-up in wages (if not backed by higher output) may well set off the wage–price spiral in the Friedman–Phelps model and lead on to further and maybe accelerating inflation.

Four sensible rules of behaviour come out of this analysis which all union leaders, shop stewards, politicians, people in the media, in fact all of us, will need to grasp if we want to cure inflation *and unemployment*. Only the recent unemployment has seemed able to cut inflation other than when incomes policies have been in force. **If we followed these four rules we would need neither high unemployment nor incomes policy to solve the problems for us.** They are:

1. **No wage increases to compensate for higher import prices.**

2. **No wage increases to compensate for a rise in taxation.**

3. **No wage increases to compensate for expected inflation.**

4. **Wages should only increase in aggregate if there has been a real increase in output.**

Let no one think me naïve enough to believe that we will follow these rules. All I am saying is that we should, and that it is because we do not that we have inflation. It is in this sense that wages are the cause of inflation, in that we do not behave sensibly in wage-bargaining. If we do not *choose* to change our behaviour, wages will go on causing inflation until economists or governments can find some way of *forcing* us to change our behaviour. It seems a shame to wait for another new medicine when we have one now that would work and which can be shown to do so in a non-controversial way.

The rest of this chapter looks at the effects on our future prospects of continuing our present behaviour patterns and policies and examines how organised labour can force up wages even when the money supply is being controlled.

## Growth

Since the labour force is virtually static we can only grow by working harder or better, or by using more machines, more capital equipment to help us get more output from the same labour force. Then we can consume more. Where is the capital to come from, and what is the incentive to invest in capital? Profit is the answer to both questions in a market economy. Most investment is financed by retained profit (some by bank-borrowing, very little by issuing new shares). Kill profits and we kill the main source of funds for investment. No one invests to make a loss. They do so to make a profit. Kill profit and we kill the incentive to invest.

As we have seen profit has been annihilated in Britain. It is not surprising then that net new investment in manufacturing is now less than one-fifth of what we spend on beer and whisky and not much more than half of what we spend on cigarettes.

No profit means no investment, means no growth, means no real wage increases. Money wage increases lead only to price increases – to inflation.

In fact the true picture is even worse. **Almost every Chancellor, faced with wages rising too fast, proceeds to deflate the economy – to drive output down and unemployment up in an attempt to slow up the rise in wages and prices**. Healey did it. Howe has done it. So will the next Chancellor and the next unless we cure the problem. The more we raise our wages, the more Chancellors deflate. The more we ask, the less we really get.

## The power of organised labour

An essential feature of monetarism is that prices should be flexible, i.e. should respond readily to changes in supply and demand. A cut in the money supply which will cut demand, will then lead to a significant fall in prices. Prices and wages are supposed to be determined by market forces – by supply and demand in properly operating goods and labour markets. Cut demand by cutting the money supply and firms lose sales and profits. Wages are cut and with them costs so that prices can be cut as well. Only if wages and prices are flexible, are responsive to supply and demand, can monetarism really work, i.e. only then will changes in the money supply work directly on prices rather than on output or employment – as we saw in Chapter 1.

Many monetarists appear to believe we are still in the world of Adam Smith – a world of many small firms where labour negotiates individually for its wage. One man goes in to the boss alone, asks for a wage increase and only gets it if the firm thinks he is worth it. If some firms pay too much they go bankrupt – become 'lame ducks' – and deter the others from following suit. In such a world monetarism might work. If there was only 10 per cent more money, wages might only rise by 10 per cent – especially if the government refused to bale out any firm that paid too much and was going bankrupt (this is the so-called 'lame ducks' policy).

What happens today is that giant unions bargain with giant firms. The unions do not argue about one man's wage. They threaten to withdraw *all* labour if the wage claim is not met. Rather than lose all its labour it pays a firm to pay up to the point where its profits are zero. This they have done. Of course, no firm wants to pay this much and will only do so if forced.

Firms pay too much because the bargaining process is not equal. A long strike makes the firm bankrupt. It does so because the firm has no output to sell and therefore no income, and yet many bills must be paid even if output temporarily ceases (wages and salaries of those not on strike, overheads, rent, rates, interest on borrowing and so on). Eventually the firm's reserves get used up and it must settle the strike and resume production, or die. For labour the situation is different. A strike involves hardship and a reduced standard of living: but if they want to enough, and if they are prepared to put up with the hardship, then workers can *survive* a strike however long it continues. They often get strike pay from the trade union, social security for wife and children and tax rebates. Many are also able to pick up some temporary work in the black economy – cash and no questions asked.

The bargaining process is tilted strongly in favour of organised labour. Workers can, if they really want to, survive a strike for very prolonged periods. No firm can. So firms tend to give in early as soon as they see the strength of feeling, or they even give in with no strike and merely settle for the best deal they can get. Why join a fight if you know you are going to lose? Not surprisingly organised labour has become very successful at raising money wages above the levels which firms would ordinarily want to pay.

It is no better in the public sector. The miners have shown that no government can take them on and win (anyone who doubts this should ask Edward Heath). If they asked for a 50 per cent rise *and really meant to have it, and struck for long enough*, any government would pay.

In 1980 workers in the steel industry forced British Steel to pay them a 20 per cent wage increase, although the Corporation was making heavy losses. What happened to the view that wages would only rise in line with the money available to pay them? What happened was that the Steel Corporation refused to pay (it offered no rise – it could not afford one). The government refused to intervene. The workers went home and stayed there for a very long time and would have stayed there a good deal longer if need be. In the end the government had to let the lame duck go bankrupt or provide the money. Since the duck was as big as an elephant and would have crushed a lot of ants if allowed to fall over, the government provided the money. It has also done so for British Leyland and many others. It will have to go on doing so because so many companies are too big to let die, the public sector is too essential in most of its forms and organised labour is too powerful for cash limits to have any real chance of working.

The public sector has recently been the main cause of inflation. There is no real restraint on it. If too big a pay rise is paid in electricity to meet a cash limit on spending, well you can always put up the price of electricity and pay the wages that way. If you are in the telephone industry you can put up the cost of a 5-minute local call by 50 per cent in one go as we have recently seen.

Local authorities are no better. Give them a cash limit and they do not meet it. Pay rises exceed the cash limit and the excess is passed on in rates to industry and the rest of us.

### Where are we going?

Public expenditure will not be controlled until the government can control wages in the public sector. The money supply will continue to rise because the government has to pay its bills.

In the private sector profits have been destroyed and with them the funds for investment and the incentive to invest. No serious efforts are being made to re-equip, to invest in growth, in raising living standards, in creating employment. Unemployment is at alarming levels. It will persist. No government dare pour money into industry, or into the economy as a whole to create demand for more output, because they know the money would be taken up in wage increases. No one dares drive the pound down to make us competitive because they know that the higher prices (due to dearer imported raw materials and dearer imported goods) will lead to more wage claims and to higher export prices, thus negating the benefit of the devaluation.

Inflation has been dropping and may go on doing so, but only because firms are on the verge of bankruptcy and unemployment is over 3 million. The new equilibrium, where wage increases at last begin to fall, is where we have 3 million unemployed, a mass of bankruptcies, no profit, no investment and no growth.

If we try to move away from this equilibrium, try to raise profits, investment and growth, we shall only start the wage–price spiral soaring again. In November 1981 even the ever-optimistic Sir Geoffrey Howe appeared to see the enormity of the problem when he said he had decided after all not to cut the employers' contribution to the National Insurance stamp because the intended help for industrial liquidity would only go out in wage increases. Just so; but then how are we ever to grow again?

We are not just destroying our own livelihoods now. As we bankrupt firm after firm in manufacturing industry the assets are broken up, sold off or scapped. The skilled teams are disbanded. A few go to other jobs, some retire early, most go on the dole. Many will never work again. Few of the firms will restart when and if the recession goes. The costs of setting up are too high. The sales needed to keep an economic size of plant busy are so large that it can take years to build up a suitable market, yet only months or weeks to destroy it. If Ford gives up production in Britain, can we ever imagine them wanting to return? So we are not just harming our own livelihoods, we are harming the next generation's too. When unemployment has been driven to 4 million, how are we ever going to get it down again? If every time profits rise we are going to remove them in wage claims, why should firms invest, build factories, create jobs?

Our generation makes its output using considerable amounts of capital inherited from the past – roads, schools, factories, machines, farms and the like. Past generations have forgone consumption so as to invest and generate growth so that their offspring – us – might be better off than they were. Now it is our turn. Even the simplest peasant farmer knows that if he eats too much of this year's crop, there will be less seedcorn to plant, less to consume next year and the year after. Yet we are behaving as though in complete ignorance of this simple fact. We have all-but destroyed profits in our greed for consumption, for more and more wages now. Profit is the incentive and the main source of finance for investment. Without it growth in a market economy must die. We are eating the seedcorn, spending less on net new investment in industry than we do on beer and whisky. If we go on in this profligate way, destroying profits and investment, in an endless search for higher and higher money wages, which is driving firms bankrupt, destroying employment, both now and in the future – if we go on in this way destroying the British economy, what will our children think? What standard of living and employment prospects are we going to leave them?

After the paper was given, on which this chapter was based, a question-and-answer session followed which brought out some useful points especially on possible future policies. It is given below:

QUESTIONS

*Question.* Supposing you are right about the problem and how bad it is, what are the solutions?
*Answer.* One possible solution would be to reduce the power of organised labour so that it cannot raise wages so fast. Another would be to strengthen firms (a state insurance scheme?). But if we make firms strong enough to face long strikes and leave trade unions as they are we will probably have more and longer strikes. So of these two possibilities weakening the power of organised labour seems the only helpful one. I doubt if it will happen though.
*Question.* Why not? Why shouldn't we reform the unions?
*Answer.* No government seems likely to want to face the possible consequences. A general strike could follow or at best massive unrest and disruption. The measures needed to make the policy work are so strong. Secret ballots, no intimidation, no social security for strikers' families – measures like these would be needed and would not be popular.
*Question.* You mean starve strikers out?
*Answer.* No. Unions would pay strike pay as they do in the other countries of Europe – up to £80 a week in some. If unions and labour bore some of the cost of the strike they might strike less often and not for so long. This policy might seem anti-worker, but it is not. By lowering the Phillips curve this policy would lower inflation and reduce the natural rate of unemployment. But, as I said, I do not think unions or many of us would accept the policy, so it probably will not happen. Only with a referendum to show popular support for union reforms do I think we could get the policy through without

serious disruption.

*Question.* So what else can we do?

*Answer.* The government could introduce an immediate pay freeze – preferably for two years. This would reduce inflationary expectations and thereby reduce our desire for higher wages. If unions are really only trying to protect members against inflation – as they so often say   then we should stop inflation by stopping wages pushing up prices. Then the need for the wage increases would have gone. Sooner or later the government must see that wages and prices are not as flexible as they had hoped. Either they must reduce the power of firms and unions to distort labour and goods markets (by a combination of anti-monopoly policy and reducing the power of organised labour) or they must accept the necessity of some form of incomes policy. If wages and prices do not respond readily to supply and demand, but are fixed by union and firm power, then monetarism cannot work directly on prices. It will cause output to fall and unemployment to rise.

Given an effective incomes policy the government could reduce the exchange rate to make us competitive and could then safely have a major injection of funds into the economy and especially to industry. Our output is low, at least partly because we do not have the same capital equipment per man as Germany, France and so on. We must invest to raise output per person. Then we can have a real increase in living standards.

*Question.* And if the government does not come forward with an incomes policy?

*Answer.* Then the TUC should offer it to them in exchange for a major injection of funds into the economy. We must have control over incomes if we want to make the economy grow. At the very least we need politicians to stop pretending whenever in Opposition that wages have nothing to do with inflation, that we do not need an incomes policy.

*Question.* When have incomes policies ever worked?

*Answer.* Every time. Under Heath's policy inflation was brought down and at the least was stopped from spiralling upwards. Under Healey the fall in prices was dramatic. Inflation ran to 27 per cent before incomes policy and after the policy was introduced, from 1976 to 1979, it fell to under 10 per cent per annum. Without it inflation would have exploded, I feel certain. Equally important, if you look at the figures in Table 2.4 you can see that output rose under Heath's incomes policy up to 1973, fell when we took it off up to 1975, rose again after Healey's conversion to incomes policy up to

**Table 2.4** *Industrial output (1975 = 100)*

|  | 1969 | 1973 | 1975 | 1978 | 1980 | 1981 |
|---|---|---|---|---|---|---|
| Industrial output (includes North Sea oil, gas, electricity, water, etc.) | 99.6 | 109.5 | 100.0 | 109.8 | 99.5 | 99.8 |

Industrial output is now at about the same level as in 1969.
Incomes policy was on from 1971–3, was off in 1974 and 1975, was on again in 1976–78/9, and has been off since the Conservatives came to power in May 1979.

1979 and has fallen ever since this government took it off. It could be coincidence (you can *prove* nothing with statistics), but I do not think so. We expand the economy when we do not fear inflation from wages; we deflate it whenever wages rise too fast – as they do whenever we take off incomes policies. The only problems with incomes policies are that as a nation we will not support them for very long, that politicians pretend we do not need them so that we will vote for them – but mainly the problem is that we keep taking incomes policies off. We need a permanent incomes policy – not temporary ones. The problem seems permanent: so must the solution be.

*Question.* What sort of incomes policy?

*Answer.* Ah, there's the rub. We need a two-year pay freeze to cure inflation, and during that time detailed study of the alternatives. In particular we should talk to the Germans and the Swedes. It's not enough to have an aggregate incomes policy – all wages up 6 per cent or whatever. It must solve the problems of individual firms and industries too. You have to pay enough to get enough nurses and policemen. It is crazy to raise wages in jobs where there are 200 applicants for every vacancy. If we do not use wage differentials to get the right number of people into each job – the number we need – then we shall have to use work permits and the like as many Communist countries do, i.e. some kind of compulsion. Personally I prefer a financial reward to force.

The kind of incomes policy I would favour would be one based on the four rules for wages on page 46. Increasing output would be the main criterion for a wage increase, that and any firms' inability to get enough workers at the current wage. In jobs where output was not easily measurable, doctors, nurses and the like, we could devise a system for them to have a share of the increase in total output, i.e. link their earnings to the growth of earnings in sectors where output can be expanded by mechanisation and productivity and where changes can readily be measured. No system will be perfect, but given a general will to succeed and co-operate it would not be hard to improve on the chaos we now have.

*Question.* Unemployment does now seem to be reducing inflation in the way described in the Friedman–Phelps model. Why not continue this policy instead of changing to the complexities of incomes policy?

*Answer.* I agree that current policy is consistent with that model. We are using high unemployment (above the natural rate) to damp down inflationary wage claims. But there are problems with that model. There is no reason why the natural rate of unemployment should necessarily coincide with any reasonable definition of full employment. It took 2½ to 3 million people out of work before inflation began falling. The costs of the policy in lost output and human misery are too high. Nor is there any reason why the natural rate of unemployment (at which wage claims cease to cause inflation) should occur at a politically acceptable level, i.e. a level low enough for politicians to have reasonable expectations of being re-elected. If the natural rate of unemployment is too high to be politically acceptable the policy implications of the model are not politically feasible in the long run. The other problem is one of time. If it has taken twenty years to build up our inflationary expectations, how long will it take to damp them down by raising unemployment and controlling the money supply? Eventually expectations of inflation may disappear – and with it wage claims that induce further inflation – but could this process be achieved in the length of a parliament or may it take ten, fifteen, even twenty years? Might it take as long to cure the problem as it took to cause it? The case for incomes policy is that if we had an effective one, if we would accept it and make it work, we could cure inflation more quickly and without unemployment or loss of output. In fact, we could increase output without inflation.

*Question.* Are you really trying to say we can only cure Britain's problems by becoming a totalitarian state on Communist lines?

*Answer.* No. There is often a clash between freedom and efficiency. My own views have always lent towards freedom. I just despair of being able to cure our present problems with all the freedom we have now.

Monetarism is dealing with the symptom, i.e. wages rising faster than output. With 3 million unemployed we may remove the symptom and stop inflation – but only while unemployment is high.

When we go back to growth and full employment the disease will re-emerge. If organised labour has the power to raise wages more than output when there is full employment won't the problem simply re-emerge? Only by reducing union power by reform, or by having an incomes policy, can we hope to solve the long-run problem.

*Last Question.* You said we could solve the mortgage problem so that the payments on a £20,000 mortgage would only be £20 per week. That's cheaper than renting a bed-sitting room. How could we do it?

*Answer.* If there were no inflation and zero interest rates the mortgage on a £20,000 house would be £20 per week, i.e. £1000 per year for twenty years. The lender pays no tax on the interest (he has no *real* income from it). The borrower tax deducts nothing. The government gets nothing. When there's no inflation this seems eminently fair and reasonable to everyone.

Yet if inflation rises to 15 per cent and interest rates to 15 per cent nothing has really changed: the real interest rate is still zero. The lender should pay no tax. But we tax his money interest rate and take away one-third of it. We let the borrower tax deduct his money interest rate – although his real rate is zero. However, we savagely penalise him in another way. When we calculate the payments we pretend inflation will stay at 15 per cent for the next twenty years and cumulate 15 per cent interest. We arrive at a huge total to repay. We divide it into twenty equal portions to be paid off each year. This year he pays for inflation we assume will be there later. But his wages are not paid like this. We do not add 15 per cent inflation to his wages for twenty years, get a grand total and pay him one-twentieth of that this year and every year – an equal amount including future inflation. He gets a low wage now that grows at the infla-tion rate: **so should his mortgage repayment be low now and grow at the inflation rate, i.e. grow in line with what he can afford as his earn-ings grow.**

To do this all we need to do is let building societies issue 'granny bonds' like the government, i.e. pay lenders the rate of inflation tax free. It's zero real interest, so no tax. The government does it on granny bonds. Why one rule for one thing and another for the rest?

If building societies could issue granny bonds and borrow at a zero real interest rate (i.e. pay investors the rate of inflation tax free) then they could lend mortgages at a zero real interest rate (plus administration charges). With no interest to pay, all a mortgagee would need to do is pay the building society one-twentieth of the price of the house purchased, plus inflation, each year for twenty years. Borrowing £20,000 would mean repayments of £1000 per year (i.e. one-twentieth of the total each year) plus inflation. If there were no inflation that is all we would need to pay. If there was 10 per cent inflation in the next year then we would pay £1000 + 10 per cent inflation = £1100. If there was another 10 per cent inflation the next year the repayment for that year would be £1100 + 10 per cent = £1210, i.e. the repayment would be £1000 per year *plus* whatever inflation occurred.

The beauty of the scheme is that payments to begin with are very low. In the first year the mortgage would be £1000 + say 10 per cent (if there was 10 per cent inflation) = £1100 or just over £21 per week. At the current mortgage interest rate of 15 per cent, the repayments on a £20,000 mortgage are now approximately £61 per week. This is far more than most can afford, so they cannot buy a house. Almost everyone could afford to pay £21 per week this year and progressively increase their payments with inflation. The mortgage would go up each year – but so would their wages (and as we have seen wages and prices go up very much in line). Home ownership would really be within the reach of almost everyone. The nonsensical distortion that a council house rent in 1981 cost on average under £12 per week and will cost under £14 in 1982, while the mortgage on a similar-quality private house would be £60+ a week would then be gone. Those who really wanted or needed to rent could do so, but the cost of buying your own for those who preferred it would no longer be prohibitively dearer and they would move into the private sector. Then those who really needed council accommodation would find it easier to obtain.

Since under this scheme lots of people would be able to buy a house who cannot now afford to do so, home building would increase (it's down to pre-war levels now). Employment would be created. Output would rise.

I would let people choose either this kind of mortgage or the present one. Lenders would gain by not being taxed on phoney money interest rates. It would cost the government nothing as it could say, if it chose, that borrowers could only tax-deduct the real interest rate. Borrowers would gain as they would have a mortgage they could afford – even if it did rise with inflation in line with their earnings. It would reduce the cost-of-living index too as mortgage repayments are a sizeable item nowadays. Can we really go on with the situation where in most towns the mortgage repayments on the cheapest houses are out of reach of someone on average earnings?

# INTRODUCTION TO CHAPTER 3

In Britain, many institutions are involved in attempting to forecast the future behaviour of the country. These range from large corporations, banks and consulting organisations to the Bank of England and Treasury. Perhaps the most interesting, however, are the forecasts which are prepared by independent bodies such as the London Business School, the Cambridge Department of Applied Economics, the Cambridge Economic Policy Group, the National Institute and the Economics Department at Liverpool University. Of these, the Cambridge Economic Policy Group has been overly pessimistic whereas the Liverpool University group has been overly optimistic. The others have been closer to the mark. The analysis used by one of these bodies, the London Business School, is very much in step with that of the current government and hence is utilised in the next chapter by David Rowan to evaluate current performance. These forecasts predict increasing levels of unemployment and high levels of inflation well into 1984. These results are in marked contrast to the public pronouncements which continue to be made and indicate a much longer period than the government envisaged for their policies to work themselves out. Indeed, although Rowan confines himself to forecasts for 1984, the year of the next election, many economists are privately forecasting that unemployment will not fall below 2.5 million before 1990 and that growth of output will average no more than 1 or 2 per cent per annum.

Rowan argues that one of the fundamental reasons behind Britain's problems is really a very old one: that politicians of all persuasions have been deluded by the idea that simple panaceas are capable of solving basic social and economic problems. He implicitly argues that politicians only listen to that analysis which reinforces their prior beliefs.

C. H. and G. M.

# 3  British Macroeconomic Policy: A Review

*by David Rowan*

## Introduction

The objectives of contemporary British macroeconomic policy have been frequently stated. They are:

(1)  to reduce the rate of inflation; and
(2)  to create conditions under which sustainable economic growth can be achieved.

Put as succinctly as possible, this chapter offers an 'assessment' of:

(a)  the progress which has been made by the Thatcher–Howe administration up to the present (September–October 1981); and
(b)  the progress which it seems likely will have been achieved by 1984.

Once we decide to eschew polemics (of which there is no contemporary or foreseeable shortage) it becomes clear that providing an 'assessment' is a complex and potentially controversial matter. For example, we need to know what is meant by 'conditions under which sustainable growth can be achieved' before we can even begin to consider whether government policy has taken us closer to (or further from) attaining them. And, of course, identifying the contribution of government policy to any observed economic events is itself no simple matter. Thus though it is common knowledge that, since Mrs Thatcher took office, the economy has experienced its most severe recession since the Second World War, it remains a difficult matter to say to what extent, if any, the recession is attributable to the Thatcher–Howe version of 'monetarist gradualism'. Because of these and other complexities, a book could be written on the issues raised by our objectives – and no doubt many such books will be written in the future.

The reader is therefore warned that the treatment here is unavoidably compressed. Some supplementary references are given at the end of the chapter and these should serve to fill out the present somewhat skeletal discussion.

The structure of the chapter is straightforward. It begins by characterising the theory on which contemporary macroeconomic policies are based. This gives a framework within which an assessment can be made. Given this framework a judgement can be made on the progress made up to the present (September–October 1981).

Applying the same sort of analysis to 1982–4 presents the additional problem that economic series for the future can only be forecasts and, since forecasting now has many practitioners, a choice must be made between alternative forecasts. Fortunately no single group's forecasts seem to be generally superior to all others. Since this is so, I have, in nearly all cases, relied on the forecasts of the London Business School (LBS).

There are a number of reasons for this. The first is that the LBS forecasts are comprehensive. The second is that they are readily available. The third is that, in general, the somewhat 'monetarist' LBS group is sympathetic to the Thatcher–Howe policy and, on the basis of its model or theory of how the British economy works, typically produces at least marginally more optimistic forecasts than some of its rivals.

This last point is of more than negligible interest. I am myself an identified critic of contemporary policy and might therefore, by the less charitable, be suspected of choosing a set of forecasts which suggest a peculiarly unappetising outcome simply in order to justify my unfavourable judgements. Reliance on the LBS forecasts disarms this criticism.

It is nevertheless the case that my arguments lead to the conclusion that, by 1984, in terms of its own stated objectives and the LBS forecasts the macroeconomic policy of the present administration will not only be a manifest failure, but also a costly one. It is for the reader to decide whether my judgement is one which reasonable men would accept.

**The present policy: economic theory**

Assuming that the form of words was chosen with care the government's statement of its own objectives implies:

(a)   that it *can* reduce the rate of inflation, but
(b)   can only *create conditions* under which sustainable economic growth can be attained.

The second and more limited formula (b) is also applied to the maintenance of 'high employment'. This seems to imply that the old notion that governments could – and should – seek to maintain 'full employment' is dead.

Rather surprisingly, however, it is typically claimed, for example by the Treasury, that these objectives are in no way novel, but have in practice been pursued by previous governments. All that is novel is the interpretation of policy in a *medium-term* rather than a *short-term* context. Thus it is over the 'medium term' which, though nowhere precisely defined, I interpret to mean 1979–84, that the Thatcher administration expects to achieve its objectives and it is on this basis that the instruments of macroeconomic policy – i.e. government expenditures, tax rates – are to be set. From this it follows that macroeconomic anti-cyclical stabilisation policies, as we have come to know them, have no part to play. There is to be no tuning – coarse or fine; and, despite official denials, this seems to confirm my earlier inference that the commitment to maintaining a high level of employment which was accepted, and typically honoured, by all governments from, say, 1946 to roughly 1973 has now been abandoned. The role of the government is now to be limited to 'creating conditions' favourable to 'high' employment. Given these conditions, 'high' employment will be attained only if there is an appropriate response by management and labour guided, or so it appears, by the benevolent 'invisible hand' of market processes.

All this is, of course, consistent with monetarist doctrine and even what is sometimes called 'new classicism'. For the principal monetarist contentions are that the rate of change of prices (the inflation rate) is determined (after a lag of some 2–4 years) by the rate of change of the money stock while the economy, if not disturbed by changes in the rate of change of money, will, through market adjustments, typically operate at what is usually called the 'natural' rate of unemployment, but is sometimes referred to as the Non-Accelerating Inflation Rate of Unemployment (NAIRU). (The reader may find it helpful to consult Chapter 1, p. 0–0, for further discussion of this point.) Thus if monetarism is correct, there is *no need* for anti-cyclical stabilisation policies since cyclical fluctuations will be mild and rapidly corrected by ordinary market adjustments. What is called 'new classicism' goes further than this by asserting that systematic stabilisation policies would, in any case, have no influence on the real economy – that is, output and employment. Though there is much more to 'new classicism' than this, in the present context the reader unfamiliar with economists' jargon can simply regard 'new classicism' as an extreme form of monetarism – albeit one which is not necessarily accepted by many distinguished monetarist economists. The central contention of both groups is of course that the labour market works in such a way that there cannot be any *persistent* tendency for the level of unemployment to be higher than its 'natural' level so that what is called 'involuntary unemployment' (arising from an inadequate level of real demand) is typically negligible: broadly speaking all who *want* to work at the existing real wage can work.

Given this theory it is easy to see why the Thatcher administration attaches so much importance to controlling the rate of growth in the money stock (defined in the British context as sterling $M_3$) and has, in fact, formulated a medium-term plan, called the 'medium-term financial strategy' (MTFS) for doing so. This envisages a *gradual* reduction in the (planned) rate of monetary expansion from 7–11 per cent in 1980–1 to 4–8 per cent in 1983–4 and though, as Table 3.1 makes clear, the actual rate and the planned (or target) rates have not coincided, the intention is plain enough: namely to bring about a gradual reduction in the rate of inflation by bringing about a prior gradual reduction in the rate of expansion in sterling $M_3$.

Why the emphasis on *gradualism?* Monetarists have always accepted that monetary action to reduce the rate of inflation will involve some costs in terms of falling output and rising unemployment (and any adverse social or political consequence that derive from these) simply because the rates of change in money wages and prices do not adjust immediately to the reduction in the rate of monetary growth which is believed (by monetarists) to determine the rate of growth of the value of goods demanded. Hence the quantity demanded falls and the result is a policy-induced recession.

**Table 3.1** The behaviour of sterling $M_3$: British monetary experience since 1979[1]

| Year–month | $M_3$ target growth rate (1) | $M_3$ actual growth rate (2) | Year–month | $M_3$ target growth rate (3) | $M_3$ actual growth rate (4) | Year–month | $M_3$ target growth rate (5) | $M_3$ actual growth rate (6) |
|---|---|---|---|---|---|---|---|---|
| 1979 J | 10.0 | 20.4 | 1980 J | 9.0 | 10.8 | 1981 J | 9.0 | 6.0 |
| F | 10.0 | 7.2 | F | 9.0 | 7.2 | F | 9.0 | 2.4 |
| M | 10.0 | −9.6 | M | 9.0 | 6.0 | M | 9.0 | 7.2 |
| A | 10.0 | 24.0 | A | 9.0 | 4.8 | A | 9.0 | 26.4 |
| M | 10.0 | 18.0 | M | 9.0 | 26.4 | M | 9.0 | 18.0 |
| J | 9.0 | 10.8 | J | 9.0 | 9.6 | J | 9.0 | 2.4 |
| J | 9.0 | 10.8 | J | 9.0 | 60.0 | J | 9.0 | 25.2 |
| A | 9.0 | 16.8 | A | 9.0 | 36.0 | A | 9.0 | n.a |
| S | 9.0 | 8.4 | S | 9.0 | 7.2 | S | | |
| O | 9.0 | 20.1 | O | 9.0 | 24.0 | O | | |
| N | 9.0 | 12.0 | N | 9.0 | 24.0 | N | | |
| D | 9.0 | 1.2 | D | 9.0 | 6.0 | D | | |
| Average for year | 9.64 | 11.8 | | 9.0 | 17.8 | | | |

*Definitions:*
Target growth rate = mid-point of target range. Range is target ± 2.
Actual growth rate = monthly percentage change in seasonally adjusted sterling $M_3$ × 12.

Source: Bank of England Quarterly Bulletin (various issues)

In an economy heavily dependent on exports of manufactures the fall in real demand may come partly as a result of a loss in competitiveness arising out of an appreciating domestic currency. Britain's experience up to March 1981 illustrates this process. But by either route, or by both, *transition costs* of this kind are certain to appear. Hence gradualism was embraced as a means of reducing the magnitude of these transitional costs while the publication of an explicit medium-term financial strategy was undertaken with the aim of influencing expectations of inflation in a manner calculated to smooth the adjustment process. This strategy is consistent with what may be called 'main stream' monetarism and was supported by many monetarist sympathisers among economists.

The government's theory, however, seems to depart from monetarist orthodoxy in two ways. The first of these, which need not detain us, consists in the adoption of a 'theory' of the determination of the money supply which emphasises the role of the Public Sector Borrowing Requirement (PSBR). This 'theory' (which has been heavily attacked) makes government expenditure and taxation decisions the primary determinant of the rate of change of sterling $M_3$.

Hence, since the rate of monetary expansion is the government's instrument of control, fiscal policy becomes dominated by the requirements of monetary policy and according to some monetarist critics, monetary control becomes ineffective – a point consistent with Table 3.1.

The second departure was more fundamental still. As we have seen, the government's theory gives it *one* instrument with which to control the economy – namely the rate of growth in sterling $M_3$. But, as we have also seen, it has *two* objectives: namely to reduce inflation and establish conditions consistent with sustainable economic growth. With only *one* instrument and *two* objectives it is usually necessary to 'trade-off' one objective against another: that is, accept (say) a rather smaller reduction in inflation as the price of approaching closer to the conditions consistent with sustainable growth. The government's view is that no such 'trade-off' is necessary, since it asserts not only that 'inflation is disastrous for output, employment and growth', but also that this relationship is a 'general rule' to which Britain is unlikely to be an exception.

Unfortunately the government gives no evidence, theoretical or empirical, in support of the 'rule'. The 'rule' is, of course, not a monetarist proposition: for it amounts to asserting that the so-called 'natural' rate of unemployment is itself dependent upon the rate of growth of the money stock – an argument not usually advanced by monetarists. Indeed monetarists commonly argue that, provided the rate of inflation is – and has been for some time – fully foreseen *both* the 'natural' rate of unemployment *and* the rate of growth in output are, as a first approximation, independent of the rate of inflation.

The warrant for the 'general rule' which the government asserts is thus far from readily apparent. Nevertheless the government's belief in the 'general rule' is of crucial importance for it is, I assume, the credence given to the 'rule' which encourages the government not only to emphasise the objective of reducing inflation, but also to aim, at least by implication, at achieving a low or even zero inflation rate.

Suppose, for example, the government had *not* believed in the existence of this 'general rule'. It might have chosen to stabilise the rate of inflation at the rate ruling when it came into office – some 9–10 per cent – and devoted its energies to extending the ability of households and firms to adjust to this rate via indexing. In this case, the transitional fall in output and rise in unemployment arising out of government policy would have been less. I conclude that it is the government's belief in this 'rule', and its implicit quantitative interpretation of the relation between inflation, employment and growth, which have encouraged it to undertake an ambitious anti-inflationary stance and accept transition costs which even its strongest supporters now regard as very severe indeed.

A further element in the government's version of 'monetarism' appears to be the implicit belief that whatever the transition costs turn out to be they are entirely transitory in the sense that they entail no harmful long-term effects on the productive capacity of the economy, on industrial relations or on the 'sustainable' rate of growth in output. What matters here is the quantitative importance of any 'permanent' or 'long-run' element in the transition costs and evidence on this point is lacking. Qualitatively, however, I find it hard to accept that a 'permanent' element will not be present since any policy induced recession must involve a slower rate of capital accumulation in both private and public sectors, a decline through disuse in the existing productive skills of the unemployed and a fairly sharp reduction in expenditure on higher education and industrial training which is, of course, simply a reduction in the rate of investment in human capital. If we add to this the probable deterioration in industrial relations and the already manifest deterioration in racial and social relations, I find it difficult to believe that the 'transition' costs do not contain a significant 'permanent' component.

From this short review I conclude that:

(i) the Thatcher–Howe policy is essentially a form of 'monetarist gradualism', but

(ii) is a 'high-risk' variant since it rests upon the dubious but crucial assumptions that:

(a) both 'sustainable growth' and 'sustainable employment' would be greater if inflation were typically lower, and

(b) however large the 'transition' costs, they contain no significant 'permanent' element.

**The present policy: objectives**

Before we can make any worth-while assessment of contemporary policy it is essential to provide a more precise interpretation of the government's two policy objectives.

At first sight the objective of 'reducing the rate of inflation' seems unambiguous. Sadly, however, there are few concepts in economics as straightforward as first appearances suggest. And 'reducing the rate of inflation' is no exception to this rule.

It is, for example, obvious that 'success' in reducing inflation cannot simply mean reducing the observed rate of inflation for almost any economist, whether of 'New Classical', 'Monetarist', 'Keynesian' or 'Post-Keynesian' allegiance, would agree that a sufficiently severe deflation, whether carried out by fiscal or monetary means, must eventually reduce the rate of change of money wages and prices if only by imposing bankruptcy on firms and increasing unemployment on workers. Whether the resulting reduction in the rate of observed inflation indicates any *permanent improvement* in the inflationary mechanism is, however, quite another matter. If and when unemployment ceases to rise, or more optimistically still begins to fall, inflation may well reappear unless some permanent change in the wage–price spiral process has taken place. Thus 'success' in the attack on inflation is to be defined in terms of permanent not transitory improvements.

This is an important and decidedly awkward conclusion. For there is no obvious way of identifying permanent as opposed to transitory effects while the observed rate of inflation, incorporating as it does temporary and non-sustainable declines in profit margins, is plainly a misleading indicator.

In these circumstances the best we can do is to argue that though a fall in the observed rate of inflation does not indicate, of itself, any improvement in the long-run position, and thus provide an index of 'success' for the government, the absence of a significant fall in the observed rate is prima facie evidence of 'failure'.

The second objective of the government is to 'create conditions under which sustainable economic growth can be attained'. Unfortunately no very clear-cut definition of what this means is available. At a minimum, however, the 'conditions' must surely embrace:

(i)   a real rate of return on capital compatible with a 'sustainable' rate of capital investment, and
(ii)  a level of 'competitiveness' *vis-à-vis* the rest of the world which is consistent with:
    (a)   the real rate of return on capital described by (i), and
    (b)   the maintenance of current account balance under conditions of growth at a 'sustainable' rate at the level of capacity utilisation defined by the 'natural' rate of unemployment.

Once again, numerical definition of the relevant concepts is virtually impossible. We do, however, know that the real rate of return on capital employed in British industry (excluding oil) fell fairly sharply between 1972 and 1980 (see Table 3.2). Indeed, by 1980 it is a reasonable inference that the rate was well below any figure compatible with 'sustainable growth' at an acceptable level of capacity utilisation.

If this is so, then a movement towards the 'conditions for sustainable growth' must entail an improvement in the rate of return on capital. The absence of any such improvement or, even worse, a further deterioration in the rate of return, is prima facie evidence of the failure of contemporary policy to bring about a movement towards meeting the first of our minimum conditions.

**Table 3.2** *Rates of return for British industrial and commercial companies**

| | | | |
|------|------|------|-----|
| 1965 | 11.2 | 1975 | 5.3 |
| 1970 | 8.6  | 1976 | 5.4 |
| 1971 | 8.8  | 1977 | 6.2 |
| 1972 | 9.3  | 1978 | 6.2 |
| 1973 | 9.1  | 1979 | 4.3 |
| 1974 | 5.2  | 1980 | 2.9 |

* Excluding North Sea activity, adjusted for inflation but before tax.

The second condition is no simpler to define, even though a number of indexes relating to 'competitiveness' are published. Typically these relate to the relative costs of manufactures at home and abroad. Probably relative costs are the most important single element in any notion of 'competitiveness' though other variables – for example, design, reliability and the degree to which delivery can be relied upon – must also be significant. Once again it is virtually impossible to identify a particular value of any 'competitiveness' index as satisfying our 'condition' (ii). However, if we regard 1979 as a benchmark which involves making the fairly strong assumptions that, in that year, the economy was operating fairly close to the 'natural' level of unemployment and, allowing for our renegotiation of Britain's contribution to the EEC, in approximate balance on *current account*, we are certainly not biasing the analysis against contemporary policy. On this basis we can argue that any deterioration in 'competitiveness' since 1979 implies a movement *away* from meeting 'condition' (ii): that is, away from creating conditions for 'sustainable' growth at 'high' employment.

**Progress and policy up to the present**

There is no unambiguously correct way of saying how far economic events since the advent of the Thatcher–Howe regime are attributable to either the government's planned policy or its actual counterpart. An estimate *can* be derived from an existing model of the economy. There is, however, a range of competing models and it is by no means clear that estimates derived from them would converge to a consensus.

My own 'guesstimate' is that some 80 per cent or more of the observed changes in economic data are attributable either to the policies actually carried out or to people's beliefs about the policies which the government planned to implement. Readers, however, should note that this estimate may well be challenged. It is a personal and not necessarily a consensus view.

It is now a commonplace that, since Mrs Thatcher took office, the economy has experienced its most severe recession since the Second World War. Gross Domestic Product in real terms has fallen by something over 7 per cent and industrial production (excluding oil) by around 15 per cent, manufacturing production has fallen by roughly the same percentage. This melancholy story is set out in Figure 3.1.

Not surprisingly, though as a series it tends to lag behind output, there has been a sharp response in both employment and unemployment. The figures are difficult to interpret because of the incidence of various official schemes which have the effect of keeping recorded unemployment below what it would be in the absence of these arrangements and also because of the failure of some unemployed to register (see Table 3.3).

Table 3.3    *Employment and unemployment,*
*Britain: seasonally adjusted*

| | | Working population | Employed* labour force | (thousands) Unemployed‡ excluding school-leavers | | Total | Vacancies notified | Short-term working |
|---|---|---|---|---|---|---|---|---|
| | | (1) | (2) | (3) | | (4) | (5) | (6) |
| 1979 | I | 26 332 | 25 070 | 1349.4 | (5.6) | 1436.5 | 233.6 | 33 |
| | II | 26 464 | 25 097 | 1305.2 | (5.4) | 1327.9 | 252.2 | 29 |
| | III | 26 551 | 25 101 | 1266.8 | (5.2) | 1438.0 | 249.1 | 42 |
| | IV | 26 445 | 25 031 | 1287.1 | (5.3) | 1359.4 | 230.3 | 61 |
| 1980 | I | 26 223 | 24 885 | 1373.9 | (5.7) | 1479.2 | 194.6 | 153 |
| | II | 26 380 | 24 696 | 1497.7 | (6.2) | 1563.9 | 159.2 | 192 |
| | III | 26 480 | 24 384 | 1699.0 | (7.0) | 1979.1 | 119.8 | 336 |
| | IV | 26 293 | 23 989 | 2019.8 | (8.4) | 2156.7 | 98.3 | 470 |
| 1981 | I | 26 029 | 23 683 | 2304.4 | (9.5) | 2455.8 | 99.6 | 491 |
| | II | 26 106 | 23 399 | 2506.4 | (10.4) | 2588.0 | 89.5 | 291 |
| 1981 | Sep*† | n.a. | n.a. | 2672.7 | (11.1) | 2998.8 | 96.9 | 181 |

Notes: * includes employers, self-employed and HM Forces.
    † Latest month for which figures are available.
    ‡ Figures in brackets are percentages of the working population.
    n.a. not available.

Sources: *Economic Trends* (various issues) for cols (2), (3), (4), (5); Department of Employment data for cols (1) and (6).

**Figure 3.1**

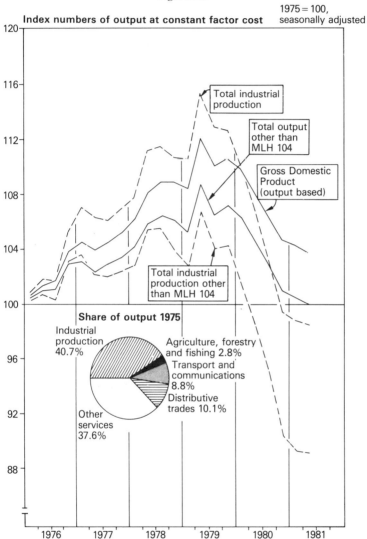

Note: MLH 104 consists of oil and natural gas.
Source: *Economic Trends* (various issues).

Neglecting these difficulties the registered unemployed (excluding school-leavers) have roughly doubled since the second quarter of 1979. Making some allowance for the incidence of the government's special schemes and for the tendency to fail to register,

**Table 3.4** *Prices, earnings, wage costs per unit of output, productivity*

| Date Year: quarter | Retail prices (all items) | | Earnings (average) | | Wage costs per unit of output all output | | manufacturing | | Output per person in manufacturing |
|---|---|---|---|---|---|---|---|---|---|
| | Index | % change | Index | % change | Index | % change | Index | % change | % change |
| 1979 I | 155.0 | 9.6 | 141.0 | 13.9 | 143.2 | 12.1 | 151.2 | 14.2 | 0.8 |
| II | 160.7 | 10.6 | 146.6 | 13.4 | 145.6 | 12.8 | 153.6 | 12.4 | 3.4 |
| III | 171.4 | 16.0 | 153.9 | 15.7 | 156.6 | 16.7 | 161.7 | 15.2 | −0.6 |
| IV | 176.2 | 17.3 | 161.8 | 18.5 | 159.7 | 16.8 | 169.0 | 14.7 | 2.4 |
| 1980 I | 184.6 | 19.1 | 168.8 | 19.7 | 167.3 | 16.8 | 178.7 | 18.3 | 0.3 |
| II | 195.3 | 21.5 | 178.0 | 21.4 | 177.3 | 21.8 | 191.1 | 24.4 | −5.2 |
| III | 199.4 | 16.4 | 188.1 | 22.2 | 188.1 | 20.1 | 201.3 | 24.8 | −3.0 |
| IV | 203.2 | 15.3 | 193.3 | 19.5 | 189.9 | 18.9 | 206.4 | 22.2 | −7.2 |
| 1981 I | 208.0 | 12.7 | 196.7 | 16.5 | 191.7 | 14.6 | 207.8 | 16.8 | −2.5 |
| II | 218.1 | 11.7 | 201.2 | 13.0 | 200.9 | 13.3 | 208.0 | 9.4 | 1.1 |

Note: Percentage changes are defined as the percentage change from the corresponding period in the previous year.

Source: *Economic Trends* (various issues).

unemployment, as usually interpreted, is now well in excess of 3 millions and is still rising by about 30,000 adults per month.

As I have tried to make clear, the appropriate interpretation of the concept of 'the rate of inflation' in the context of the government's objectives is a matter for debate. Table 3.4 brings together a number of relevant series.

If we think solely in terms of prices then, on an annual basis, the current rate of inflation is *above* that ruling when the present administration came into office. The rate is, however, substantially below the 22 per cent to which the Chancellor's increase in VAT and other measures had raised it by the third quarter of 1980. Not too surprisingly a similar pattern holds for both average earnings and for wage costs per unit of manufacturing output.

A simple-minded interpretation of these series leads inexorably to the conclusion that, after 2¼ years, the Thatcher–Howe experiment with 'monetarist gradualism' has just about neutralised the inflationary impetus provided by the Thatcher–Howe attempts to shift from direct to indirect taxes. Even this, however, may somewhat overstate the case since profit margins have certainly fallen in manufacturing so that the inflation of prices does not fully reflect the inflation of costs.

On the other hand, it is a familiar monetarist proposition that the rate of inflation responds to monetary restraint only with a long and ill-defined lag. We should therefore look to the forecasts for 1982–4 to give us a better idea of the degree of 'success' the authorities have achieved in reducing the actual rate of inflation.

It is, of course, a matter of judgement as to whether the price–wage mechanism in Britain has been favourably modified during the last 2¼ years. My own assessment of this, which is really the crucial issue, is that it is far too early to say. It follows that, if the reader is prepared to accept my agnosticism on this point, the Thatcher–Howe regime cannot yet claim any 'success' for its anti-inflationary policy.

**Indeed, there has been no significant fall in the rate of inflation since the Thatcher–Howe administration took office and there is therefore no 'success' with the government's primary objective to offset the 5½–6 per cent fall in Gross Domestic Product and the 12–13 per cent decline in industrial production which, on the basis of my 'guesstimate', can be attributed to macroeconomic policy.**

**Typically, of course, GDP grows at some 'trend' rate. Contemporary fashion among economists puts this 'trend' at the very low**

**figure of 1.5–2.0 per cent per annum.** Clearly, since **1979:ii this 'trend' growth has been lost so that, in relation to 'trend', policy has reduced output by some 9½–10 per cent and industrial production by around 16–18 per cent. This is probably a better estimate of what the so-called 'transition costs' in terms of lost output have been thus far.**

As against this record – which is scarcely reassuring – has there been any 'progress' in 'creating conditions for the attainment of sustainable growth'?

Measuring the real rate of return on capital employed in industry and commerce (excluding oil) is – as usual – not free from ambiguity. In nominal terms profits in this area (excluding stock appreciation) are likely to be between £1¾ and £2¼ billions *below* 1979, which was some £0.9 billion *below* 1978. Thus nominal profits look like falling by around 16–18 per cent between 1979 and 1982 and by more than 20 per cent since 1978. Putting the rise in prices as low as 30 per cent suggests that, in a little over 2¼ years, real profits must have fallen by over 45 per cent and the real return on capital by a similar percentage. In 1979, according to the Bank of England, the pre-tax real rate of return was 4½–5 per cent. On this calculation it cannot now be much above 3 per cent and may even be lower.

Thus the rate of return, already unacceptably low in 1979, has been sharply reduced by government policy, which has, as a result, moved the economy further from any rate of return compatible with 'sustainable' growth.

The behaviour of 'competitiveness' is set out in Figure 3.2 in terms of the usual indicators calculated by the Control Statistical Office.

No extensive comment on Figure 3.2 is required since it is only too plain that:

(a)   'competitiveness' (defined in terms of relative normal unit labour costs) has declined considerably since the second quarter of 1979

while

(b)   a significant part of this decline has been due to the movement of the 'effective exchange rate'

According to the econometric model of the British economy constructed by the Treasury *both* the 'effective exchange rate' *and* the index of 'competitiveness' are highly responsive to British monetary policy. It thus seems reasonable to attribute 80 per cent or so of the

**Figure 3.2**

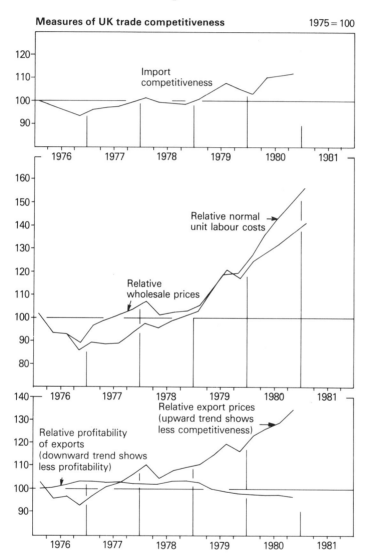

Measures of UK trade competitiveness      1975 = 100

Source: *Economic Trends* (various issues).

exchange-rate behaviour to government policy. Hence, to a significant but admittedly disputable extent, policy must have caused 'competitiveness' to fall from what it was in the second quarter of 1979 to a figure which is certainly below any level which could be regarded as consistent with 'sustainable' growth at a 'high' level of employment. Given the present position, even a small rise in output would sharply reduce the *current account* surplus.

Overall, therefore, what may be called the government's 'half-term' report, is decidedly dispiriting, for its policy has produced no gains in terms of reduced inflation while imposing extremely severe costs in terms of lost output and increased unemployment. At the same time the British economy, again as a result of policy, is even further from a level of 'competitiveness' and a rate of profit compatible with 'sustainable' growth at 'high' employment.

In short, if, as some would claim, the government's policy has been a success what, one wonders, would define failure?

**The shape of things to come: the prospects for 1982–4**

If the 'half-term' performance of the government's economic policy is, as we have argued, the reverse of successful, what are the prospects for the remainder of this Parliament? Ministers and their numerous apologists are currently arguing not only that all recessions are eventually followed by recoveries (a truism of bewildering unimportance), but that the recession is now (Sept–Oct 1981) virtually over. The future (it seems) is for a steady recovery culminating in some sort of 'economic miracle'. Unfortunately, ministers' forecasts are not very relevant. In what follows we rely upon those of the London Business School – a well-established research organisation which, as we have seen, is broadly monetarist in its approach to economic modelling and is typically sympathetic to the Thatcher–Howe experiment with monetarist gradualism. What is our future as the LBS foresees it? The more important elements in its forecasts of June 1981 are set out in the Table 3.5.

To remind readers of the limitations of economic forecasting Table 3.5 not only gives the latest available forecast (June 1981), but, for comparative purposes, the forecasts made in October 1980. As the reader can see, the revisions have not been negligible. Moreover, they have typically been in a pessimistic direction. Since most of the 'news' between June and September 1981 has been unhelpful, it seems very probable indeed that the next round of LBS forecasts (which will appear at the end of October) will incorporate further pessimistic revisions. (Since this chapter was written, the

**Table 3.5** *London Business School: economic forecasts, 1980–4*
SELECTED SERIES

| Variable | 1980 F.1 | 1980 Actual | 1981 F.1 | 1981 F.2 | 1982 F.1 | 1982 F.2 | 1983 F.1 | 1983 F.2 | 1984 F.1 | 1984 F.2 |
|---|---|---|---|---|---|---|---|---|---|---|
| Real GDP % change | -2.5 | -3.0 | -0.6 | -1.7 | 2.4 | 2.8 | 1.9 | 2.0 | 1.8 | 1.4 |
| Industrial prod. (index) | 108 | 105 | 107 | 100 | 110 | 103 | 111 | 104 | 112 | 104 |
| Unemployment, G.B. (excl. school-leavers) 000s of persons | 1547 | 1574 | 2000 | 2424 | 2174 | 2563 | 2226 | 2576 | 2266 | 2639 |
| Consumption goods prices % change | 16.9 | 15.6 | 12.0 | 10.5 | 8.5 | 8.9 | 6.5 | 8.1 | 6.4 | 8.8 |
| Average earnings % change | 16.7 | 17.8 | 12.8 | 10.8 | 11.0 | 9.2 | 7.5 | 9.7 | 7.6 | 10.6 |
| Labour cost per unit of output % change | 17.0 | 22.7 | 11.9 | 7.9 | 8.1 | 5.9 | 5.4 | 7.4 | 5.8 | 7.4 |
| Effective exchange rate % change | 9.2 | 10.0 | -6.9 | 2.2 | -4.7 | -6.1 | -4.1 | -6.4 | -4.1 | -6.7 |
| Current account balance £ millions | 121 | 2737 | -1379 | 3851 | -1412 | 1698 | -1521 | 1725 | -2645 | 1710 |
| Company profits* % change | -7.1 | 0.5 | -25.7 | -9.2 | 10.6 | 26.7 | 18.6 | 13.8 | -2.1 | 7.2 |

Definitions:  F.1 denotes forecasts published in October 1980.
F.2 denotes forecasts published in June 1981.
Actual denotes observed out-turn.

Note: * Excludes stock appreciation and North Sea oil.

Sources: *LBS Economic Outlook* (Oct 1980 and June 1981).

LBS forecasts for October 1981 have appeared. They do incorporate such revisions.) In short, Table 3.5 is probably an 'optimistic' version of our economic future as this is forecast by a marginally 'optimistic' forecasting group. As they stand the forecasts are depressing enough. Suitably discounted for probably excessive optimism, they offer very little comfort indeed.

Consider, for example, the government's overriding inflation objective. The rate of inflation is forecast to fall to close to 9 per cent in 1984. But, since this forecast was made, the prospects for inflation have worsened and the typical expectation is now for 'double-digit' inflation in 1982–4. If we give this its minimum value of 10 per cent then five years of monetarist gradualism will have left the observed rate of inflation virtually unchanged. This hardly suggests a policy 'success' – unless, of course, it is maintained that the famous lag in the response of the inflation rate to monetary restraint has simply proved to be rather longer than was originally believed. On this reading 'success' has only been delayed and will appear, if not in 1985, 1986 or 1987, then 'eventually'. This argument may comfort monetarist true believers. To others it may sound as unconvincing as I find it myself.

Between October 1980 and June 1981 and LBS revised *downwards* its forecast for growth in GDP and revised *upwards* its forecast of adult unemployment. It will be surprising if this type of revision is not repeated. For example, an output fall of only 1.7 per cent between 1980 and 1981 looks like an underestimate, just as growth of 2.8 per cent between 1981 and 1982 looks like an overestimate. But it is worth noting that, even if the LBS's June forecasts are accepted, unemployment (as defined) is forecast to rise by 200,000 by 1984. In this sense, therefore, the recession is forecast to become deeper and the level of output to fall further below capacity.

To summarise these forecasts rather crudely they suggest that five years of 'monetarist gradualism' will have, by 1984:

(i)     brought *no reduction* in the observed rate of inflation; but
(ii)    entailed a severe loss in output; and
(iii)   rather more than doubled the level of recorded unemployment – a statistic which contemporaneously understates the increase in the unemployed.

Thus though the transition costs have been very considerable, the transition to a lower rate of inflation is not forecast to occur until some future as yet unspecified date.

The LBS forecast for the value of profits (excluding stock appreciation) suggests that over 1978/9 to 1984 they will rise by some 30 per cent while prices will have risen by about 70 per cent. Hence real profits (excluding oil) will be 40 per cent or a little less lower in 1984 than in 1978/9 and, since the real capital stock has shown some increase, the real rate of return rather more than 40 per cent below its 1979 figure. Thus, by 1984, the pre-tax real rate of return will still be only about 3 per cent even though it seems likely that a rate more than twice this would be required to generate a rate of investment consistent with 'sustainable' growth at 'high' employment.

The LBS measures 'competitiveness' slightly differently from the Central Statistical Office. Very roughly its June 1981 forecasts suggest that, by 1984, international competitiveness will still be 15 per cent or so worse than in 1978 and perhaps 10 per cent worse than in 1979.II. Again very roughly, the level of 'competitiveness' will be close to what it was just prior to the Wilson–Callaghan devaluation of 1967 – a level demonstrably incompatible with 'sustainable' growth at any acceptable level of capacity utilisation and implying severe balance-of-payments (or exchange-rate) problems if the economy moved along such a path.

It is, of course, possible that the LBS's conditional forecasts convey a misleadingly pessimistic impression. But on recent experience this seems unlikely. My own forecasts would be more pessimistic about both growth (which I believe that the LBS overestimates in both 1982 and 1983) and unemployment (which I believe it underestimates). Equally it is quite possible that, precisely because 1982–4 looks so unappetising, macroeconomic policy will be significantly revised so that the LBS's forecasts, which are conditional upon its being maintained unchanged, are rendered irrelevant. But unless this happens I do not expect output in 1982 to grow at much above 1 per cent. The Treasury (November 1981) forecast, which has just been published, forecasts 1 per cent growth.

**However, if the LBS's estimates are even approximately correct, the only possible conclusion is that monetarist gradualism – at least as interpreted by the Thatcher–Howe administration – will, by 1984, have proved itself to be an unambiguous and extremely costly failure.**

The judgement, it should be noted, harsh as it is, takes no explicit account of the fact that not all the costs imposed by the policy are

*transitional*. Some must have a 'permanent' or 'long-run' component in the damage done to both real capital (in particular the roads,
the railway system and the housing stock) and human capital. Con-
ceivably there will also be additional damage to the country's
already appalling industrial relations. These 'long-run' costs are
unquantifiable. But this does not mean that they are not highly
significant.

### Conclusions

If the economic forecasters are approximately correct, it is impossible to escape the conclusion that five years of the Thatcher–Howe
version of monetarism will have achieved, at very considerable
costs, (a) no progress in its attack on inflation and (b) negative progress in its attempt to establish conditions consistent with 'sustainable' growth at 'high employment'. Additionally, the economy will
not be operating at 'high employment' but (probably) with close to 3
millions unemployed. Pressing understatement to the very limit if
not beyond I have categorised this outcome as a costly failure.
Others less dedicated to describing a bloody shovel as a spade might
call it as a disaster. But whatever it is called, our present prospects
do raise an important question: how did such a policy ever come to
be accepted?

The answer to this question really requires a sizeable monograph
rather than a few short paragraphs. Nevertheless I would argue that
the adoption of Thatcher–Howe monetarism is simply one more
illustration of the intellectual (and moral?) bankruptcy of the
British establishment and its consequential attachment to panaceas.
At the political level, the rise of the SDP has some of the same
characteristics since its main appeal, at least at the moment, is that it
is *not* either of the two intellectually bankrupt major parties.

The attachment of the British establishment to panaceas is notori-
ous. In the immediate post-war period the fashionable panacea was
'socialist planning'. From 1951 to 1961/2 this was replaced by
'market processes' and 'the salutary discipline of interest rates'. As
these gradually failed to produce the magical miracle cure, the
fashionable dogma became 'indicative planning', even though it was
never entirely clear precisely what this was. By the beginning of the
1970s 'indicative planning' was losing ground. 'Market processes'
were back in favour and these, plus entry into the EEC (even on

dubious terms) were to produce the promised economic miracle. None of these – like their more familiar successors – came even close to meeting expectations. I believe that this is because none of them reflected a coherent and empirically well-grounded analysis of Britain's economic problems and a serious attempt to grapple with them. Rather, like the late Mr Maudling's 'dash for growth' or the later Heath–Barber monetary explosion, they were attractive short-term expedients which could, at a pinch, be defended on the basis of some currently fashionable doctrine even though there might be little empirical evidence to support it.

I believe that the main function of these panaceas was evasion. Their purpose was to sustain the illusion that Britain did *not* have deep-seated and long-run problems which were difficult to diagnose and even more difficult to treat. For what the 'panacea approach' essentially asserted was that provided we adopted 'indicative planning' or 'EEC entry' or 'monetarist gradualism' or whatever the current panacea happened to be, there was no need to do anything else. Those who suggested the contrary were alarmist and irresponsible.

Thus we were expected to believe – and many of us did believe – that with a panacea and a prayer – and, of course, the leadership provided by the 'establishment', our problems, whatever they were, would go away. Unfortunately they did nothing of the kind. They remained and, in many cases, got worse.

I believe that Britain's contemporary macroeconomic policy is primarily one more example of the same sad tradition. Thatcher–Howe 'monetarist gradualism' is no less a dogmatic evasion because, unlike most of the previous panaceas, its immediate consequences are unpleasant. The obsession with inflation is a useful means of persuading otherwise sensible people that it does not *really* matter that we have an overvalued pound, a non-viable rate of return on real capital, abysmal (and probably worsening) industrial relations, inadequate standards of management, a deteriorating infrastructure and an economy operating with around 15–20 per cent of excess industrial capacity. All we have to do is to control sterling $M_3$ hard enough, drive unemployment high enough, keep the Public Sector Borrowing Requirement down enough, pray fervently enough and do all three for long enough and *this time* the magical miracle cure *will work* and our problems *will* go away.

Without wishing to be unduly cynical, I must record that I doubt it.

## Bibliography

Readers who wish to supplement the discussion in this chapter are recommended to consult the following sources:

1. Official Reports
   House of Commons Treasury and Civil Service Committee
   3rd Report on Monetary Control
      Vol. I.   Report (713–I) of 1979–80.
      Vol. II.   Appendices (713–II) of 1979–80.
   Memoranda on Monetary Policy, Vol.  I (720   ) of 1979–80.
   Memoranda on Monetary Policy, Vol. II (720–1) of 1979–80.
   3rd Report on Monetary Policy
      Vol.  I   Report on Monetary Policy (163–1) of 1980–1.
      Vol.  II   Minutes of Evidence (163–2) of 1980–1.
      Vol. III   Appendices (163–3) of 1980–1.

2. For continuing analysis, commentary and forecasts
   HM Treasury Forecasts, each November and accompanying the Budget.
   *National Institute Economic Review* (quarterly).
   *Economic Outlook* (published by the London Business School) (quarterly).

3. For commentary, analysis and statistical material
   *Bank of England Quarterly Bulletin.*
   *Midland Bank Review* (quarterly).
   *Economic Trends* (published monthly by HMSO).

## INTRODUCTION TO CHAPTER 4

It may seem from previous chapters – and for that matter from the one that follows – that economists at Southampton are a fairly pessimistic lot. Although their lines of argument are slightly different the authors are unanimous in their belief that economic policies have, more often than not, been based on misguided ideas or formed with insufficient supportive evidence.

This theme is particularly apparent in the next chapter, by Michael Wickens. He argues that some economists have been too keen to advise governments to implement policies when there was only scant evidence on the likely outcome of such policies. Equally, governments have been too keen to implement radical policy changes with little idea of how the market mechanism operates, a theme already prominent in the previous two chapters. Of course, there are differences. Wickens is sceptical about the efficiency of incomes policies, advocated in Chapter 2 by Hawkins. He believes that increases in the money stock have generated the current inflation whereas Hawkins believes that the cause has been claims by workers for higher wage settlements.

This conflict of views is not based on a difference of logic. Wickens argues that given the way we *do* behave, incomes policies get little support and therefore are not very successful at holding down wages and prices. Hawkins argument is that we should seek ways to *change* the way we do behave, to gain support for incomes policies, which could then cure our underlying economic problems. Alternatively he argues that governments could reduce the power of organised labour so that it was less able to frustrate the working of incomes policies.

An important contribution of Wickens's chapter is a further clarification of the Keynesian approach to economic policy and the subdividing of the monetarist school into two groups: (a) the gradualists and (b) the so-called modern classical school.

C. H. and G. M.

# 4   What Inflation has Revealed about the Formulation of Economic Policy

*by Michael Wickens*

> As the new year looms one should spare a thought for the Chancellor
> of the Exchequer, Sir Geoffrey Howe, who has an unenviable task.
> He has to think up a new economic policy. And fast.
>
> (*The Guardian*, 29 December 1981)

### Introduction

The role of the state in economic life has fluctuated over the
centuries, but our present attitude to government intervention in
the economy is largely a result of Keynes's analysis of the 1930s
depression. Observing the failure of the economic system to eliminate unemployment sufficiently rapidly, Keynes provided a
rationale for government intervention designed to stabilise the
economy more quickly. Although Keynes was principally concerned with the maintenance of full employment, governments are
now also charged with the responsibility for controlling inflation,
achieving a steady growth of the standard of living and preserving
the value of the currency.

With the benefit of hindsight the early years of the application of
Keynesian demand management policy, in the 1950s and the beginning of the 1960s, now appears to have been remarkably successful.
However, from the mid-1960s onwards a number of problems have
arisen with the performance of the economy which have led to the
search for alternative policies; monetarist policy is one such alternative. Dissatisfied with both Keynesian and monetarist policies,
recently a number of economists have begun to question the feasi-
bility of governments to stabilise the economy by active intervention. Although it is too early to come to a definitive judgement on

the merits of this sceptical view of government's ability to control the economy, an understanding of how and why previous policies have failed will help us to appreciate better the reasons for such a radical reappraisal of stabilisation policy and may provide some lessons for the future conduct of policy.

In this chapter I shall examine the proposition that excessive reliance has been placed on the government's ability to control the economy. A more realistic assessment of the role of government would recognise our lack of knowledge of how the economy works, especially in the short run, and would recognise that governments lack the means to control the economy. Accepting such a proposition implies that we should no longer bestow office on the party which makes the most exaggerated promises of rapidly changing the course of the economy in order to achieve full employment, economic growth and the control of inflation. It does not, however, imply that there is no role for government. At a minimum, government is required to promote the efficient performance of the economy by, for example, legislating against monopoly and pollution and by providing collective (or public) goods such as defence, education and health. It should also temper economic efficiency with justice by providing social welfare. Nor does this view preclude government from carrying out some degree of stabilisation; it simply asserts that less intervention will probably be better for the economy than the level that has prevailed for the past thirty years.

I shall illustrate this argument by a detailed examination of inflation and its control. The importance attached to the control of inflation has varied considerably over time, as have the economic explanations of inflation and the choice of anti-inflation policy. I shall, however, begin by examining Keynes's analysis of the 1930s, the reasons why he advocated interventionist economic policies and how this legacy influenced post-war economic management.

As some of the economics in this chapter has been introduced in Chapter 1, the reader will need to read that first.

## The legacy of Keynes

Before the present government, all British post-war governments have given priority in economic policy to maintaining full employment. The present Conservative government are the exception in giving priority to controlling inflation. In its evidence to the Treasury and Civil Service Committee on Monetary Policy in June 1980, the Treasury stated that

> governments themselves cannot ensure high employment, so that it would be misleading to present the change of emphasis in objectives as 'ending the post-war commitment to high employment'. Governments can create the *conditions* in which it can be achieved, but *whether it is* achieved depends on the responses of management and labour.

Laying responsibility for the maintenance of full employment on governments is usually associated with the economics of J. M. Keynes. Writing in the 1930s, with the experience of the great depression in mind, Keynes concluded that the economic system will not by itself eliminate unemployment and that government intervention was required. According to Keynes unemployment is due to a lack of demand for labour rather than to voluntary withdrawal from work. In a self-stabilising economic system prices, wages and interest rates would adjust in such a way – probably downwards – that it would become profitable to increase employment levels. Keynes argued that prices and wages, in particular, were not sufficiently flexible downwards in the short or medium term to permit such an automatic adjustment. Moreover, even if they were flexible, uncertainty about the future would deter increased investment.

**Due to the stickiness of prices and wages and to uncertainty, Keynes recommended that the government should intervene by raising aggregate demand through increased public investment**. This would then generate higher employment. He doubted the effectiveness of tax cuts to raise aggregate demand sufficiently because the public would be likely to assume they were only temporary. Moreover, he rejected the use of monetary policy because he saw the transmission mechanism as operating through lower interest rates inducing higher investment and he doubted whether this would be a very effective way of increasing investment in a slump for two reasons. First, Keynes thought it would be difficult to reduce interest rates sufficiently, since in a depression interest rates are low and people tend to expect interest rates to rise. Hence increases in the supply of money will simply be hoarded by people in the expectation of being able to make speculative gains after the rise in interest rates. This phenomenon is known as the Liquidity Trap. Second, and more important, uncertainty about the future in a depression tends to reduce the responsiveness of investment to changes in interest rates. Keynes thought that monetary policy would be more likely to be effective in controlling investment in a boom by inducing high interest rates.

Keynes's analysis of the failure of the economic system to be self-stabilising, his conclusion that governments should intervene to restore full employment and his recommendation that this intervention should consist of the management of aggregate demand through public capital expenditure has provided the intellectual foundation for nearly all of British post-war economic policy and, to a lesser extent, for the economic policy in most other developed economics. Subsequent refinements have led to a policy of continuous intervention – known as fine-tuning or, to use one of the currently popular nautical metaphors, a touch of the tiller – and to a broadening of policy instruments to include public expenditure on consumption and services, variations in tax revenue through changing direct and indirect tax rates and investment allowances and grants.

Prior to 1967 demand management appeared to be remarkably successful in reducing the size of economic fluctuations. From

**Figure 4.1**  *Unemployment in Britain*

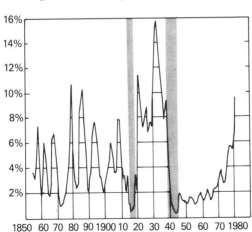

Figure 4.1 it can be seen that, in contrast to the years preceding 1940, the unemployment rate in Britain in the post-war years was approximately 2 per cent or less. During this period total output grew at an average rate of 3 per cent per annum and, apart from 1951 and 1952 – a period influenced by the Korean War – it can be seen from Figure 4.2 that inflation did not exceed 5 per cent per annum. Not surprisingly in the mid-1960s, large-scale unemployment was regarded as a thing of the past. Having solved the problem of unemployment it was thought that economic policy should concentrate on refinements which would prevent the 'stop–go' cycle. If the economy recovered too fast from the recession under the stimulus of frequently mistimed and excessive injections of aggregate demand, then because domestic output was unable to increase sufficiently quickly to satisfy the increased demand, imports grew faster than exports leading to a net drain on international reserves. This precipitated a balance-of-payments crisis and necessitated a reverse of policy to one of deflation in order to reduce imports and thereby preserve the value of the currency.

At the present time it is difficult not to look back on the success of the post-war British economy prior to 1967 with a certain envy and nostalgia. But after 1967, shortly after the Keynesian hegemony had extended to the USA in the Kennedy–Johnson years, Keynesian economic policy began to break down. The interesting question is whether this period of stability was due to the choice of economic policy or to the absence of large shocks to the domestic and world economies.

## The problem of inflation

The principal sources of dissatisfaction with economic policy in the late 1960s and early 1970s were the failure to achieve sustained economic growth due to the 'stop–go' cycle and the failure to control inflation. One of the contributory factors to the 22 per cent inflation rate in 1975 was the determined attempt by the Heath government to achieve long-term growth in the early 1970s – the so-called 'dash-for-growth'. As the economic experience of the 1970s accumulated inflation came to be seen as the dominant problem. The present Conservative government's priority for controlling inflation is an outcome of this process.

In large part the cause of inflation in the 1970s may be traced back to Keynes's diagnosis in the 1930s. When Keynes was writing *The*

87

**Figure 4.2** *British and US inflation percentage (annual rates)*

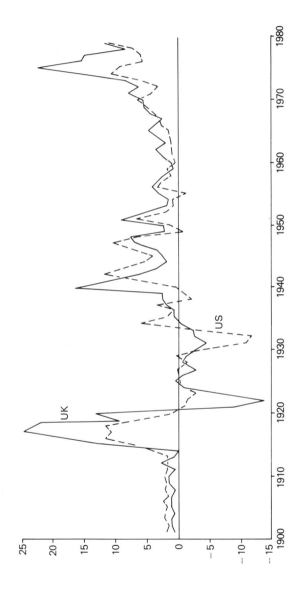

*General Theory of Employment, Interest and Money* unemployment was the dominant issue, not inflation; in general prices were falling in the 1930s, not rising. For Keynes the main economic problem was that aggregate demand was not sufficient to employ all those who wished to work. As a result of the inflationary experience of the last ten years and the low levels of output growth over this period, emphasis has moved towards interpreting the problems of the British economy as the result of a failure to supply goods at the right price and at the right time. Figure 4.3 shows how since 1973 most of the increase in total (*nominal*) expenditure has been due to a rise in the price level rather than to a rise in output. Thus one of the main weaknesses of the analysis of Keynes as seen from the perspective of the post-war years is his almost entire neglect of the supply-side of the economy.

**Figure 4.3**    *The price level and GDP in Britain*

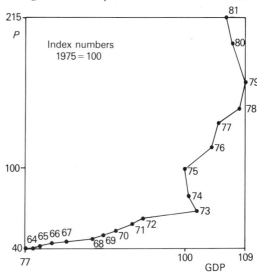

In most of his writings Keynes assumed that inflation was only likely to occur if the economy was operating at or near to full employment. Since this was not a likely contingency in the 1930s Keynes did not concern himself with the problem of inflation. He was willing to accept the prevailing theory known as the Quantity Theory of Money which asserts that at full-employment inflation is due entirely to the growth of the quantity of money in the economy. In *How to Pay for the War* (1940) Keynes argued that in a fully employed economy inflation was due to an excess of (nominal) demand over supply with the implication that the control of inflation requires a reduction in the pressure of demand. Keynes did not therefore provide a theory of inflation when the economy was operating at less than full employment.

**The Phillips curve**

The gap in the theory of Keynes caused by the absence of an explanation of inflation was filled in 1958 by A. W. Phillips, who showed that an empirical relationship could be found between the rate of growth of money wages and the rate of the unemployment based on data for the period 1861–1913 and this provided a very good explanation of the corresponding data for the period 1919–58. Figure 4.4 illustrates the 1861–1913 relationship (the Phillips curve), with the data for the later period also plotted for comparison.

**Figure 4.4**   *The Phillips curve from 1861 to 1913 and data 1923 to 1958*

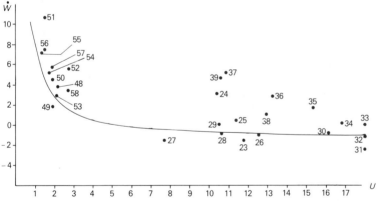

The curve should be interpreted as implying that the greater the rate of unemployment, the lower the rate of wage inflation. Unemployment was assumed by Phillips to reflect pressure on the demand for labour relative to the supply of labour, i.e. unemployment measures the 'tightness' of the labour market. The connection between aggregate expenditure and the unemployment rate is viewed as follows. Increased expenditure on goods would increase the supply of goods and hence the demand for labour to produce these goods, which in turn would reduce unemployment. In this way increased expenditure can once more cause inflation.

This remarkable empirical regularity stretching over a period of nearly one hundred years has proved to be one of the milestones of post-war economics. Not only did it provide the link missing in Keynes's work between the real and nominal sides of the economy (i.e. between output and prices), but it also appeared to demonstrate the extraordinary power of empirical methods in economics and confirmed the possibility of providing a sound statistical basis for economic knowledge. Under the influence of the methodology of Popper, R. G. Lipsey recast the Phillips curve as a testable scientific theory whose predictions were not falsified by the data. In doing so he gave impetus to the claims of economics as a science and to policy-making as an activity requiring careful measurement.

The policy advice drawn from the Phillips curve was that inflation could be controlled by selecting the appropriate rate of unemployment. It was argued that this could be achieved by the management of the aggregate demand for goods, i.e. of total expenditure. But at the same time as it opened one gate the Phillips curve closed another, for it also implies that only certain combinations of wage inflation and unemployment are attainable, namely those combinations on the curve. In particular, lower wage inflation *and* lower unemployment rates are unobtainable. Nevertheless, from time to time, governments have, through the use of incomes policy, attempted to improve on the trade-off and achieve lower levels of both. More will be said about these attempts later.

The Phillips curve implies that there is no other influence on wage inflation than the balance of demand and supply in the labour market and this can be satisfactorily measured by the unemployment rate. It was shown by Lipsey, however, that wage inflation would not only be influenced by the level of unemployment, but also by the rate of growth of commodity prices, i.e. by price inflation. According to Lipsey, at each rate of unemployment, a rise in the rate of price inflation would increase the rate of wage inflation. This implies that there is a separate Phillips curve for each rate of price inflation.

It may be helpful to illustrate these arguments using a diagram. In

Figure 4.5 the axes are $\dot{W}$, the rate of change of money wages (a dot over a variable denotes that it is the rate at which that variable is changing that is being represented), and $U$, the unemployment rate. The line $AA$ represents the Phillips curve and depicts attainable combinations of $\dot{W}$ and $U$. Following the argument above, each Phillips curve is associated with a different level of price inflation, $\dot{P}$. The line $AA$ is the appropriate Phillips curve when the rate of inflation is $\dot{P}_A$ and the line $BB$ is the corresponding curve when inflation is $\dot{P}_B$ – note that $\dot{P}_B$ is assumed to be greater than $\dot{P}_A$ (i.e. $\dot{P}_B > \dot{P}_A$). Thus the higher the rate of inflation, the further to the right (or the further above) is the Phillips curve. Put another way, an increase in the rate of inflation will shift the curve to the right.

**Figure 4.5** *The effect of price changes on the Phillips curve*

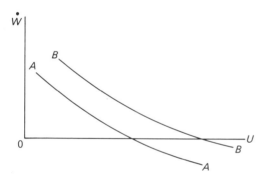

Having drawn a distinction between wage and price inflation it may seem from the amended Phillips curve that wage inflation can be controlled by a suitable choice of price inflation. Attempts to hold down nationalised industry prices and the setting up of government bodies to watch over prices are examples of policies that appear to be based on this principle. These policies are, however, doomed to failure except in the very short run. If costs are rising, then, unless firms can use factor inputs more efficiently through increased productivity, the need to maintain profit margins (or avoid losses) will force up prices. Nationalised industries often find that as a result of government policy to hold down their prices, they have large trading losses which are then met out of the Exchequer, i.e. out of taxation or by reduced public expenditure elsewhere or by increased government borrowing.

This suggests that the interrelationship between wages and prices is more complicated than first thought. Not only may wage changes be influenced by price changes; price variations may at the same time be influenced by wages. Assuming that the principal sources of costs are wage costs and imported raw materials, it is possible to explain price inflation as the combined result of wage inflation and the rate of change of import prices. Since wage inflation is determined in part by price inflation, and price inflation is determined in part by wage inflation, an increase in *either* wages *or* prices, from whatever source, will raise *both* wages and prices, setting up what is sometimes called a wage–price spiral.

A flow diagram may assist in following this interdependence and also in seeing how changes in unemployment and the rate of change of import prices affect wages and prices. Figure 4.6 depicts the basic Phillips relationship and indicates that wage inflation is determined by unemployment. The arrow shows the direction of causation.

**Figure 4.6**    *The Phillips curve*

Lipsey's amendment to the Phillips curve includes price inflation as an additional determinant of wage inflation. This is depicted in Figure 4.7.

**Figure 4.7**    *Lipsey's relationship*

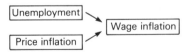

Price inflation is determined by wage inflation and the inflation of import prices and this is depicted in Figure 4.8.

**Figure 4.8**    *Price determination*

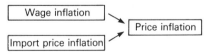

The interdependence of the determination of wage inflation and price inflation can be represented by combining Figures 4.7 and 4.8 to give Figure 4.9.

**Figure 4.9**  *Joint determination of wage and price inflation*

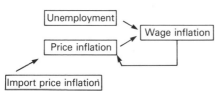

Figure 4.9 shows that a change in the rate of unemployment changes wage inflation, which in turn changes price inflation and this once again changes wage inflation, thereby setting up the wage–price spiral. A change in import prices begins the spiral by causing a change in commodity prices when then changes wages, etc. Thus unemployment and import prices are the underlying determinants of both wage and price inflation. **Failure to understand the interdependence of wages and prices has led to much wasted effort trying to identify whether it is changes in wages which cause changes in prices or vice versa**. Having apparently identified which causes which, a legislative constraint is then often imposed on the offender. As the analysis above has shown, however, neither is the ultimate cause of the other; in the end they are both the result of changes in other factors.

This point can be illustrated first by considering the way rising import prices may have caused inflation. A common explanation of the high levels of inflation in 1974 and 1975 is the rise in import prices in 1973 and 1974 following a general rise in commodity prices and especially in oil prices. The rate of change of import prices jumped from 5 per cent in 1972 to 28 per cent in 1973 and to 46 per cent in 1974. Oil prices rose by 337 per cent in 1974 and other commodity prices rose by 72 per cent in 1973 (also oil prices rose by 112 per cent in 1979). On the face of it there would seem to be little doubt that this explanation of inflation in Britain in 1979 and 1975 was justified. Yet a note of caution should be sounded because the very fact that all commodity prices more or less rose together suggests that commodity prices, whilst not necessarily under the control of any one country, and certainly not Britain, are nevertheless responding to something else. More will be said about this later.

The influence of unemployment on inflation is more complicated. It was explained earlier that the unemployment rate is a proxy for the tightness of the labour market and it has been shown that an increased tightness of the labour market reduces unemployment and hence increases both wages and prices. It was also explained that the labour market will tighten if there is an increase in the demand for labour relative to supply due, say, to an increase in the demand for goods and services for which more employment is required to help the supply of goods to meet the increased demand. In general these factors can be summarised as demand influences on inflation because they are transmitted through the demand for labour. There are, however, corresponding influences which are transmitted through the supply of labour.

It is a common view that trade unions cause inflation by excessive wage claims. Whatever the merits of this view, it has to be analysed very carefully because there are many pitfalls for the unwary. Within the analytic framework developed above there are two ways in which trade unions can cause inflation. First, they can alter the rate of unemployment by reducing the amount of labour supplied at every wage rate. In this way, the supply of labour may influence the rate of inflation. Second, they can affect inflation directly by acting as a third factor independent of and in addition to the other two factors, the unemployment rate and the rate of change of import prices. The trap into which it is easy to fall is to argue that just because unions appear to be more active in pushing wage claims this is necessarily an independent cause of inflation. Much of trade union activity in seeking rises in wages is simply a response to rising prices and is designed to preserve the real wages – living standards – of its members. Such behaviour cannot be regarded as a cause of inflation, but simply a response to it; they are part of the process by which price rises are transmitted to wages. In terms of the above analysis, following a shift in the demand for labour associated with the rise in the price level, unions cause a corresponding shift in the supply of labour which leaves unemployment more or less unchanged.

If trade unions are to be shown to be a cause of inflation rather than a part of the transmission process, then it must be established that they have an influence either on unemployment or, for example, directly on the Phillips curve. Since this issue is pursued in some detail in Chapter 2, it is not necessary to dwell further on it here. My own view is that there is little evidence to support the existence of an independent trade union influence operating through either of these two channels. Although it can be shown that strike activity is positively correlated with inflation, it is difficult to find well-corroborated evidence that strikes, or any other measure of union 'pushfulness', has an *additional* influence on inflation in the Phillips-curve function. The reason for this is that such measures of union activity appear themselves to be almost entirely a response to prevailing market forces which have already been represented in the Phillips curve. In contrast, unions seem to have had more influence on the distribution of income; stronger unions such as the NUM are better able to maintain and increase real wages than weaker unions. There is, however, no evidence that these distributional changes have greatly affected the general level of price increases.

To summarise the argument up to this point, anti-inflation policy within the Keynesian economic framework has been based largely upon the Phillips curve and its extension. According to this view there is a stable long-run trade-off between inflation and unemployment. The principal means of controlling inflation is seen to be through demand management of the rate of unemployment. Nevertheless there may be external forces such as rising import prices which are driving up inflation and which the government can do little about. Thus with the addition of the Phillips curve Keynes's economic theory is complete. Through demand management persistently high levels of unemployment can be prevented, but choosing too low a level of unemployment will cause unacceptably high levels of inflation. Provided the chosen combination is compatible with the Phillips curve, the particular choice is a political matter.

**Monetarism**

If the Keynesian view of the world is correct, how then did high levels of inflation and unemployment occur simultaneously? How did the economy move from unemployment rates of 2 per cent or less and inflation rates of 5 per cent or less which prevailed prior to 1967 to unemployment and inflation rates both over 10 per cent in 1981? Was it due (1) to mismanagement of the economy, (2) to using the wrong economic theory, or (3) to a change in the behaviour of the economy possibly induced by the changes brought about by the economic policies themselves? There are proponents of all three views; indeed some hold the three views at the same time. It is only too easy for economists to blame mismanagement since this places the responsibility on others. Whilst this may have some part to play, I propose to focus attention on the other two causes, both of which are due mainly to lack of understanding about how the economy works.

At the present time the principal alternative to Keynesian economics is monetarist economics. There are many different versions of monetarism, but in volume 1 of its *Report on Monetary Policy* published in 1981 the Treasury and Civil Service Committee identified two broad strands which it called gradualism and the New Classical School. The two groups share the view that unemployment is not a failure of demand but of supply, and that inflation is primarily due to excessive growth of the money supply. However, they differ in their policy prescriptions.

*Gradualism*

The basis of the gradualist position is a denial of the Keynesian proposition that a government can reduce unemployment by increasing its expenditure. According to the gradualists the outcome would be higher inflation with unemployment unaffected. They argue that there is no long-run trade-off between inflation and unemployment of the sort envisaged by Keynesians. In so far as such a trade-off exists, they claim it is only in the short run and is due to workers' misperceptions about the inflation rate. In terms of the previous analysis of the Phillips curve the gradualists would replace actual price inflation as a determinant of wage inflation by expected price inflation and argue that it is expected and not actual price inflation that determines wage inflation. In the short run, due to misperceptions, expected inflation will typically lag behind actual inflation, i.e. people adjust their expectations slowly as information becomes available.

In order to illustrate the difference between the gradualist and the Phillips-curve analysis consider the effect of an attempt by the government to reduce the rate of unemployment. For convenience assume that initially the rates of wage inflation, actual price inflation and expected price inflation are all zero. The Phillips curve corresponding to these assumptions is depicted as the line $AA$ in Figure 4.10.

**Figure 4.10** *The Phillips curve and the natural-rate hypothesis*

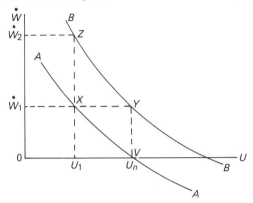

The rate of unemployment, initially at $U_n$, is reduced by the government to $U_1$ causing a rise in wage inflation from zero to $\dot{W}_1$. Thus the economy moves from point $V$ to point $X$. The rise in wage inflation will cause an increase in price inflation as before; in turn this will cause expected price inflation to rise and will shift the Phillips curve to the right.

When expected equals actual inflation, i.e. when inflation is fully anticipated, it is assumed that the Phillips curve will have shifted to $BB$. If the government abandons its attempt to reduce unemployment then the economy will settle down again at point $Y$, at the original level of unemployment but a higher rate of wage inflation $\dot{W}_1$ and by implication a correspondingly higher rate of price inflation. If, on the other hand, the government maintains its desire to reduce unemployment to $U_1$ then wage inflation will rise to $\dot{W}_2$. This will induce a further upward shift in the Phillips curve. Continuation of the policy of maintaining unemployment at $U_1$ will simply result in an ever-accelerating inflation rate. Eventually the government would probably be forced to abandon this policy and allow unemployment to return to $U_n$, but by then inflation would be very much higher and would be permanent unless policies are introduced to reduce it. Thus in the long run the Phillips curve is vertical at $U_n$, i.e. there is no trade-off in the long run, the unemployment rate has no permanent effect on inflation.

The level of unemployment to which the economy returns is called the *natural rate of unemployment*, hence the name given to this theory of inflation, the *natural-rate hypothesis*. The natural rate of unemployment is assumed to be roughly constant and to be due largely to workers searching for acceptable jobs. Thus unemployment is assumed to be voluntary and not involuntary as argued by Keynes.

**Figure 4.11**   *Wage change and unemployment, 1964–81*

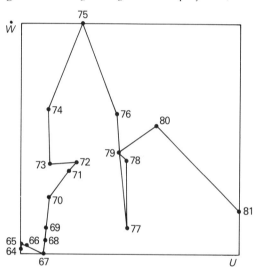

How well does the natural-rate hypothesis explain inflation in Britain? In Figure 4.11 the rate of wage inflation is plotted against the unemployment rate for the period 1964–81. It is apparent that there is no discernible long-run trade-off of the sort found by Phillips for the previous one hundred years. For the period 1964–75 the Phillips curve appears to be vertical in the way described by the natural-rate hypothesis. However, after 1975, unemployment has risen markedly in a way not consistent with the natural-rate hypothesis; to be consistent with it this rise would need to be attributed to an increase in the natural rate of unemployment when the vertical line in Figure 4.10 moves to the right. This is in fact the claim of proponents of the theory. But such a recourse would seem to destroy the very basis of the theory, because if the natural rate of unemployment rises more or less in line with the actual rate of un-employment then there is little value in the concept.

In a speech to the Labour Party Conference in September 1976, following the period 1964–75 when the natural-rate hypothesis seemed to hold best, the Prime Minister, Mr Callaghan, said

> We used to think that we could just spend our way out of a reces-sion, and increase employment, by cutting taxes and boosting government spending. I tell you in all candour that that option no longer exists, and that in so far as it ever did exist, it worked by injecting inflation into the economy. And each time that hap-pened, the average level of unemployment has risen. Higher inflation, followed by higher unemployment. That is the history of the last 20 years.

A similar position was adopted by Sir Keith Joseph in a speech in Preston in 1975. He argued that post-war policies have tried to maintain full employment by expanding demand through deficit financing without giving sufficient consideration to supply factors such as wage levels, labour mobility, productivity, efficiency, pro-fitability and competitiveness. As a result full employment had been maintained only temporarily. Shortly after an expansion of demand, shortages appear which drive up prices, increase imports and lead to a fall in employment. Continued attempts to maintain full employment by expanding demand in this way, without the requisite attention to supply simply result in accelerating inflation with no alleviation of unemployment.

The power of economists to influence government thinking can hardly be better illustrated than this. The political complexion of the party seems to be no barrier to the influence of economic ideas.

The gradualists replace the Keynesian explanation of inflation by a modern version of the Quantity Theory of Money (see p. 15), which asserts that inflation is due to excessive monetary growth even when the economy is at less than full employment. The classi-cal Quantity Theory of Money subscribed to by Keynes assumed full employment. The principal architect of the modern version is Milton Friedman. According to Friedman:

> Inflation occurs when the quantity of money rises appreciably more rapidly than output, and the more rapid the rise in the

quantity of money per unit of output, the greater the rate of inflation. There is probably no other proposition in economics that is as well established as this one. (Milton Friedman and Rose Friedman, *Freedom to Choose*, Penguin, 1980, p. 299.)

Friedman maintains that although there is no one-to-one correspondence between the rate of monetary growth and the rate of inflation

there is no example in history of a substantial inflation that lasted for more than a brief time that was not accompanied by a roughly correspondingly rapid increase in the quantity of money; and no example of a rapid increase in the quantity of money that was not accompanied by a roughly correspondingly substantial inflation. (Friedman and Friedman, p. 300).

Friedman's policy prescription for inflation is as uncompromising as his diagnosis:

The cure for inflation is simple to state but hard to implement. Just as an excessive increase in the quantity of money is the one and only important cause of inflation, so a reduction in the rate of monetary growth is the one and only cure for inflation. (Friedman and Friedman, p. 316).

One of the reasons why Friedman attributes more influence to monetary effects than did Keynes is because Friedman does not share Keynes's view that the transmission mechanism of monetary policy is mainly via the effect of lower interest rates on investment expenditures. Whereas Keynes saw money as an alternative to holding *financial assets* Friedman regards expenditure on *goods* as an important alternative to holding money. Thus for Friedman excess money balances are spent directly on goods thereby raising aggregate demand very quickly. Keynes believed that excess money balances will drive down interest rates and induce increased investment expenditure. As it takes on average eighteen months for investment to respond to a change in the cost of capital, Keynes's transmission mechanism of monetary policy is too slow for short-term stabilisation of the economy and, as was argued earlier, in a recession is too uncertain.

The focus of attention of Keynes's analysis is the goods market and in particular on aggregate demand. In contrast, Friedman emphasises the role of the money market. He argues that the demand for money is more stable than the demand for goods and that the supply of money is an exogenous variable under the control of the government. An increase in the supply of money will cause money supply to exceed money demand and the excess money will be spent. Temporarily output will then increase, but in the longer run the whole effect will be felt by a rise in prices. The rise in prices will raise the demand for money and equate demand with supply once more but now with a higher price level. Thus continuous injections of money will simply cause inflation.

**Table 4.1** *Money growth and inflation in the major industrial nations 1975–80*

| Country | Annual rates of money growth[1] | Annual rates of inflation[2] |
|---|---|---|
| | % | % |
| Italy | 20.5 | 17.1 |
| United Kingdom | 12.3 | 13.7 |
| France | 10.0 | 10.7 |
| West Germany | 7.8 | 4.1 |
| USA | 7.5 | 9.1 |
| Canada | 7.5 | 9.0 |
| Japan | 7.2 | 6.3 |
| Netherlands | 6.8 | 5.8 |
| Switzerland | 5.3 | 2.5 |

[1] $M_1$ for all countries execpt the USA, where a slightly different measure used.

[2] Consumer price index used as a measure of inflation.

There is a considerable amount of evidence in support of this version of the Quantity Theory of Money. Two pieces of evidence will be offered here. The first is Table 4.1, which shows the average annual rates of growth of the money supply and the corresponding rates of inflation in nine major OECD countries over the period 1975–80. This evidence suggests that over fairly long periods a country's inflation rate is highly correlated with its rate of monetary growth (the correlation coefficient is 0.89). The second piece of evidence is Figure 4.12. This refers to Britain alone and shows the rate of growth of the M₃ definition of the money supply and the inflation rate. The figure shows that there is, as Friedman claims, a lag of approximately two years between changes in the rate of money growth and changes in the inflation rate.

**Figure 4.12**    *Money growth and inflation in Britain*

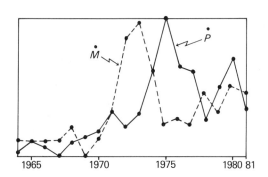

It is interesting to ask two questions at this point. If it were true that inflation is caused by excessive monetary growth how is it that an excess demand for labour would cause inflation even temporarily? And how can inflation be due to rising import prices? In so far as the excess demand for labour is due to excess money balances being spent on goods there is no conflict. The short-run Phillips curve simply reflects the transmission of monetary influences. If, on the other hand, excess demand for labour is caused by a reduction in the supply of labour at the old wage rate due to higher wage claims, then wages will actually rise only if firms are able to borrow more money to pay for the wage increase. This will be possible if the government 'validates' the wage rise by increasing the supply of money.

It can also be argued that rising labour costs only cause inflation in so far as there is an accommodating increase in the supply of money. A demand for higher pay can be interpreted as a decrease in the supply of labour at the existing level of wages. Such a decrease in the supply of labour will cause an excess demand for labour, and hence an increase in wages and the inflation rate, as before. The difference here is that in order to pay for the wage increase firms may need to borrow money from the banks. If banks supply money to firms to pay the wage increase then there may be an increase in the supply of money. Whether there is an increase in the demand for money depends on the government's response. If the government permits an increase in the money supply then it is said to have 'validated' the wage rise by excessive monetary growth, thereby providing once more a monetary explanation of inflation. If the government prevents the money supply from increasing by, say, increasing interest rates, this will tend to offset the inflationary effect of the wage rise by causing a contraction in expenditure on goods and hence a decrease in the demand for labour.

The extent to which rising commodity prices are passed on to domestic prices depends upon what happens to the exchange rate. If the exchange rate is fixed then virtually the whole of the import price rise will be passed on to domestic prices. With fixed exchange rates the money supply is tied to the maintenance of the parity since, in effect, the Bank of England must supply, however much sterling is required to fix the price of sterling. A rise in import prices will raise the domestic demand for sterling. In an open economy with fixed exchange rates, this will necessitate a corresponding increase in the money supply. With floating exchange rates the government can choose to allow the exchange rate to appreciate, thereby in part offsetting the rise in the price of imports and preventing the full impact of the import price rise from being felt by domestic prices. Another consequence is that the money supply need not be increased by as much as it would with fixed exchange rates. In the extreme case the exchange rate could be allowed to appreciate sufficiently to completely insulate the domestic economy from foreign inflation. The problem with this strategy is that it would maximise the loss of competitiveness of British goods and, by making exports more expensive, would cause a reduction of output.

Over the period 1977–80 the exchange rate against the dollar appreciated by approximately 44 per cent; admittedly this was from a sharp trough in 1976. Between spring 1979 and January 1980 the exchange rate against all currencies (i.e. the effective exchange rate) rose by about 25 per cent. Appreciation of the currency by these magnitudes severely reduces competitiveness. It has been estimated that between the end of 1976 and 1981 competitiveness declined by about 65 per cent. The output costs of using exchange-rate appreciation to control inflation are not hard to imagine.

It was mentioned earlier that world commodity prices rose dramatically in 1973 and 1974, and this may have contributed to inflation in 1974 and 1975. During this period the exchange rate against the US dollar was more or less constant, implying that domestic prices did bear most of the burden of adjustment. However, the fact that domestic inflation is caused in part by 'exogenous' – outside – influences does not mean that the commodity price rise itself is inexplicable. Prior to the rise in commodity prices the rate of growth of the world money supply rose from about 5 per cent in 1970 to roughly 15 per cent for the period 1971–73 intimating that the Quantity Theory of Money holds at the world level too.

Although the above arguments suggest that there is a strong association between money growth and inflation such that if money growth is reduced, inflation will fall, they do not prove that the money supply can be controlled. Professor Kaldor, for example, has asserted that the high correlation between money growth and inflation just proves the *ineffectiveness* of monetary policy. His argument is that the money supply cannot be controlled and that it is determined *by* money demand. The desire to increase expenditure will raise the demand for overdrafts and hence the demand for money. As soon as the loan is granted both the money supply and expenditure are increased. Kaldor's policy recommendation is therefore that inflation be controlled by demand management rather than by monetary means.

If true this theory would appear to offer a different explanation of the connection between money growth and inflation. There are, however, two difficulties with Kaldor's theory. First, it seems to be more appropriate for the narrow $M_1$ definition of money than for $M_3$, the measure used above, and, second, the timing of money growth and inflation must be more or less contemporaneous if Kaldor's theory is true. The evidence seems to show that while there is no systematic connection between the rate of growth of $M_1$ and of inflation in the same year, there is a systematic lag of inflation behind the rate of growth of $M_3$ of about two years. Thus Friedman's view seems to be more consistent with the evidence than Kaldor's. (For definitions of $M_1$ and $M_3$, the reader should consult Chapter 1.)

Despite this, however, the issue of whether or not the money supply can be controlled is still very relevant for the effective implementation of gradualism. Both the previous and the present governments have failed to achieve their monetary targets as Table 4.2 shows. The period since November 1979 has been particularly

**Table 4.2** *Monetary targets and the money supply*

| Date | £M$_3$ target range % | £M$_3$ actual growth rate % |
|------|------------------------|------------------------------|
| Dec 1976–Mar 1977 | 9–13 | 7.7 |
| Apr 1977–Mar 1978 | 9–13 | 16.0 |
| Apr 1978–Oct 1978 | 8–12 | 10.9 |
| Nov 1978–June 1979 | 8–12 | 13.3 |
| July 1979–Oct 1979 | 7–11 | 10.9 |
| Nov 1979–Mar 1980 | 7–11 | 17.8 |
| Apr 1980–Mar 1981 | 7–11 | 22.2 |
| Apr 1981–Oct 1981 | 7–11 | 18.1 |

£M$_3$ is sterling M$_3$. All growth rates are on annual basis.

unsuccessful. Various explanations for this have been offered. They include the argument that monetary restrictions introduced in 1970 and recently abolished distorted the money supply figures, especially in 1979 and 1980. The restrictions inhibited the growth of M$_3$ and their removal caused a sudden surge of M$_3$ as people switched their forms of borrowing. More generally, it is argued that the public can switch between assets of different degrees of liquidity more or less at will and therefore render any single measure of money such as the narrow definition M$_1$ or the broader measures M$_3$ and PSL (private-sector liquidity) meaningless. Certainly, the broader the measure of liquidity (i.e. the more types of assets included such as cash, bank deposits, building society deposits and short-term Treasury Bills) the more difficult it is to control. The Civil Service strike during which money-supply figures were not available is cited as another problem for monetary control. Partly as a result of these problems new methods of monetary control are in the process of being introduced. It remains to be seen whether these are more successful than pervious methods, but a certain degree of scepticism is not entirely unjustified.

## *The new classical school of monetarism*

This is the other main strand of monetarist thought and is more recent than gradualism. At the core of the New classical school (NCS) is the belief that the public acquires and processes information very efficiently and rapidly with the result that government stabilisation policy is made ineffective. The gradualists assume that information is obtained inefficiently with the consequence that inflationary expectations are slow to adjust and monetary influences on the economy take some time to work their way through. The NCS argue that expectations about inflation and other economic quantities are formed 'rationally'; that is, using all of the available information including their perception of how the economy works. This is not to say that the public have perfect information. Unanticipated events occur which, until the public learns about them may be very influential. Moreover, due to costs of adjustment the effect of these shocks on the economy may persist for some time; the NCS explain the business cycle and prolonged periods of unemployment as the result of shocks whose influence have not been eliminated.

The implications of the NCS for economic policy are very profound. According to the NCS interventionist economic policy implicitly assumes that the government is better informed about the state and structure of the economy than the private sector which 'is sunk in the passive stupor of abysmal ignorance' (Brunner). Through such asymmetries of information, and, in particular, through having privileged information, the government is able to fool the public and thereby make their policies work. However, because the public is smarter and is better informed than the government realises, it soon takes steps to counteract and offset the policy, thereby rendering it only temporarily effective. The brief period of effectiveness of the policy is due to creating unanticipated shocks for the private sector. These shocks upset the public's calculations and cause them to make mistakes which are not in their self-interest. The conclusion is, therefore, that the proper role for government is to minimise these shocks by announcing clearly in advance any change of policy.

The government's medium-term financial strategy in which target rates of growth of the money supply are announced several years ahead are clearly just the sort of policy that the NCS advocate. Recently budget changes have been leaked in advance causing the public to stock up goods before tax increases which again should please the NCS.

Thus the NCS attribute the failure of many government policies to have permanent success not to incompetence on the government's part, but to a misunderstanding of the way the economic system works. There are many examples in the field of anti-inflation policy which can be cited in support of these claims. A few of these will suffice.

(1)   Dissatisfied with the Phillips-curve trade-off, most post-war governments have tried to lower both inflation and unemployment by introducing an incomes policy. Although the rate of inflation has often been reduced after the introduction of the incomes policy – 1972 and 1976 are good examples of this – at no time has the inflation rate been within the norms laid down by the policy. Moreover, research has failed to show that many of these reductions in the inflation rate can be attributed solely to the incomes policy. Governments usually accompany the incomes policy with policies designed to deflate the economy by restricting aggregate demand. These policies have the effect of raising unemployment and, through the Phillips curve, reducing wage and hence price inflation. If the effects of rises in unemployment are separated from the effects of the incomes policy, then the incomes policy alone is rarely found to have any significant effect. An exception to this is 1972, and possibly 1976, when incomes policy did significantly reduce inflation beyond the decrease caused by the rise in unemployment. However, even in 1972 further research has shown that as soon as the incomes policy was withdrawn, inflation increased once more, completely offsetting the gains made while the policy was in operation. This can be interpreted as the result of workers trying to restore their real incomes or living standards. The solution may seem to be not to remove the incomes policy. However, the abandonment of incomes policy is not usually a voluntary act by the governments concerned. They were simply bowing to public and

trade union pressure. Hope is still triumphing over experience, however, as economists are even now searching for new incomes policies which will work permanently.

(2)   Before governments were aware of the Phillips curve it had existed for one hundred years. Within a short time of trying to exploit the relationship for policy purposes it appears to have disintegrated. This is exactly what the NCS would predict.

(3)   One of the principal pillars of monetarism is the existence of a stable demand function for money. Such a relationship appeared to exist up to about 1970. After 1970, when monetarist policies began to be used, the demand for money function started to breakdown. Whether this was because it was misspecified or due to monetary policy changes is still not clear.

(4)   The centrepiece of Keynesian economics is a stable consumption function. From the mid 1970s onwards it was noticed that existing consumption functions failed to explain the rise in the ratio of savings to income. This has been attributed to the effects of inflation, and efforts are being made to reformulate the model to take better account of high inflation rates.

The failure of empirical relationships to remain stable when they are used for policy purposes has been expressed colourfully by Charles Goodhart of the Bank of England. He has said that:

> any statistical regularity will tend to collapse once pressure is placed upon it for control purposes. . . . In 1970 it was believed that there were a number of important economic regularities which could be manipulated for quite short-term control purposes – the Phillips curve, the demand for money function, the consumption function. During the early 1970's these regularities became unstuck one after the other. They are regularly glued together again, down in the econometric workshops, but they no longer carry the same bright conviction (*The Times*, 8 February 1980).

In volume 1 of the *Third Report* from the Treasury and Civil Service Committee on Monetary Policy the NCS was dismissed with some dispatch on the grounds that through the rapid acquisition of information, prices would be flexible in the short run and hence monetary policy would work far more quickly than gradualists supposed. This is not, however, a necessary implication of the NCS's position. It is only *well-announced* changes in the money stock which work rapidly through to prices when they are implemented. Unanticipated changes can take much more time. Moreover, through unanticipated fluctuations in the exchange rate, prices and output will continue to adjust slowly.

## Conclusions

One of the reasons for such a detailed examination of anti-inflation policy in Britain in recent years is to provide evidence in support of my contention that an excessive reliance on the efficacy of government intervention is misplaced due to our lack of knowledge about how the economy works. It is clear that there are several theories about the causes of inflation and there are even more proposals for controlling it. None of the theories has universal support and none of the proposals has worked very well.

For the last thirty-five years all governments in Britain have shared the view that one of their principal tasks is to manage the economy by active intervention. They have been encouraged in this by an electorate willing to bestow office on the party which promises most and by economists flattered to find patronage for their latest theory. In the last few years it has been recognised increasingly that the performance of the British economy has fallen far below the promises of successive governments. The result of this has been a widespread disillusionment with economics and with economists. Surprisingly, however, it has not diminished the public's desire for interventionist macroeconomic policy. The failure is usually attributed to an incompetent government pursuing a defunct economic theory the remedy for which is a new government carrying out a different and often diametrically opposed economic policy. As the promise of early success fades after about two years in office, it is not uncommon for a government to alter its economic policy to one very similar to that of the previous government. Unfortunately, it is easier to change policy than for the economy to recover.

Some of the blame for this situation must lie with the economics profession for encouraging the view that the remedy lies in adopting a different interventionist policy and for claiming more for the success of this policy than a realistic assessment of current economic knowledge would permit. In so far as economic knowledge rests on evidence, it is based on models which are very much first approximations. Thus policies designed to alter radically the structure of the economy or to move the economy into territory very different from that previously experienced can derive little support from existing empirical economic knowledge. Moreover, even where we have good explanations of how the economy has behaved in the past it cannot be taken for granted that the economy will continue to behave in the same way after a policy change.

Criticising economists in their role as political economists does not imply that one should be disillusioned with economics itself though it may require an adjustment about the way in which our economic knowledge should be used. However poor our present economic solutions the problems themselves will not disappear; nor is it probable that better solutions will be found by other means. What is required is a greater sense of realism about what is known and what is not. Macroeconomic policy which is based on an over-optimistic assessment of current economic knowledge will simply prolong the failure of the economy.

## INTRODUCTION TO CHAPTER 5

There are two main reasons why economists may be led to different conclusions about the state of the economy: (a) Lack of complete information about important economic processes, forcing them to 'guesstimate' and (b) different political objectives. In the next chapter Kenneth Hilton picks up this second theme by arguing that how we see economic problems and their solutions depends very importantly on what we wish to achieve. In other words, what are our objectives? However, finding out our objectives is only part of solving the problems at hand. A realistic assessment also requires us to answer the question: what can we actually achieve? While we often have to ask and answer both questions as individuals, too often when we look at the outside world we forget that there are limits to what we can achieve. For example, consider two problems which recur in various forms in this volume.

1. Most of us want to have more money and to be better off. Yet unless we increase output, if we are to be paid more, someone else must be paid less or, indeed, become unemployed. What we want to achieve may involve substantial costs.
2. As part of the 1979 election programme the Tory party announced that its objective was to reduce the rate of inflation. Many would agree with this objective. However, we must also ask: what can we actually achieve? Less government spending and higher interest rates may reduce aggregate spending and hence lower the rate at which prices are increasing. But less aggregate spending may also reduce output and employment.

The message is: there is no such thing as a free lunch. We must not only make clear what it is that we want to achieve. We must also consider what our priorities are in recognition of the fact that resources are not unlimited.

C. H. and G. M.

# 5   What is Britain's Economic Problem?

*by Kenneth Hilton*

> The material means of achieving ends is limited. We have been turned out of Paradise. . . . Everywhere we turn, if we choose one thing we must relinquish others. . . . Scarcity of means to satisfy ends of varying importance is an almost ubiquitous condition of human behaviour. (Lord Robbins, *An Essay on the Nature and Significance of Economic Science*, 1932)

Defined in this manner an 'economic problem' is something that is not simply akin to Britain in the 1980s. It is something that mankind has pondered since the days of Adam and Eve. Indeed, it is highly likely that the 'economic problem' will exist until the demise of the species *homo sapiens* (and most likely will be the ultimate cause of that demise).

Such words as these and those of Lord Robbins while accurate representations of the state of man are, in truth, very superficial. On the one hand, they may lull us into the false belief that Britain or indeed *homo sapiens* in general has no control over his current or future environment. On the other hand, such phrases grossly over-simplify the nature of the problem.

Most of us are prone to some form of day-dreaming. Some of us may dream of owning a Mediterranean villa, others may dream of a fast sports car, others of a peaceful country cottage. The difficulty is that the facts of life, or rather the 'economic problem', render it impossible for us all to make all our daydreams come true. There are simply not sufficient resources for *all* of us to fulfil *every* possible wish. We cannot all afford that villa or cottage or all else we desire. We must choose within the limited resources that exist in the world, and within the world's resources, from those available to the particular individual concerned.

We all have objectives which we wish to achieve, whether at

home, at work or at leisure. But not all these objectives are feasible. The 'economic problem' becomes one of setting priorities and weighing up one objective against another. Of course, such decisions are extremely difficult to make in a consistent fashion although in practice we make them many times a day. One of the most all-pervasive difficulties is that of *uncertainty* as to the likely outcome of any of our actions. We may undertake something which we expect to be feasible and then after much time and effort find that it is not. Dealing with economic problems, then, not only consists of setting objectives which we hope will be feasible, but of developing responses when our expectations prove to be incorrect.

The above considerations are phrased largely in such a way that they seem relevant only to a single man or woman living in isolation from the rest of society. However, in reality each are part of a broader society; and our society in turn is part of a broader international world.

We now find Robbins's economic problem becoming more and more complex, but this is inevitable: human behaviour and human systems *are* complex. It is interesting to note that the famous physicist, Max Planck, is reported by Keynes as giving up the study of economics for physics, because economics was too difficult! Unlike the physical or even biological sciences, economists cannot identify laws which appear to be immutable for long periods of time. We need to take account not only of the variability of the behaviour and objectives of individuals, but also of the changes in the objectives as a result of their achievement or failures. For society, at large, there is the complex problem of determining the objectives of that society when individual objectives can vary so much.

For example, some commentators have been arguing that those who possess political power are today often in conflict with those who possess economic power in terms of the aims or objectives that they respectively seek. Trade unions and big businesses may well hold the economic power while the political parties and the Civil Service hold the political power. Unless there is some reconciliation of these objectives a conflict will arise. What is apparently an economic problem may in some instances develop from political disagreements.

Other writers, such as J. K. Galbraith in his *Affluent Society* (1958) and *New Industrial State* (1967), have gone further than this and argued that, far from having an economic problem, Britain has been one of the first countries to solve the economic problem of the last quarter of the twentieth century: it is merely that we have not recognised it as such. These are arguments which were put into sharper focus by Nossiter, who argued that

> The lack-lustre performance of our dark satanic mills should be regarded as a sign of health rather than a symptom of sickness [for he argues that it is a reflection of a difference of objectives, and it is the case that] Britons . . . appear to be the first citizens of the postindustrial age who are choosing leisure over goods on a large scale. Of course almost everyone, everywhere all the time would welcome extra income, command over more goods and services. . . . But many appear to have arrived at a level of income at which they regard the extra effort to obtain extra income as not worthwhile. (*Britain: a future that works*, 1978).

How valid are such arguments as these? Before we can go on to examine them we need to look at the performance of the British economy.

**The facts**

(or lies, damned lies and statistics)

How can we measure whether or not a country is in a bad way in economic terms? Consider the selection of statistics shown in Table 5.1. These illustrate various aspects of the improvement in economic welfare (and the associated social well-being) that have occurred over the past twenty-five years. Naturally we could find other measures from similar sources that provide a bleaker picture (the incidence of violent crime for instance) and even those quoted (car ownership, for example) may not be regarded with complete equanimity by all.

Because of the difficulty of 'adding up' these kinds of measures, the economist's starting-point is the derivation of aggregate (or total) measures. Such aggregate measures are only a starting-point, and few would suggest they represent the whole picture. As they are subject to many defects, both conceptual and practical, they need to be used with care. None the less, they do provide indicators.

**Table 5.1**  *Selected indicators of change in
living standards*

|  | *c.* 1955 | *c.* 1980 |
|---|---|---|
| Life-expectancy    at birth | 72 | 76 |
| (female)              at 70 | 81 | 83 |
| Rate of infant mortality | | |
|    (per thousand live births) | 26 | 12 |
| Number of students at | | |
|    universities (thousands) | 101 | 330 |
| Number of telephones | | |
|    (million 'stations') | 6 | 25 |
| Percentage of manual workers | | |
|    entitled to at least three | | |
|    weeks' holiday with pay | 2 | 99 |
| Number of cars registered | | |
|    (millions) | 4 | 15 |
| Percentage of households | | |
|    without own toilets | | |
|    (millions) | 7 | 1 |
| Colour television licences | | |
|    (millions) | – | 13 |

If one adds up all incomes (allowing for the double counting that
may arise if, for example, a child's pocket money from a parent is
counted as 'income'), or adds up all expenditure, one can obtain a
global measure of well-offness. Such measures as Gross Domestic
Product (GDP) or Total Personal Incomes can be adjusted to make
an allowance for change in price levels to derive what are called real
(as compared with money) measures.

The result of deriving such a time series is shown in Figure 5.1
depicting the growth of real GDP over the past fifty years; other
aggregate measures, such as industrial output (even excluding
North Sea oil and gas), provide a similar though not identical picture. But note how relative things are. At first glance, Figure 5.1
gives the impression of remarkable improvement and success over
the past fifty years. Yet closer examination reveals the failure or
problem of the decade of the 1970s. Industrial production has fallen
dramatically in the recent past, as illustrated in Figure 5.2, something which did not occur on this scale even during the Great
Depression of the 1930s.

Some would say we ought to be most concerned about the poorer

**Figure 5.1**    *Britain's gross domestic product 1931–81 (at 1975 prices)*
          *Britain's industrial output 1931–81 (at 1975 prices)*

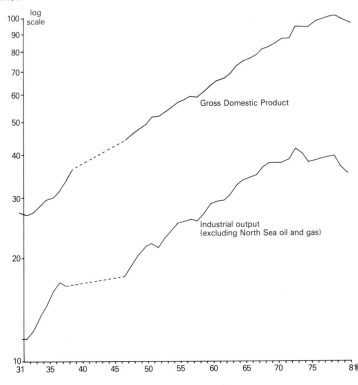

members of the community; but the Royal Commission on the Distribution of Income and Wealth did find that (so far as they could draw any conclusions from the statistics) there had been some movement of the share of total income away from the very rich and none away from the poorest members of society. An indication of this is shown on Figure 5.3 where estimates of the real value of the old-age pensions are shown, together with the real average weekly wage of male manual workers. Poverty has many dimensions. Yet the data do suggest there have been great gains in terms of physical well-being; and comparisons with male manual workers suggest some improvement in the position of old-age pensioners relative to this group; and relative to other groups a similar picture emerges.

**Figure 5.2** *Industrial output (excluding North Sea oil and gas) 1970–81*
*(index of industrial production: base 1975 = 100)*

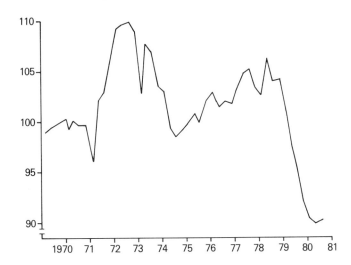

But what of inflation and what of unemployment?

The change in the value of the pound sterling in terms of its purchasing power and the level of unemployment are shown on Figure 5.4 and here the picture is indeed less satisfactory. Inflation has been a persistent feature of post-war Britain, which far from going away has become worse. Yet one may ask why there is concern about price changes? It can be persuasively argued that price rises *per se* are not necessarily evil: some (low) price inflation was regarded by Keynes, for example, as useful. Even with larger rates of price inflation the principal argument is that such inflation redistributes incomes in an unsatisfactory manner: it is clear that this economic problem is a political one, too. Arguments about the rate of exchange of sterling with other currencies, and the lack of competitiveness of British manufacturers are (at least in a naïve form) difficult to sustain in the face of large fluctuations in the exchange rate (also shown against the US dollar in Figure 5.4) without any obvious correlation with the rate of price inflation.

Similar though much less persuasive arguments could be made in respect of unemployment. None the less, it is clear that many people are concerned about price rises and unemployment; and it is probably these indicators that people look at first in their criticism

**Figure 5.3**    *Real value of retirement pension and of average earnings of male manual workers (£ per week at 1980 prices, 1948–81)*

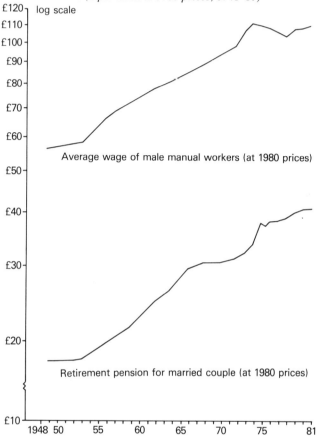

of the performance of the British economy. Yet, before the 1980s, **in no year in post-war Britain was the unemployment rate as high as the** *lowest* **rate experienced in the 1930s. Even in 1982, the unemployment rate will not reach the average experienced in the 1930s.** Even for those unemployed living standards are much higher today than those for the average employee of the 1930s. Few would want to return to the 'good old days' of the inter-war period. Harold Macmillan summarised this in 1957 when, as Prime Minister, he said: 'Let us be frank about it: most of our people have never had it so good.'

**Figure 5.4** *Inflation, unemployment and the exchange rate 1931–81*

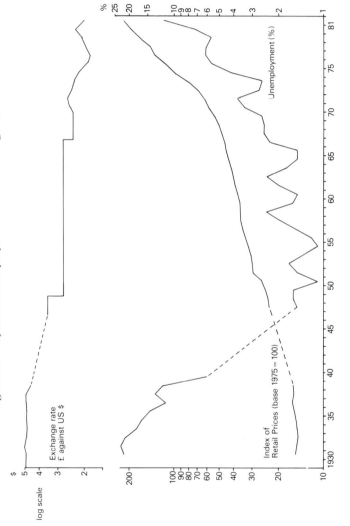

**The Rest of the World**
(or No Man is an Island)

The above argument suggests that Britain does have economic problems, but when compared with the past, the British people are not doing badly in economic terms. But what of the rest of the world?

Broad comparisons of per capita national income between countries in 1979 have been made by *The Economist* (*The World in Figures*, 1981). Out of 213 countries of the world, 170 countries were estimated to have a *lower* average income than Britain and only 40 countries had a higher average income. Income per head in two-thirds of the countries of the world is less than a half than in Britain. In the extreme cases of Cambodia and Laos income per head is estimated at less than one-tenth of that in Britain. Given the imperfections in such data, such comparisons must be treated with caution, but the general picture is clear: relative to the majority of the world's population, the British people are rich, very rich.

It is, however, not such countries as these where the majority of the world's population resides with which comparisons are most frequently made, but with a group of advanced industrialised countries. The comparisons then become less impressive. Some recent measures are shown in Table 5.2. Industrial growth has been less, inflation and unemployment higher, in Britain than in most of the other industrialised countries listed. But does this represent failure? Is this an economic problem? Some would say what does it matter what happens in the rest of the world. Of what relevance is it to us? Let us pursue this argument further. We need to consider what is 'success' and how we can judge performance, and to explain this we have recourse to two simple examples.

First, consider the problem of defining an objective for an individual or group of individuals with a common aim. We may envisage the decision-taking and evaluative process in the way described in Figure 5.5.

For example, a manager of a football club in the second division may have the aim of achieving promotion to the first division. If his team does so he would be regarded as being a 'success'. But in the following year his objective will change. No longer will the supporters be satisfied merely with staying in the first division; and

**Table 5.2**   *Comparisons with other industrialised countries*

| Countries (in descending order of income per head, 1979) | Annual industrial growth % | | Annual inflation rate % | | Standardised unemployment rate % | |
|---|---|---|---|---|---|---|
| | 5 years to 1980 | 25 years to 1980 | 5 years to 1980 | 25 years to 1980 | 5 years to 1980 | At mid-1981 |
| West Germany (£5200) | 3.4 | | 4.0 | | 3.4 | |
| | | 4.4 | | 3.5 | | 4.8 |
| USA (£4500) | 4.6 | | 8.8 | | 6.6 | |
| | | 3.7 | | 4.5 | | 7.2 |
| France (£4500) | 3.2 | | 10.4 | | 5.6 | |
| | | 4.6 | | 5.8 | | 9.3 |
| Japan (3500) | 7.3 | | 6.6 | | 2.0 | |
| | | 10.6 | | 5.5 | | 2.0 |
| UK (£3000) | 1.4 | | 14.4 | | 6.1 | |
| | | 1.9 | | 6.5 | | 12.6 |
| Italy (£2400) | 5.4 | | 16.6 | | 3.9 | |
| | | 5.9 | | 7.0 | | 5.0 |

Sources:
*Income per head:* National income per head at 1979 exchange rates, from *The Economist*, The World in Figures, 1981, p. 11.
*Annual industrial growth:* Linked indices of industrial production, from UN *Statistical Yearbooks, 1961, 1967, 1977*, and UN *Monthly Bulletin of Statistics* (Oct 1981).
*Annual inflation rate:* Linked consumer price indices – source as for industrial growth.
*Unemployment:* Unemployment as % of workforce adjusted to US definitions, as described in UK Department of Employment *Gazette* (Aug 1980). Sources: Department of Employment *Gazette*, various issues up to Nov 1981.

demotion to the second division, a state which would have been regarded in a neutral way in the previous year, will now be regarded as a 'failure'. In brief, our objectives are conditioned by our past achievements. If we can achieve a particular target on one occasion we can surely achieve it again, or so the feeling runs. This is reflected in a common practice in the business world: this practice involves setting targets based on last year's results. Production managers are judged on whether they have exceeded last year's out-

**Figure 5.5**

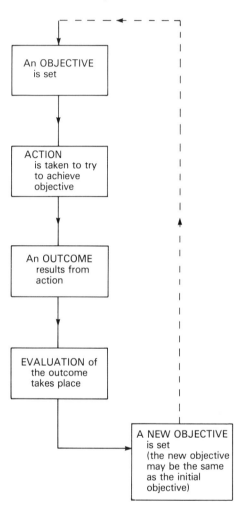

put; salesmen on whether they have improved on their sales figures
. . . etc.

The example of the football team manager does draw attention to
another kind of comparison frequently used in respect of economic
performance: that of ranking countries by some performance
measure. It is worth reflecting that as in football league tables, in
international comparisons, except in an Alice-in-Wonderland

world, all the competitors cannot be winners. Some *must* do worse than others.

The issues are even more complex when an individual has more than one objective. How can we judge performance when there is a conflict between objectives? Let us explain this further by reference to a simple gardening example. Two gardeners, Margaret and Ronald, each grow tomatoes and cucumbers in their greenhouses. Their (hypothetical) results are shown in the Table 5.3 below for each of three years.

**Table 5.3** *Yields for two imaginary gardeners*

|      | Margaret | | Ronald | |
| --- | --- | --- | --- | --- |
|      | Tomatoes lb. | Cucumbers lb. | Tomatoes lb. | Cucumbers lb. |
| 1970 | 100 | 50 | 90 | 60 |
| 1975 | 130 | 45 | 140 | 40 |
| 1980 | 160 | 40 | 200 | 30 |

If we look in isolation at Margaret's performance over time in respect of tomatoes we might conclude that she had done pretty well. Yet if we take into account her cucumbers as well, how do we judge her performance? The difficulties of evaluation are compounded when we know of Ronald's performance, for in respect of the output of tomatoes he has performed better than Margaret: but worse in respect of cucumbers.

And what of outside influences? The weather may have been different in each of the years, being more or less favourable to cucumbers or tomatoes. Margaret's greenhouse may have been damaged by a freak storm that affected only her garden and not Ronald's. There could be many such outside influences. Ronald may have had (or chosen to build) a bigger greenhouse initially. Margaret may find that the oil needed to heat a greenhouse is provided so cheaply by a kind uncle that she can sell some to Ronald in exchange for some of his tomatoes. As a result she may not bother with her tomatoes. Indeed for other reasons Margaret may have different objectives to Ronald. Margaret's family may prefer to see more of her at home rather than have her spend her time in the greenhouse, etc.

Too much should not be made of crude analogies between the USA in the form of Ronald, and Britain in the form of Margaret. Yet with countries as with people, before we can judge performance we must have some idea

not only of *objectives*

but also of *what can be achieved*

Only then can we make any attempt at judgements.

In the long term what can be achieved may be determined in part by natural resources, by climatic conditions, geographical features, etc. There is little evidence to suggest that Britain is defective in these regards. Arguments about the benefits of wartime destruction in Germany, and about attitudes in Britain are dependent basically on the lack of will to change in Britain. These are arguments about objectives. It is to these we now turn.

### Social welfare
(or tomatoes, cucumbers and leisure)

The objectives for individuals may be hard to define. What of those of a country? Are they changing? Are they compatible? Who sets these objectives? Is there yet some truth in the Nossiter argument quoted above? How can we find out whether or not the British people really want more material goods at the expense of other things?

Some recent studies based on the opinion poll ratings of politicians in power have been developed in various countries. One study suggests that with the levels of inflation, unemployment and change in incomes that were experienced up to the late 1970s, the factors which individuals regarded most important in judging politicians' performance were related to these three factors. Overall the results are difficult to interpret in a simple way, but in crude terms the results of one investigator, Pissarides, suggest that a 1 per cent rise in the rate of inflation (e.g. from 15 per cent to 16 per cent) reduces a government's lead in an opinion poll by 0.6 per cent; a 1 per cent rise in unemployment reduces the lead by 6 per cent (but with diminishing effects as unemployment becomes higher): and a 1 per cent rise in the growth of incomes increases the lead by 0.8 per cent

*Economic Journal*, 90, 1980: 569–81). Similar arguments about incomes are discussed in Butler and Kavanagh's work on the *British General Election of 1979* (Macmillan, 1980). Thus, one could conclude that if politicians are judged on how far they achieve these objectives people regard the objectives as important. But all these results, particularly those relating to unemployment and inflation, must be regarded as provisional.

Other pointers come from reports of the causes of strikes – more than half are reported to be a result of disputes over wages – from the matters raised with MPs by their constituents – predominantly about matters which would be improved with higher incomes or higher public expenditure – and from matters referred to social workers – who are often expected to provide financial advice and funds, etc.

Material goods *do* appear to matter.

It is this last sentence which is crucial to an understanding of the economic problem. If British society as a group prefers leisure, then they must be willing to accept the consequences of this objective.

It would be comforting to believe that Britain's poor record in the last decade was due to a sudden change in objectives – to a conscious decision to opt for less growth, and more leisure; but the evidence of available studies seems firmly set against this view. In addition in opinion polls in recent years members of the public consistently put reducing inflation and unemployment as the top two objectives that governments should have. Lastly, those who feel we have *chosen* less growth and more leisure might wonder why we haven't arranged a shorter working week as a general rule, instead of having a zero working week for the 3 million unemployed – most of whom want more work, not more leisure.

### Conclusions

(or what is the answer . . . what is the question?)

This chapter has attempted to introduce some of the dilemmas associated with macroeconomic analysis. The nature of the economic problem which Britain has is related to the objectives which are sought or perceived to be sought by the British people.

Sometimes one can observe that 'failure' occurs because the objectives have been inconsistent or because aspirations have been

raised by politicians anxious for power. Judgement is involved no
only in assessing the extent to which Britain has failed to achieve the
objectives set for itself, but also in the extent to which the objective
exist, are consistent, or realistic.

The emphasis of the other chapters in this volume is naturall
enough on the recent problems of the British economy; and indeed
on most criteria one cares to choose the British economy has no
done well in the recent past. Although the economic growth
between the 1930s and the early 1970s has made us better off ir
material terms, British economic performance of the last ten years
in terms of *improvements* of living standards, in terms of unemploy
ment, in terms of price inflation has been decidedly poor from
almost any standpoint.

None the less it is important to bear in mind that many of the discussions of economic policy rely on assumptions, implicit or
explicit, about the *objectives* of the policy. It is not merely a question
of whether we can give up material goods for leisure, but also
whether we want to do so; it is not only whether we can give up some
of our natural environment for economic growth, but whether we
want to. . . . The choices are many: we need to know which choices
are possible, or exist, and which do not. But we also have to make
that choice.

Many of the disputes between economists are not about the
means but about these objectives. Policy choices relate to an uncertain future, and the choice will normally be between the *risk* of one
outcome (associated with one objective) and the *risk* of another outcome. The policy choice may rely not just on the respective likelihood of these two events happening, but also on the relative desirability in the eyes of the policy-maker or theorist. The complexity of
the real world is immense.

Some commentators, even some economists, use this very uncertainty, this very complexity, to confuse the real issues. Some will
have particular preferences, particular value judgements, which
will appear implicitly and not explicitly in their arguments. When a
politician suggests that the course he advocates is the only course of
action possible on economic grounds. . . . The statement 'only by
reducing inflation can we solve Britain's economic ills' involves not
just assertions about the nature and workings of the economic
system but a series of value judgements. Some in society will prefer
the risk of marginally higher rates of inflation to the risk of higher

unemployment or lower growth; some will prefer to risk higher unemployment to reduce the possibility of higher inflation, assuming
such a trade-off exists. Such value judgements should be brought
out, made explicit where possible. Only if the objective, or set of
objectives, are always explicit in any economic analysis can one
hope to achieve any kind of rational economic policy. *That* is the
primary lesson of the analysis offered in this chapter.

## INTRODUCTION TO CHAPTER 6

Most of us at some point in the working day begin to look forward to taking a break or a relaxing pint at the local in the evening. As Friday approaches we begin to plan our weekend activities. Some of that leisure time may be spent thinking of a week skiing in Austria or a longer holiday on a sun-drenched beach on the Mediterranean. Leisure, and planning for it, absorb a lot of our time. But does that mean that we should want to spend all of our time away from work? Would you want to be permanently unemployed? Probably not. We need to work in order to obtain the money to enable us to go on holiday (and also to buy food, clothing, housing). Besides, most of us would get rather bored sitting around all day with nothing to do.

The above considerations are crucial for understanding the problem of unemployment as David Heathfield emphasises in the next chapter. When we *choose* leisure we are unemployed. It is a decision of our own making. The problem is that the statistics do not distinguish between such individuals and those who want to work but cannot find work. In this sense, unemployment statistics overstate the problem. On the other hand, people who are on short time because the demand for the goods they produce is low are counted as employed. There is thus a sense in which the unemployment statistics may understate any imbalance. Consider the following example. A firm's sales fall by, say, 50 per cent. They could lay off 50 per cent of their workforce with the result that recorded unemployment increases. Or all workers could work half-time, in which case recorded unemployment remains unchanged.

The question is: If we do not know what unemployment is, how can we design policies to reduce it?

David Heathfield's discussion extends beyond the realm of statistical definitions to the identification of various types of unemployment. He concludes, somewhat provocatively, that not all forms of unemployment are 'bad'. And even if some forms are considered to be undesirable, they may not be susceptible to government action.

C.H. and G.M.

# 6 Unemployment: Too Much of a Good Thing

*by David Heathfield*

## Introduction

It is not unusual to hear someone say that work is a curse yet in the same breath claim 'the right to work'. On the one hand work is something from which the lucky leisured class has escaped and from which the young, elderly and infirm should be protected. Yet on the other hand we seem to want to create and maintain jobs – even dirty and dangerous jobs like coal-mining. But there is more to work than simply doing a job for money. It also has social and psychological significance so that although with one part of ourselves we find it irksome with another part of ourselves we welcome the discipline and the sense of identity and worth which it bestows.

It is not difficult therefore to understand why often confused and conflicting accounts of unemployment are commonly given by individuals and trade unions alike. What is less easily explained is the widely held view that unemployment is largely, if not exclusively, a matter for the government rather than for the individual to deal with.

There are indeed some economic theories which suggest that some kinds of unemployment are amenable to government economic policy. But other forms of unemployment are not amenable to policy or alternatively need no remedial action. The consensus of the 1950s, 60s and 70s seems to have been that all unemployment can and ought to be remedied by government action. The question in those days was to decide to what extent full-employment policies were to be pursued when they had unwanted side-effects – say, for example, increased inflation. But what is the story today? Is the current bout of unemployment largely or solely the responsibility of the government, and if so what should they do about it?

130

The purpose of this chapter is to outline some of the ways in which unemployment comes about and to see what, if anything, the government should and could be doing about it.

## Work and leisure

We begin by considering a very simple world comprising just one man on an island – a Robinson Crusoe economy. Of Crusoe's many activities some will be carried out for the pure pleasure of doing them. Others will be done not because he likes doing them, but because they lead to better things. He may, for example, fear heights and yet still climb trees, in order to get at the coconuts.

Some activities may be both enjoyable and productive, but for our present purpose it is convenient to assume that every activity can be classified as either enjoyable or productive, but not both. All productive activity will be regarded as work. We can therefore gauge Crusoe's level of employment by the time he spends on productive activity – time spent otherwise is leisure.

## Full employment, unemployment and underemployment

Crusoe is fully employed when he works as many hours as he wants to; he will want to work another hour only if the reward for working is greater than the pleasure he gets from leisure. If an extra hour in bed brings him more enjoyment than the fish he could catch in one hour then he will stay in bed. Full employment therefore is not some known fixed number of hours per man per week. It differs among men, varies with wage rate, and changes as individuals' attitudes to work change. *Under*employment is working fewer hours than one wishes and *over*employment is working more. Our *un*employment statistics refer only to those with no work at all.

## Flexitime and work-sharing

Those in employment have very little control over the number of hours they work so that some employed workers are obliged to work more hours than they wish and others are obliged to work fewer. There are perhaps good reasons for this inflexibility of the working week, but it means that we become solely concerned about unemployment rather than about the wider problem of under employment. It also rules out one possible way of ameliorating the unemployment problem; that of changing hours rather than employees when work is scarce. When output is cut by 10 per cent then, typically, the workforce is cut by 10 per cent rather than maintaining the workforce and everyone working fewer hours. Negotiating flexihours is surely a matter for the workplace rather than for the government. But the government does have a role to play. It could so arrange the taxes on employment that the employer gains no benefit from cutting men rather than hours. At the moment there are quite heavy taxes levied *per head* of workforce and hence are independent of the number of hours worked. In such circumstances it clearly makes good economic sense to employ as few people as possible and work them for as long as you can.

### Necessary unemployment and voluntary unemployment

It may seem on first sight that underemployment (or overemployment) is not possible on Robinson Crusoe's island since he alone decides what he will do. A moment's reflection, however, will suggest otherwise. Crusoe's plans to dig his vegetable patch may be thwarted by bad weather. His choice would be to work, but he is prevented from working. He is therefore involuntarily unemployed. His unemployment is, however, *necessary* and *unavoidable* since no one can control the weather. His unemployment is due neither to the government nor to the 'system' and cannot be avoided by any employment policy. There are seasonal and other unavoidable cyclical forms of unemployment in a modern economy too.

### Waiting for the 'right' job

It could, of course, be argued that Crusoe could find something else to keep him busy: he may be prevented from digging but not from working. Similar arguments have been advanced about the unemployed in our economy. They are told to accept any job which must be offered and to 'get on their bicycles and look for work'. Others would argue that it is unreasonable to expect the unemployed to accept any job or to move house in order to get a job. Even when the unemployed are prepared to move, the difficulties of finding somewhere to live are often insurmountable. There can be little doubt that local-authority housing encourages immobility and that something more could be done for those anxious to move. What is not quite so clear is what constitutes a 'reasonable' argument for not accepting a job. Do we wish to decrease the number of registered unemployed by insisting that they move to find work and accept jobs which they consider to be unsuitable? There can be little doubt that as we have grown richer we have come to expect less and less of the unemployed. And, it could be argued, quite rightly so. It is not easy to assess the community view about what is 'just', but it is something we must do before we can decide whether such unemployment is 'voluntary' or 'involuntary'. The correct policy may well depend on such a judgement.

**Another view of full employment**

Unemployment of a different kind may occur if the rewards of working are uncertain. If, for example, Crusoe expected poor weather or pestilence he may not plant crops. But if, in the event, the weather were favourable and the pests failed to materialise, he would regret not having done the planting. He cannot, of course, avoid the disappointments of this kind, he must decide before hand, given the risks, how much work he will do and will occasionally make mistakes. In our economy the effort of doing the work and the risks of not getting any output are borne by different people. He who provides the labour (the employees) may wish to work more hours than thought appropriate by the man bearing the risk (the employer). If the workers and employer disagree about how many man hours should be worked then some workers will see themselves as being *unnecessarily* prevented from doing work which they want to do and are capable of doing.

This is one source of conflict between the two sides of industry, but the answer lies in gaining a better understanding of each other's point of view rather than in more government action.

**Technical change**

In order to deal with the implications of technical change we have to introduce another castaway (Defoe) on an island close enough to permit them to trade. Imagine that Defoe is particularly good at collecting nuts and that Crusoe excels at fishing. It would clearly be in the interests of both for Defoe to specialise in nutting and Crusoe to specialise in fishing and for them to exchange nuts and fish at some agreed price. If subsequently a device or invention appeared which made Crusoe able to collect nuts for himself then he may choose no longer to trade with Defoe. In such circumstances Defoe would surely try to prevent the introduction of the device. He would be worried not only about the loss of his 'job', but also at the weakening of social links derived from trade and so on.

Crusoe may indeed agree with Defoe and either suppress the device or perhaps give it to Defoe to use. In the extremely complicated modern system of production and exchange it is simply not possible for even the most benign Crusoe to adopt such an attitude. He is so divorced from those who produce the things he buys that he can have no idea at all of the ultimate consequences of his buying nuts or buying nut-gathering gadgets. It is doubtful whether even the government could gather sufficient information and expertise to inject social and moral considerations into market behaviour. 'Big' systems seem to be very productive, but also become more and more difficult to manage. Some argue that we have already gone too far, and should return to small-scale economies.

*Structural unemployment*    In the event of his being excluded from trade, Defoe is materially no worse off than he was before trade began and he is not unemployed; he can go back and cultivate his own backyard. But in our economy withdrawal of exchange amounts to a withdrawal of livelihood since self-sufficiency is simply not possible. Reducing the demand for some kinds of work will, because of specialisation, reduce the income of those who do it. It is not that there is too much leisure, it is rather that it is all visited upon one group of workers. This kind of unemployment is called 'structural' unemployment and is an inevitable consequence of social and technical change. If there is no demand for horseshoes there will be no demand for farriers and there is no case for the government maintaining the farrier industry. The government can seek to control the pace of change, but foreign competition often limits our power to do even that. What has been attempted is man-power planning and government-sponsored retraining programmes. Some would question the ability (or desirability) of the government to carry out such programmes satisfactorily. A counter-proposal is simply to see that labour (and capital) does not 'specialise' in one particular task and is not led to expect a lifetime's employment in it.

Some ideas of the extent of structural change may be gleaned from Figure 6.1, which shows the changing pattern of employment in Britain's manufacturing industries. This reached a peak of 8,600,000 in 1961 has fallen since then to 6,000,000 in 1981. The losses from manufacturing have been taken up in the service sector so that overall employment has not followed the pattern set by manufacturing. But the transition from manufacturing to services usually involves a spell of unemployment.

*Market power* Imagine next a third unfortunate castaway (Plomley) on an island close enough to those of Defoe and Crusoe to trade. Let Plomley be very good at hunting. He and the other two castaways exchange nuts, meat and fish and each specialises in one form of production. If 'Nuts' Defoe now invents something which allows him to hunt more efficiently than 'Meat' Plomley, then he may no longer wish to trade nuts for meat, which robs Plomley of one customer, but Defoe may also coerce 'Fish' Crusoe into not trading with Plomley. Defoe, being now able to supply both nuts and meat can insist that Crusoe trades only with him on pain of his withdrawing both meat and nuts from their exchange. Plomley is thereby excluded from trade altogether and is rendered unemployed by this exercise of Defoe's market power. The point is that some unemployment is *unnecessary* and *involuntary* and due to some economic agents selfishly wielding their market power. This same kind of power can be used to prevent others from adopting new techniques. For example, Defoe (in the absence of Plomley) could insist that Crusoe abandon his nut-gathering device on pain of losing both nuts and meat which Defoe exclusively supplied.

This seems to be a matter for the government, if at all, only in the sense of the government as law-giver rather than in its role as an economic enabler. Protecting the rights of the weak has meant introducing laws aimed at strengthening labour in its unequal struggle against capital. Some would say that what is needed now is law to protect some workers from the unequal power of other workers.

**Figure 6.1**   *Employment in British manufacturing industries (m.)*

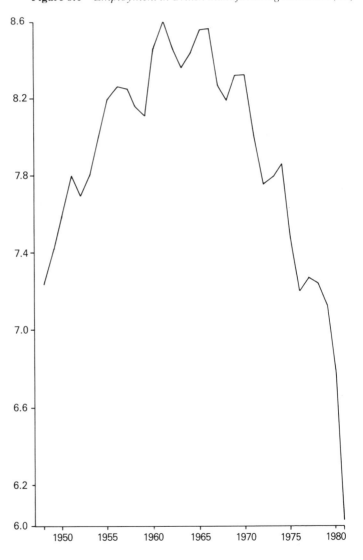

## The need for capital

If now instead of there being three islands our three castaways were thrown up on the same one, then the first to arrive (Crusoe) would colonise it. The second (Defoe) could live only if he had access to the 'means of livelihood'. If Crusoe confines him to the beach then his choice of employments is greatly reduced. If he is given equal rights with Crusoe, then Crusoe must suffer a decline in his 'productivity'. The advent of Plomley will require a further division of the best nut trees and best fishing-pools, etc., so as to further reduce the productivity of Crusoe. In a modern economy it is access to plant and machinery rather than plots of land which is important. The more 'capital' each labourer has access to, the higher will be his earnings; thus it seems to be in the interest of an individual worker to drive up his capital/labour ratio. This means that, unless there is an increase in capital (which comes from savings), other workers will have lower capital/labour ratios and lower incomes. They may even have no capital at all because others insist on having all the capital allocated to themselves. This is another example of the exercise of market power in an anti-social way.

One implication of this need for capital is that a baby boom will, on reaching school-leaving age, require large amounts of new capital if renumerative work is to be found for them. Those already in work have some claim to their jobs and can effectively keep the youngsters out of employment. The Employment Protection Act, designed to protect workers from employers, also protects the employed from the unemployed.

There are perhaps three ways of easing this kind of problem. First, we could share what capital there is by job-sharing. Second, we could encourage some workers voluntarily to leave the labour force so as to make way for newcomers. There are no obvious candidates for 'early retirement': certainly there is no clear case for forcibly retiring older workers simply because they are older – but some workers might *choose* unemployment if the terms were right. And, third, we could encourage saving so that more capital is available for everyone. The government could replace voluntary saving with a tax designed to raise the amount of capital required, but this gives it a very great deal of control over the way industry develops. The view taken by the present government seems to be to make investment funds available to the private sector by restricting the amount of private savings taken by the government. That is, they wish to reduce the Public Sector Borrowing Requirement so as to make room for private borrowing and investment.

Some statistics may be helpful here. The share of national income going to investment has been falling fairly steadily since 1968 (see Figure 6.2) having reached a peak of 23 per cent in 1968 it fell to 18.5 per cent in 1981. It is not easy to see why this should be so. Perhaps the rewards going to those who save are not attractive enough. Perhaps parsimony has given way to profligacy as a private and social virtue.

*Low producers*

Not everyone can, of course, make use of capital. It may be that Plomley, washed up on to the same island as Defoe and Crusoe and given equal access to the 'means of production' is nevertheless incapable of supporting himself. No matter how hard or long he works he is slowly starving to death. Crusoe and Defoe may offer to help by supplementing Plomley's earnings so as to give him some leisure and still have enough to live on. In our economy Plomley could be employed only if he accepted a less than subsistence wage (assuming his wage was equal to his production). Thus he would not be employed at all since such wages are simply not paid. We have the notion of a fair wage and anyone incapable of producing that amount is not employed at all. These unemployed wish to work, can work, but are excluded from work because we believe that no one should be asked to work for 'too low' wages. One way of moderating this 'all-or-nothing' effect would be to introduce a 'negative' income tax so that low wages can be supplemented without stopping work altogether.

**The effects of unemployment benefit**

There are many ways of arranging for the support of Plomley, but all have the inevitable consequence of redistributing goods away from those who produced them. When this is done voluntarily it is called charity and nowadays carries a distinct opprobrium. The preferred method of redistributing incomes is through some state agency

**Figure 6.2** *Investment as a share of national income*

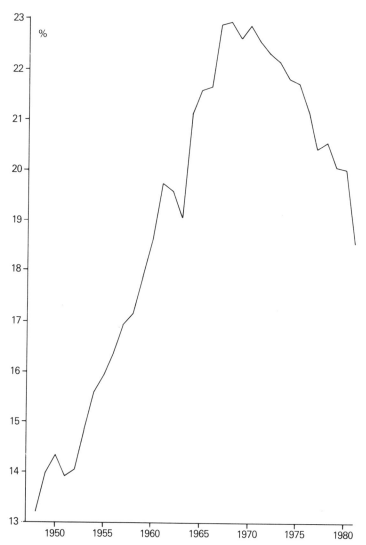

which raises its funds through taxation and distributes them according to a set of rules prescribed by Parliament. Those who argue against this method do so on the grounds that whereas Defoe and Crusoe may well be prepared voluntarily to work a little harder and give some of their produce to Plomley they may well resent the imposition of say a 30 per cent tax on their production by a central authority. This may cause them to work less rather than more since they now receive only 70 per cent of what they produce. Some workers, it is argued, who are on the borderline in the sense that they can only just produce enough to live on will stop work altogether and switch to the dole themselves. Centrally organised financial relief for unemployment is therefore likely to increase voluntary unemployment by the two devices of reducing the reward for labour and raising the reward for leisure. This is the kind of reasoning which lies behind the calls, increasingly heard, for a reduction in unemployment benefit. The argument is that many of those currently registered as unemployed are *voluntarily* unemployed and choose the dole to the pay packet. Reducing the dole would 'force' them back to work. This argument is reinforced by the claim that others registered as unemployed are in fact earning in the 'black' economy. This means that they avoid taxes and duties and receive the dole as well as their 'black' earnings.

It is no doubt true that some claimants abuse the system. The question is, when should the government say enough is enough and inflict upon perfectly innocent victims of unemployment a further cut in income? The plain fact is that we have very little evidence to say who is *involuntarily* unemployed and who is not. This makes it practically impossible to know how best to determine unemployment benefit or any other policy aimed at tackling the recorded levels of unemployment.

**Uncertain facts and alternative interpretations**

One would expect that in a wealthy and growing economy the amount of work would be declining, that there would be a great deal of structural unemployment, that the unemployed would be supported for long enough to find a job of their choice and that more and more people would fall below the minimum employable wage category. We would, in short, expect some forms of unemployment to increase not as an avoidable social evil, but as evidence of a humane, growing economy. If we decide we can no longer afford to have people picking and choosing jobs or if we no longer want to contribute to those incapable of supporting themselves then we could say we have too much unemployment. This, however, is from the point of view of those who are taxed to support the unemployed. From the point of view of the unemployed, there is too much unemployment when they feel unjustly excluded from certain kinds of jobs, obliged to stand a disproportionately high part of the cost of structural change, forced to accept a job which is well below their expectations or are unable to find employment at all. It is not always possible to avoid these forms of unemployment, but some compensation will be expected and can be offered in terms of unemployment benefits.

What is clear is that in order to say anything sensible about unemployment it is necessary to know what kind of unemployment is being recorded. Our official statistics simply record the number of those registered for work but unable to find it. Some of these will not be looking for work, but register in order to claim benefit, some though genuinely looking for a 'proper' job will nevertheless be 'unofficially' employed whilst registered. Those not eligible for benefit may not register even though they are unemployed and looking for work. Some people in employment will feel underemployed and be seeking other jobs although not registered as unemployed. Thus the measure of unemployment which informs our policy-makers is an entirely inadequate measure of the nature and extent of *unnecessary, involuntary underemployment.*

## Unemployment v inflation

A great deal of the current economic debate about unemployment is concerned not with what the government can do to increase labour mobility or moderate the rate of technological change; rather it is to do with how the government causes unemployment by pursuing a tight money policy.

In order to introduce this part of the debate it is necessary to conjure up yet another island inhabited by Ben Gunn, who has access to a treasure comprising one thousand pieces of gold. Our original three islanders now decide to use money in their exchanges rather than pure barter. They each bring their goods to Treasury Island once a month and sell them to Ben in exchange for gold pieces. Say one hundred objects of equal value are traded and that Ben allows only one hundred pieces of gold to leave the island.

Clearly each object will exchange for one gold piece and Defoe, Crusoe and Plomley will return to their islands clutching in total, one hundred gold pieces. During the coming month they pay visits to Treasury Island and buy back the goods they deposited there. At the end of the month all the gold pieces are returned to Ben and all the goods used up. The process then begins all over again.

If, at the beginning of the next month, Ben decides to use two hundred gold pieces (rather than one hundred as before) for this trade then there still being only one hundred objects each will now attract two gold pieces. Prices will have doubled and the islanders return home with two hundred gold pieces between them. They may feel much better off, but clearly when they come to buy back the goods from Ben they get back exactly the same as before. All incomes and prices have doubled and no one is any better or worse off. This leads some economists to argue that inflation is really of no consequence. What is important is how much is produced, not how many gold pieces there are.

Those who insist that inflation is a 'very bad thing' rarely answer the point that money is 'neutral' and price level irrelevant.

## The effects of issuing more money

In a world of this kind the only way for an islander to claim goods from Treasury Island is first to deposit some goods there. First he produces, then he sells, then he buys and finally he consumes. What he gets back is of exactly equal value to what he deposits.

If, however, we change the rules slightly and allow Ben to increase money supply whenever he wishes then he may choose to increase the number of gold pieces in circulation after the islanders have sold him their goods. Since he now has both the new money and the goods this new money can only be put into circulation by Ben spending it or giving it away. If he spends it then he is allowed to have some of the goods produced by the islanders even though he produced nothing. If he gives the money to Plomley, then Plomley can buy a greater share of the goods then he supplied. Prices will again double since there are two hundred gold pieces being spent on one hundred objects, but in this case there will be distributional effects of issuing new money. In the real world there seems to be no way of issuing new money without these redistribution effects. And the objection to inflation is that it is the result of someone who has not produced being allowed to purchase goods as if he had produced. Purchasing power is created by allowing him access to newly printed money which, by definition, he did not 'earn' by producing goods.

This arbitrary redistribution of goods may cause the islanders to doubt the value of trading via Ben and they may cut down production a little, but that is not the main influence of money supply on output and employment.

## Bargaining up prices

If we imagine that the islanders have some control over prices they may, by competing between themselves, bid the prices of all goods up. That is to say when they bring their goods to Treasury Island they are each trying to get the highest possible price. They know, of course, that if all prices double then they will neither individually nor as a group be any better or worse off. Nevertheless each of them knows that unless he bargains hard he will get less than the others. In the absence of a prices and incomes policy they will jointly force prices up.

Ben may respond by drawing from his treasure whatever number of coins he needs to buy all their goods at the new prices. He knows he will get all the coins back at the end of the month. If he does issue money then prices will continue to rise as long as the islanders compete for higher prices for their goods. They will not, however, be any better or for that matter any worse off whatever may happen to prices.

If, on the other hand, Ben decides that he cannot, or simply will not, issue any more coins then when the islanders double prices he can buy only half their produce. They thus return to their islands with some of their produce unsold. They will then produce less in future, feeling there is no demand for what they produce. In this case, when no new coins are issued prices will double and output and employment will halve. This is 'stagflation' such as we currently have. Ben Gunn is arguing that the solution is for the islanders to moderate their bargaining. The islanders argue that Ben need only to issue more coins and all would be well.

### Gainers and losers

It would seem from this that the success of a tight money policy in bringing inflation under control depends crucially on price and wage bargainers understanding the effects of their actions on unemployment *and* being able to reach some agreement on prices and wages which does not result in price increases.

As we have seen in the real economy, it is not the case that all workers reduce their hours, but rather that some workers have no hours at all. It is as if instead of Defoe, Crusoe and Plomley each accepting a one-third reduction in their working hours, Defoe and Crusoe continue working full time and Plomley is prevented from working at all. In so far as this is true there will be very little reason for Defoe or Crusoe to moderate their claims – it is not they who will lose their jobs. The 'discipline of the market' is thus greatly weakened if the penalty for vigorous bargaining does not fall on all the bargainers equally.

The present government therefore seems to be relying on the fear of the *possibility* of being unemployed rather than the *certainty* of being underemployed. It is not clear how strong that possibility would appear to be to most strong bargainers. The government's case for pursuing a tight money policy at all must be either that inflation is bad *per se* or that the distributional aspects of increasing money supply are unavoidable and unacceptable. There has been very little work done on this latter point: it is not known how to increase money supply without redistributing income and wealth.

### Non-labour costs

If, as is the case with oil, some price increases are beyond the control of the labour then the only way to make do with a fixed supply of money is to cut wages as oil prices increase so as to hold constant the overall level of prices. This downward flexibility of money wage rates may turn out to be very difficult to achieve. Money supply must therefore be increased if unemployment is to be avoided.

Again some statistics may serve to illustrate this point. Figure 6.3 shows output rising, with only the occasional hiccough, fairly steadily since 1948. In 1979 there was a marked reversal of this trend – output falling four percentage points over the next two years. Year-

**Figure 6.3** *Gross domestic product evaluated at 1975 prices*

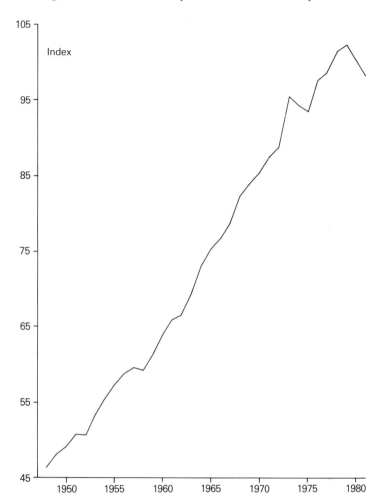

on-year price changes are shown in Figure 6.4 and even a cursory inspection shows no appreciable correlation between prices and output. This makes it difficult to argue, as the government does, that inflation *inevitably* leads to falls in employment and output. There is, however, evidence to suggest that the tight money policy introduced in 1979 did adversely affect output without bringing prices under control. Figure 6.5 shows how the rate of unemploy-

**Figure 6.4**   *Rate of inflation*

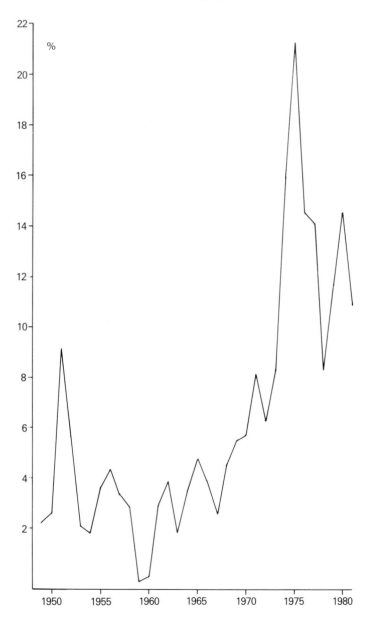

**Figure 6.5** *Unemployment rate*

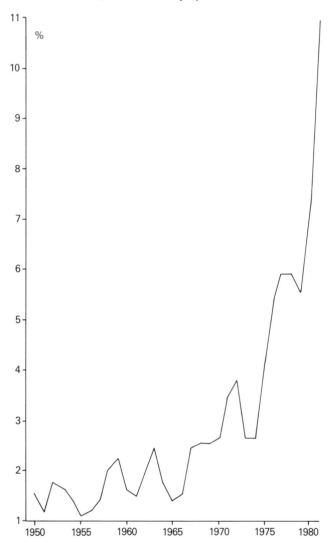

ment has changed over the last thirty years. Beginning at about 1.5 per cent it has been rising ever-more steeply to reach 10 per cent in 1981. The very sharp jump after 1979 again corresponds to the introduction of the tight money policy. The 5 per cent jump in unemployment also corresponds very closely with the 4 per cent fall in GDP showing that the reduced output involves laying off men rather than reducing hours of work. What is meant by a tight money policy and whether or not the government can ever successfully control money supply are issues taken up elsewhere in this volume. The point being made here is that a shortage of money can result in *unnecessary, involuntary* unemployment.

## Summary and conclusion

Unemployment, the scourge of the 1930s, was once conquered but now is back with us again. Is it merely a recurrence of the 1930s strain of chaos, requiring the same treatment as before? Or is it immune from old remedies? Is it a new strain or a mixture of strains requiring a more discriminating approach? The aim of this chapter has been to separate out various forms of unemployment to see which are suitable cases for treatment by the central government. Not all forms of unemployment are to be regarded as 'bad' and of those which are, not all are susceptible to government action. To some extent the classification of unemployment into these various types is a subjective matter, depending more on the point of view of the observer than on the facts of the case. But even if we did all agree on matters of opinion we still lack the facts necessary to formulate appropriate policies.

The government could moderate the harmful effects of technological change by controlling the pace of change and helping labour to be more mobile – both professionally by retraining programmes and geographically by easing the difficulties and expenses of moving house.

The unequal distribution of unemployment could be eased by encouraging a rather more flexible working week. This would mean that hours rather than men would be reduced when output fell and everyone would suffer a small fall in income rather than some suffering all the reductions. This could be helped along by the government reducing the fixed costs of using labour and by introducing a negative income-tax rather than a pure unemployment benefit. The spirit behind these recommendations is one of encouraging everyone to make what contribution he can to the country's economic well-being. The present system prevents and discourages some potential contributors.

When unemployment is due to a shortage of capital, the government may wish to force or encourage extra saving by taxation and exhortation. At the moment suppliers of capital and employers of labour are not highly valued.

Legislation aimed at moderating the behaviour of economic agents is typically designed to protect the employee from the employer (e.g. The Employment Protection Act). Unfortunately this also has the effect of protecting the employed against the unemployed. Those without work have no way of influencing wage bargains simply because they are not allowed to compete with existing workers.

Particular attention has been paid to the supposed 'trade-off' between unemployment and inflation. This is the main bone of contention in British politics. It is suggested, by the theory and the facts, that the pursuit of low inflation by restricting the money supply will adversely affect the level of output and employment.

# INTRODUCTION TO CHAPTER 7

The old hawker's call, 'Round and round it goes; where it stops nobody knows', applies beautifully to 'money'. We have very little knowledge of where our pound notes or cheques go, as they are used to purchase goods and services and finance transactions, and as Chris Hawkins and Michael Wickens argued, this is critical to the understanding of inflation. This is the problem which David Heathfield and Ivor Pearce attempt to come to grips with in the next chapter. They find it curious that much of our macroeconomic policy should be devoted to the control of money (as discussed in each of the previous chapters) when it is inherently uncontrollable under present institutional arrangements. Heathfield and Pearce argue that we should have some form of automatic adjustment mechanism which determines the amount of money available in relation to prices. For example, consider the following example. If prices should rise for some reason, it would be desirable if the amount of money in circulation were to fall. This in turn would reduce spending and cause prices to fall back. Since, as Heathfield and Pearce argue, governments are frequently undisciplined, it is necessary that the control mechanism should be automatic. And the mechanism should work both ways. If prices should fall, there should be an automatic increase in the money stock.

In current circumstances such a proposal is bound to seem radical and new. However, it has a well-known historial antecedent. For a period in the late nineteenth century and early twentieth century many countries operated under a system called the gold standard. Ideally it was supposed to operate something like this. If a country was experiencing inflation consumers would switch from purchasing goods at home to purchasing goods manufactured in countries where prices were constant (or the rate of inflation lower). As a consequence this country would find itself spending more abroad than foreigners were spending on its goods. A balance-of-payment deficit would occur. To settle this deficit the country would have to pay foreigners, using some of its stock of gold. This would reduce the amount of gold left to circulate in the home economy, i.e. reduce the money supply and cause a downward pressure on prices. There was thus an automatic mechanism tending to adjust the money supply and inflation via the balance of international payments. Heathfield and Pearce argue that their automatic scheme will create an environment in which prices adjust efficiently without unduly affecting employment levels. This approach contrasts with Hawkins, Rowan and Wickens, who are considerably more sceptical about the speed with which the price mechanism operates. We have come now to a fundamental issue where economists are only beginning to scratch the surface. It is certainly an area where considerably more data and analysis are required.

C.H. and G.M.

# 7   A Tract on Sound Money:  Why and How

*by David Heathfield and Ivor Pearce*

## WHY

Trying to conduct economic affairs in terms of money, the purchasing power of which changes at an ever-changing rate, is as absurd as trying to develop an engineering project with instruments which recalibrate themselves erratically from day to day. Sanity can be preserved only if changes in the unit of measurement are predictable; but it is not in the nature of inflation that its progress should be predictable. Those who argue that it is possible to 'get used' to inflation are observing only that, since we have no alternative, almost any degree of misery can be endured. It cannot be a question, should inflation be halted? it can only be a question of when and how.

Does it not seem strange that at the present time we go to enormous lengths to preserve unchanged the meaning of the words 'metre' and 'gram' but we care not at all about the meaning of 'one pound sterling?' It was not always so. Generally speaking, throughout the five thousand years of recorded history much more attention was paid to the unit of value than to the unit of length. Apart from one or two brief and disastrous experiments the meaning of the pound sterling has always been strictly fixed. The legend 'I promise to pay the bearer on demand the sum of one pound' which appears on our banknotes finally became ridiculous only in 1932.

In the past fifty years we have developed a very odd way of doing things. No longer does our base money have a real cost of production. It can be had simply for the cost of printing notes. No longer does it have an intrinsic 'scarcity' value. To compensate for this we try to control the supply of money. This goes against nature in the sense that suppliers who can earn abnormal profits by evading controls will never be entirely suppressed. Nothing which costs nothing to produce can ever be worth anything in the long run.

Nor is this the worst of it. In order to maintain the value of money it is not sufficient merely to keep the supply constant. Supply must be kept in line with demand. If demand increases, so must supply – if demand falls so must supply. Yet we have no universally agreed theory which allows us to calculate the demand for money. The essence of the dispute between monetarists and others concerns the nature of the demand for money and the extent to which it might be affected by variations in interest rates. We do not therefore know how to determine the precise supply of money which will preserve a fixed value. The present British government is following current conventional wisdom in controlling the rate of interest in the hope, supported by an uncertain theory, that this will control the demand for money in the hope, supported by a still more uncertain theory, that this will control the value of money. Nobody any longer is entirely satisfied that the government will be successful. Our currency is becoming unacceptable.

Is it not time that economists made some effort to find a way to re-establish *direct* control over the value of money? If we could be sure that the value of money was fixed we might then allow the supply of money to take care of itself. Whatever scheme is devised it must be simple, call for minimum knowledge of parameters, which are hard to measure accurately, and require no government controls. It is easy to generate ideas. What is not easy is to generate the right idea appropriate to our time. In the hope that it might provoke discussion we propose one possible plan. We urge that points we have overlooked should become the starting-point for further discussion rather than an excuse for rejecting a principle which we believe cannot, in the long run, be evaded.

**HOW**

Our starting-point is the well-known economic maxim that nothing can command, for long, a price much different from its supply costs. This, combined with the fact that governments can print money (at practically no cost) and issue it (at its face value) in any quantity, suggests that the value of money will, in the long run, decline until it reaches printing costs.

The essential idea behind this chapter is that the Issue Department of the Bank of England should stand ready to either buy or sell £1 notes for the current retail price level, as measured by the Retail Price Index. This means that should the index fall below 1.00, say to 0.90, then anyone can 'buy' £1 notes for 90p each from the Bank of England. Conversely when the index stands above 1.00, say 1.10, then anyone can sell £1 notes to the Bank of England for £1.1. In the first case, when £1 notes are sold by the Bank of England the revenue (derived from selling notes) must be put back into circulation either by paying off government debt or by the government simply spending it. Conversely, when £1 notes are sold to the Bank of England they must be destroyed. The revenue necessary to buy them must be raised by borrowing from the public or by increasing taxes. The Bank of England must not print notes unless the public buy them, nor must it destroy notes unless the public have sold them.

## Making profit by selling money

It would not do, of course, for someone to take £1 to the Bank when the index is high and demand £1.1, and then at once offering the £1.1 for £1.21 and so on indefinitely. We have to ensure that the profit to be made from selling money is not to be had for nothing. By imposing a (say thirty days) delay between the surrender of a note and receipt of the payment for it would ensure that capital is tied up in the money selling business as in any other business.

## Effective laws are never invoked

Notice first, that the pound note could never for long be diminished in real value. If prices were to rise, the holder of each note could, within thirty days, compensate himself for his real loss by selling it to the Bank of England. Indeed it might not be necessary even to do this, for shopkeepers, as well as noteholders, would observe the index to have risen. To the shopkeeper this could mean extra profits since by the sale of goods for notes he earns both the notes *and* the rights of noteholders. The mere observation that prices in general have risen, could be sufficient reason for putting prices down again if competition were severe. The index reverts to its proper level, with scarcely any delay.

**Decreasing the quantity of money**

Furthermore it is easy to see that destroying notes necessarily reduces the total amount of high-powered money in circulation. Any note sold to the Bank of England is physically destroyed and the note and coin given by the Bank of England in exchange came, not from an unused store or from new printing, but, from the sale of bonds or from taxation, i.e. from money already in circulation among the general public. Accordingly, as the quantity theory of money tells us, prices must fall, the cost-of-living index reverting to its proper level (unity) at which point it becomes unprofitable to destroy money further.

**Action through interest rates**

It is not desirable, in this brief account, to trace in full the transmission mechanism from a reduction in the quantity of money to the fall in prices, but a number of points might be made. First the mechanism must be quick in operation or the market would be unstable. Not more than thirty days are allowed for prices to adjust. On the other hand, whenever the index is seen to stand above 1, some pound notes would be switched from their normal usage to make a profit in the money-selling business. To hold on to high-powered money, clearing banks (Barclays, Lloyds, NatWest, Midland) would need to pay a rate of interest on all deposits so as to give a return in thirty days equal to that which could be earned by the surrender of a note. This would imply an annual rate of interest of 24 per cent for a mere 2 per cent rise in the index. It would be necessary therefore for clearing banks to charge a similar rate on loans. Any businessman having a bank loan or, for that matter any outstanding loan of any kind, would be bound to reduce his indebtedness by selling goods out of stocks (thereby reducing prices) and/or by cutting wages and prices, so driving the index back to its base level. It is doubtful if, with such a system, the index could ever rise by much more than 2 per cent and even then only momentarily.

## Expectations

Consider also the role of expectations under such a system. Once the community got used to the new institutions everyone would be expecting prices to fall whenever the index stood at a level greater than 1. It would appear profitable to sell any goods, held for whatever reason, if only because it would be understood that they could be repurchased almost immediately at a lower price.

## Increasing the quantity of money

If more money should be needed, any individual or institution would be able to require the Bank of England to print notes upon payment, in notes, of a sum of money equal to the amount to be printed multiplied by a cost-of-living index. The payment for the printing of notes should be used immediately by the Bank of England to buy bonds. This means that the high-powered money supply will increase when the index is below 1. No one, of course, will want to have money printed when the index stands above 1 for this would imply that the buyer finishes with less money than he started with. The cost of money creation would exceed the value of the money created.

If, on the other hand, the index stood at 0.8 it would be possible to but a £1 note for 0.80p. There would be a powerful incentive to create money if and when prices fall.

## Making profits by buying money

Once again, of course, we have to ensure that the market is stable. There must be an effective mechanism to ensure that prices will rise sufficiently quickly on the creation of extra money to prevent too many notes appearing too soon.

The following is a possibility. The purchase of new money might be allowed only after thirty days' notice of intent, at the same time, it might be necessary to require payment for new money to be made at a price determined by the value of the cost-of-living index on the day of payment rather than on the day on which notice of intent is given. This will introduce an element of risk for the buyer.

**Interest rates again**

Just as in the case of money annihilation, payment for money printing must be made when notice of intent is given rather than on
delivery of the new notes. The Bank of England must at once use the
money from these payments to buy bonds from the general public.
This will have two effects. First, it will tend to reduce the rate of
interest. Second, it will return immediately to the banks all the notes
lost in consequence of the payments to the Issue Department.

In contrast with the money annihilation case there would be no
loss of notes by the commercial banks. On the contrary, as new
notes come to be printed after the thirty-day period, commercial
banks would find themselves in possession of more notes than before. Nor within the thirty-day period should they find themselves
with fewer notes for any appreciable time. There should be no need
for commercial banks to *raise* their interest rates paid to depositors.

**Expectations again**

To rely entirely on a fall in the interest rate to stimulate demand for
labour and goods and hence price rises, however, it might well be to
rely on a mechanism which is too slow. What might be needed is
some device for translating rapidly the profits, earned by those who
bought new money, into the hands of manufacturers or holders of
goods. If expectations were rational, of course, there would be no
need for such a device; for with an index standing at 0.8 and the
whole world expecting it to return to 1 no holder of goods would be
willing to sell. Prices would rise and with them profits and wages.

**Perverse expectations**

If prices were not expected to rise, it is conceivable that the expanding money supply, whilst causing interest rates to rise, would be
used simply to make a profit out of buying more and more new
money. That is, the new money, instead of pushing up prices, would
be ploughed back into buying more notes. Eventually there would
be a spill-over into the goods purchased causing the index to move.
But the accumulation of new money would have been too great so

that the index would overshoot the value 1. An unstable cycle of price fluctuations could develop.

All this should not be a matter for great concern. Lengthening of the thirty-day period of notice with its consequent increase in uncertainty may well prevent instability at the cost of a longer period of low prices. This is a matter for further consideration and experimentation.

## International trade

Once the value of the pound is fixed it might become very much in demand internationally. Unless similar schemes were introduced by other countries it is likely that the pound would very quickly replace the US dollar and even, perhaps, the Special Drawing Rights as the unit of international account. This could lead to difficulties in the absence of a countervailing force.

## Exchange rates

In particular, individuals and institutions domiciled abroad may very well wish to hold sterling as a hedge against inflation in their own countries. There would then be an inflow of foreign currencies for conversion into pounds.

This demand for sterling, over and above the demand for other currencies, would lead to a rise in rates of exchange in favour of sterling.

## Exporting money

Sterling will look attractive whenever a foreign country's interest rate falls below its inflation rate. Britain should therefore expect, from time to time, an inflow of 'hot' money. This will cause a movement in exchange rates too favourable to sterling. There will be a shift in British production away from internationally traded goods to those which do not enter into trade if, that is, producers can be induced to maintain full employment. Otherwise British production and employment will fall. Imports will rise above the value of exports until the imbalance of trade is equal to the abnormal inflow of foreign currency. A new balance will be reached in international *payments* (but not trade). What will happen is that the 'hot' money flowing in, will induce the British to consume more than they produce, and import more than they export. The British will be exchanging their good currency for foreign imports.

There are two problems which arise. The first is that inflows of hot money (and perhaps outflows) are intermittent phenomena dependent on what is happening overseas. We are therefore liable to suffer continual change in our pattern of production, with consequent dislocation and losses. These bouts of unemployment would be generated by the failure of foreign countries to equip themselves with a satisfactory currency.

### The repatriation of sterling

The second problem arises out of the liabilities which we would incur precisely because the value of the pound sterling is guaranteed. It is pleasant to enjoy the consumption of more goods than we produce especially when we pay for these with money which we have, after all, only printed. But it is not so pleasant when the day comes for us to take back our printed money and give back goods.

### A remedy

The philosophy which we have been pursuing is one of 'no controls', 'let the market work!' But there is one thing we must control and that is the effect upon us of our neighbour's folly. In the country of the blind the one-eyed man is not king unless he modifies his behaviour to take account of everyone else's blindness. If everyone had a proper currency no control would be needed; but where we are forced to trade in currencies without intrinsic value we have to deal with the problems created. Even so the last thing to choose is non-convertibility or quantitative exchange controls. We need to make the market work in spite of its weakness.

One way to achieve the desired result is to set up a permanent Trade Commission to watch the balance of trade as opposed to the balance of payments. Whenever we show signs of importing more than we export, the Commission should sell bonds in Britain for sterling and use the proceeds to buy foreign currency. The foreign currency in turn is used to acquire assets abroad. This will allow the growth in the foreign holding of sterling to continue, but the consequent inflow of foreign currencies would be repatriated in exchange for foreign assets. The exchange rate is therefore unaffected by 'hot money'.

The operations of the Commission would ensure that the foreign accumulation of sterling balances were matched by our holdings of foreign assets. The excess of imports induced by the foreign 'hot' money would take the form of an acquisition of foreign real capital hedged against foreign inflation. British 'good' currency would be swapped for 'good' real capital abroad and not for goods to be consumed. Foreign-held sterling would be properly backed by foreign real capital. Our exchange rate would cease to be affected appreciably by foreign capital inflows. There need be no artificially induced changes in the pattern of British production. Home industry would be protected against unnaturally favourable exchange rates; the British economy would be insulated from the shock of flights of currency.

**Banking**

The principal difference for the commercial banks would be that each would have to accept responsibility for the maintenance of its own solvency. At the moment the Bank of England in its role of lender-of-last-resort stands ready to issue whatever quantity of notes required by the commercial banks for their solvency. Under our scheme, banks which were short of notes might be able to borrow or sell bonds, but there would be no bottomless pit available at the Bank of England. Commercial bank credit could, as now, be created by expanding chequing accounts, at will, simply by raising deposits and entering a counterpart loan. But if the creation of this credit raised prices above 1.00 then notes would be offered for destruction and the stock of money would be reduced. Loans would have to be called in by the commercial banks. The rate of interest would rise sharply.

As in the days of the gold standard there would be the risk of a 'run on the bank'. This is not necessarily a bad thing. It is precisely the risk of collapse which keeps banks from behaving irresponsibly. No doubt it would be proper to arrange 'insurance' to protect depositors and it might be the responsibility of the Bank of England to oversee this. The risks taken by commercial banks should be assessed, by examination of their accounts, and their insurance premiums varied accordingly. To require the Bank of England to act as lender of last resort is equivalent to confessing that commercial banks *do not know* the level of their own reserves. How can any bank behave prudently if it does not, in the last analysis, know what its reserves are?

## The bond market

Although in principle anyone can offer notes for destruction or buy notes from the Bank of England, we imagine that will be carried on almost entirely by institutions, particularly the commercial banks and the discount houses.

Under the scheme proposed here, money is no longer irredeemable interest-free government debt. It becomes instantly transformable into thirty-day 'bonds' whose price is the level of the price index. Thus the discount houses for example may choose to put some of their funds into Treasury Bills and some into the money-selling business for realisation in thirty days. This thirty-day 'bond' may be traded like a Treasury Bill for which it becomes a close substitute, the principal difference being, of course, that whereas the return on Treasury Bills is negotiable, the return on the Money Bond is set by the retail price index.

This substitutability of Treasury Bills and our Money Bonds means that price fluctuations yielding less than the Treasury Bill rate will leave the quantity of money unaffected since no one will use money to create or destroy notes if they can make a higher return by investing in Treasury Bills. But any persistent drift in the price index will, however small, eventually lead to a level of prices which renders Money Bonds more attractive than Treasury Bills whence corrective movements in the supply of money will occur.

This 'substitution' is of course substitution in the eyes of the holder of the assets. As far as the government is concerned Treasury Bills and Money Bonds are substitutes only if the price index is falling. Treasury Bills represent government borrowing and are unambiguously a source of funds, but the notes accepted in return for Money Bonds must be destroyed when the price index stands above 1.00 and the Money Bonds subsequently redeemed with borrowed funds or with tax revenue. Thus a rise in the price index results in a decrease in the demand for government debt coupled with an increase in its supply, thereby lowering Treasury Bill prices (i.e. raising interest rates). If the index stands below 1.00 the notes received have to be used to pay off debt or to finance a budget deficit – they are subsequently redeemed by printing new notes. This results in an immediate switch from Treasury Bills to Money Bonds (leaving the net debt holding by the public unchanged) and to an eventual increase in notes and a reduction in Money Bills when they are redeemed thirty days later with newly printed notes. The net result in this case is a reduced supply of Treasury Bills and an increased supply of money; thereby raising Treasury Bill price and hence lowering interest rates.

## Conclusion

We offer here a scheme for maintaining a sound money. The essential feature is that notes issued by the Bank of England may be at any time exchanged for Money Bonds, which in turn after a fixed time period must be redeemed by the Bank at a price determined by the retail price index. Notes may be neither printed nor destroyed except through the mechanism of the Money Bond. A detailed comprehensive account of any such scheme as this would be neither possible nor at this early stage desirable, but we have attempted to hint at some of the implications of the scheme for the behaviour of the central and commercial banks, the bond market and the exchange equalisation account. Whatever the merits or demerits of these speculations might be we would not want the scheme to stand or fall by them.

Any scheme, whatever its intrinsic merit, directed at maintaining a sound money, will to some extent succeed or fail depending on whether or not people believe in it. One of the merits of this scheme is that anyone can, in principle, exchange his £1 note for its original worth whatever the rate of inflation might be. With this kind of guarantee it is probable that wage bargaining and price setting would no longer be fired by expectations about inflation rates and thus would, by being themselves moderate, contribute directly to the stability of prices.

Finally we have argued throughout that this is a means of maintaining a sound money, which is not quite the same thing as attaining a sound money. It might well be felt that the immediate adoption of a scheme such as this would cause considerable disruption of not only the money markets, but also the real side of the economy. The means and timing of introducing any such scheme must, as must the details of its operation, be the outcome of a wide and informed debate. The object of this chapter is to invite discussion and to offer a line of thought to inform rather than dictate current policy.

# INTRODUCTION TO CHAPTER 8

Not surprisingly, most of the previous chapters have commented upon the government's attempts to reduce the rate of inflation by concentrating on control of the money supply. There are many methods which have traditionally been used in the past and there is no one approach which is used throughout the world. However, the fulcrum upon which monetary policy is based is the commercial banking system, for here resides the potential for increasing or decreasing the level of deposits held by businesses and households. A simple example will serve to illustrate this point. Suppose that you take £50 which you have been holding and deposit them in your current account at a commercial bank. This sets in motion a quite amazing sequence of events. The bank lends the funds to someone who wishes to buy some item, say an inexpensive television set. The television dealer then deposits his receipts in his current account. The money supply has increased. And it will increase even further. The commercial bank will make an additional loan with the newly deposited funds. And the chain will continue to grow.

One procedure for controlling the rate of growth of bank deposits (part of $M_3$ as defined by Chris Hawkins in Chapter 1) is for the government's agent, the Bank of England, to require commercial banks to hold a proportion of the funds on deposit as idle reserves. This ratio is about 1 per cent in Britain as compared with the USA or West Germany where it lies between 10 and 20 per cent. A second method is for the Bank of England to buy or sell government debt to households and businesses. This has the effect of increasing or decreasing the funds on deposit at the banks.

Whether these or other methods are utilised in an attempt to control the level of $M_3$, there is some uncertainty as to the effects these actions will actually have upon the level of economic activity. In the famous Radcliffe Committee Report of 1958 it was pointed out that the wider the variety of assets which compete with commercial bank deposits, the more difficult will it be to implement an effective monetary policy. This is the theme which George McKenzie develops in the next chapter on international banking. He first takes the reader through simple examples based on the activities of building societies, which, he argues, tend to increase the velocity of circulation, $V$ (refer to Chapter 1 again). Then he shows that exactly the same thing has occurred with the rapid growth of international banking over the past decade. Consequently, as the monetary authorities attempt to control $M_3$, there may well develop offsetting changes in the velocity of circulation, $V$.

C.H. and G.M.

# 8 Is there an International Banking Crisis?

*by George McKenzie*

Any mention of international banking is bound to conjure up very picturesque images in most people's minds. Well-dressed men briskly walking down one of the streets in the City to a meeting where some multi-million pound deal will be clinched. The proverbial gnomes of Zurich rapidly moving funds around the world to take advantage of the most recent changes in interest rates. Central bankers smoking large Cuban cigars and drinking brandy after an emergency meeting in Washington or Basle. The world of high finance and espionage depicted in the best-selling novel of Paul Erdman *The Crash of '79* (1976). It is an image of a highly technical world tinged with clouds of mystery and perhaps a little adventure.

No doubt there is some very small element of truth in this widely held image. In reality, however, international banking activities are undertaken by men and women of high principle whose motives are not terribly different from those of any worker or executive: to achieve financial reward for work done. It is true that many of the transactions which are entered into by banks are highly complicated. However, as we shall see in this chapter, the basic principles of international banking are quite simple to understand. Indeed this chapter provides me with the opportunity to discuss some of the mechanics of the financial sector which have been implicit in previous chapters.

International banking activities are a very important component of the British economy. First, as can be seen from Table 8.1, approximately two-thirds of all deposits held at British banks (including foreign-owned banks) are in terms of foreign currencies. International banking is thus an important source of funds and hence of profits for these institutions. Second, over the past decade, both the private and public sectors have increasingly sought loans denominated in foreign currencies. Thus in 1980 approximately 20 per cent of such borrowing from banks was of this form. This raises an important policy question. In a world of free trade in goods and financial items (such as shares, bonds and bank deposit funds) is it possible for the Bank of England to influence the money supply in such a way as to affect economic activity or will banks and corporations simply obtain the required funds elsewhere? Third, at a time when most monetary authorities throughout the world have been attempting to carry out policies designed to cool down the international economy, international bank loans have grown at a fantastic pace. The result has been that these institutions have sought customers that they would have turned down in the past. As we shall see, loans to many developing and Eastern-bloc countries have risen dramatically. The question is: is this a viable situation?

**Table 8.1**    *Total deposits at British banks (£ million)*

|  | Sterling | Foreign currencies |
|---|---|---|
| 1981 | | |
| (third quarter) | 79 155 | 226 148 |
| 1980 | 70 643 | 152 027 |
| 1979 | 57 451 | 132 666 |
| 1978 | 48 634 | 109 947 |
| 1977 | 43 351 | 93 833 |
| 1976 | 38 510 | 90 770 |
| 1975 | 35 515 | 66 174 |
| 1974 | 33 901 | 49 397 |
| 1973 | 30 628 | 39 892 |
| 1972 | 24 013 | 25 755 |
| 1971 | 19 310 | 17 650 |

Source: *UK Financial Statistics.*

In order to be able to explain all these issues it will be helpful if we first answer the question: what do banks, and, in particular, international banks, actually do? The answer is that the basis of international banking is not much different from that of the traditional high-street bank or building society. To appreciate this rather fundamental point let us turn back the pages of history several centuries to a time when the main form of money was metal coinage. At the time most people probably believed that the value of the coins stemmed from the market value of gold, silver, copper or other metal used in the minting. However, this need not be the case. The real value of money stems from the quantity of goods which can be purchased by a pound, dollar or Deutsche Mark. The real value of money stems from the willingness of consumers, businesses and financial institutions to accept the particular form of money used, either on the basis of custom or law. Given that this is the case, it is not too surprising that an important innovation took place in the seventeenth century. Coins of whatever form were then, as they are today, a cumbersome means of payment. They had to be transported from place to place for the purpose of carrying out transactions. There was always the risk of loss or indeed of theft. As a consequence, goldsmiths initiated the practice of accepting customers' gold coins for safekeeping. Since they always maintained stocks of gold for their own work, they had to provide storage facilities for themselves. Consequently, the provision of storage facilities to others was a logical extension of their existing business.

The goldsmiths quickly realised that, despite periodic withdrawals by some depositors, there were generally offsetting new deposits by others such that the stock of gold on hand was always some positive amount. This provided a further profitable opportunity: they undertook to loan a proportion of their deposits to other customers who required funds to finance some business venture. Provided that the goldsmiths maintained adequate reserves they would be in a position to withstand (a) a reasonable amount of net withdrawals and (b) the possibility that a proportion (hopefully small) of borrowers actually defaulted on their loans.

Inherent in the activities of the goldsmiths are the basic characteristics of modern banking. First and foremost, it is clear that banks enable an economy to make better use of available financial resources. Suppose that they, or, in our example, the goldsmiths did not exist. Those individuals with savings, e.g. holdings of gold coins, would be forced to keep them idle. Those individuals short of funds necessary to undertake a potentially profitable investment would remain frustrated. Suppose that I wanted to borrow funds in order to build a house. You, the reader, would no doubt be very wary of lending me the required funds. I might be dishonest or I could lose my job, a possibility particularly strong during periods when business conditions are weak.

Banks, on the other hand, are in a position to get round these two difficulties provided that two extremely important and fundamental assumptions are fulfilled.

1. There is a *low* probability that a large proportion of depositors will withdraw their funds.
2. There is a *low* probability that a large proportion of borrowers will default on their loans.

If the word *low,* italicised above, is changed to *high,* then not only the banks but the economy as a whole is in considerable trouble. If the high probabilities become a reality, then the bank will be unable to meet the withdrawal requests of the remaining depositors. Technically it will be bankrupt. If this situation is widespread throughout the economy (as it was during the Great Depression) the entire financial system will appear to be overextended. People's assets will be wiped out and economic activity will decline.

There is a very real trade-off between the greater efficiency which banks and other financial institutions bring about and the potential for instability that they engender. Of course, it must be emphasised that during normal times the probability of any difficulties arising will be very low. However, the fact that banking crises have occurred in the past has led to the development of the central bank. In general central banks have very close connections with the government of the day, although in many economies they are semi-autonomous. In most countries the job of the central bank is to regulate the money supply, to ensure the stability of financial markets, to help the central government raise money by borrowing and to oversee the operation of commercial banks. In this last capacity the central bank acts as a watchdog or policeman.

Although the public relations managers of leading commercial banks may suffer from cardiac arrest upon reading this, it is indeed the case that banks are 'gamblers'. They are betting very heavily that the two fundamental assumptions listed above will be fulfilled. However, when one thinks about this in greater depth, there is really nothing wrong with 'gambling' at all. Virtually every moment of our lives we take decisions which involve gambles. As we drive to work we assume that there is a very small probability of being hit by a heavy lorry whose breaks have failed. More to the point, managers and directors of companies take a gamble every time they invest in a new project designed to increase profits. If the project fails, the company could go bankrupt with all the attendant consequences for both management and the workforce. The stakes are thus very high. Similarly when we invest our savings in the shares of individual companies we are gambling that they will be successful, or equivalently, we are gambling that they will not fail. Risk-taking or gambling is thus part and parcel of everyone's life. This is widely accepted and thus we do not expect to be protected every single moment of our lives against the likelihood that something may go wrong. Indeed, risk-taking is part of the dynamic of a modern and prosperous economy.

The question then arises, you say, why should we be so concerned with the risk-taking or gambling activities intrinsically associated with the operation of banks? If risk-taking is such a normal part of our everyday life why should we single out banks for special consideration? Why should central banks, as they do in one way or another, take such interest in the viability of commercial banks. The basic answer lies in the fact that if banks were to fail the consequences would not only affect the workers, managers and directors of those banks. The failures would affect everyone. Current account deposits in all major industrial countries fulfil the role of money or media of exchange. This is a far cry from the days of the goldsmiths when the coins utilised possessed some intrinsic value. In contrast the intrinsic value of the pages in your cheque book (or indeed of any pound note) is virtually nil. Their value arises from the widespread custom that virtually everyone is willing to accept these pieces of paper in exchange for the provision of goods and services. (The bank card, of course, provides an extra incentive; in particular, it protects any shop against fraud.)

The point of this discussion is that banks act as much more than intermediaries who accept deposits from savers and provide loans to others. The accounts which they create act as money and hence, if banks should fail in any substantial number, depositors would lose, less money would be available and economic activity would be severely affected. For this reason, central banks are ever watchful that such circumstances do not arise. They may simply monitor the activities of banks and other financial institutions. If a bankruptcy occurs they may arrange for other banks to take over the business of the failed institution. Or the central bank could simply act as a lender-of-last-resort. That is, the central bank could lend money to the commercial bank in difficulty in the hope that this would enable it to meet all its obligations and provide it with sufficient time to get its house in order.

To sum up this part of the discussion we note the following points:

1. Banks enable available resources to be utilised more efficiently.
2. Like all businesses, banks are risk-takers.
3. However, unlike other businesses, their deposits act as money; hence, central banks, such as the Bank of England, act as watchdogs to ensure that banks do not get into difficulties which would hinder their role as creators of money.

One more step is required before we can fully appreciate the implications of international banking. Deposits at high-street banks are used as money, as we have just emphasised. However, there exist other important high-street institutions which are very similar to banks, but whose deposits cannot physically be used as money. These are the building societies. Like your current account balance at a commercial bank, you can easily withdraw funds from a building society. However, unlike your current account balance you cannot write a cheque against your building society account. You must first obtain pound notes or arrange for funds to be transferred to your current account at the bank up the street. This fact has some rather interesting implications, which are best explained by examining a simple example. In particular, let us examine what happens when you decide to transfer, say, £100 from your current account to a building society account. In Table 8.2 we show hypothetical balance-sheets for these two institutions. The columns labelled 'liabilities' record the amount of money which they owe to you as depositors. On the other side of the balance-sheet are recorded the assets of these institutions; that is, the loans and investments which they undertake.

Thus under the liabilities side of the high-street bank's balance-sheet is recorded your withdrawal of funds. There is then a corresponding increase in the liabilities of the building society as soon as you deposit your funds there, say, into a share account. A very crucial thing happens next. The building society loans out your £100 in the form of a mortgage, say to John Smith. The latter, in turn, purchases a home from Peter Jones, who, in turn, deposits the

**Table 8.2**

Balance-sheet of High-street Bank

| Liabilities | Assets |
|---|---|
| Your current account<br> deposit<br> – £100 | |
| Peter Jones's current account<br> deposit<br> + £100 | |

Balance-sheet of Building Society

| Liabilities | Assets |
|---|---|
| Your share account<br> + £100 | Mortgage loan to John Smith<br> + £100 |

John Smith purchases a home from Peter Jones, who deposits the funds at the high-street bank.

---

funds in his account at the high-street bank. The final situation is as depicted in Table 8.2.

Two points stand out for consideration. First, the overall level of deposits and loans of the high-street bank remain unchanged. Peter Jones's deposit of £100 just offsets your withdrawal of £100. There is no need for the bank to alter the level of its loans. However, deposits and loans at the building society have both increased. How is this possible, you ask? It is almost as if something has been created from nothing.

The important issue to appreciate here is that the assets and liabilities created by the building society are somewhat different from those created by the bank. We have already noted that cheques cannot be written against the deposits of the building society. But offsetting this is the fact that such deposits yield interest, which is not the case with your current account deposit. Then, on the asset side, the two institutions compete head-on but in different ways. The building society offers long-term loans (e.g. twenty-five years) for housebuilding, something that banks have been very reluctant to do until recently. In contrast, banks have preferred to make reasonably short-term loans and investments (up to five years). The two institutions thus offer differentiated products. And in the process, the building society brings about an even more efficient utilisation of resources than would otherwise have been the case. By providing services that other financial institutions have preferred not to provide, a higher level of economic activity is achieved than if there were only banks in existence. Of course, like the banks themselves, the building societies are gamblers, making exactly the same assumptions that the banks do. That is, they assume that there is (a) only a *low* probability of substantial withdrawals, and (b) only a *low* probability of widespread default among borrowers.

As a consequence, widespread failure of building societies would have similar implications as a widespread failure of commercial banks. Many individual depositors would lose a substantial proportion of their savings. Spending levels would be reduced and this would lead to similar changes in the levels of output and employment. Despite this apparent similarity with commercial banks, building societies do not possess any lender-of-last-resort. Instead there exist arrangements which are really of the form of gentlemen's agreements. If a particular building society gets in trouble, that institution may be helped out by its colleagues in the Building Societies Association, by commercial banks or, if need be, by the Bank of England. There are, however, no formal arrangements.

We may now summarise the argument of this section as follows. In addition to banks there are other institutions, such as building societies, which increase further the efficiency with which resources are utilised. They do this by competing directly with the high-street banks in terms of the services provided. However, deposits at such institutions are not money in the sense that they cannot be directly used for the purpose of carrying out transactions.


**International banking**

We are now in a position to analyse the mysteries of international banking. In point of fact, what is involved is not terribly different from the activities undertaken by high-street banks and building societies. Indeed, no new points of principle arise in our subsequent discussion. Only the details will appear to be different.

The origins of international banking are really the origins of banking itself. The Italian word *banca* means bench, which in this case refers to the bench at which foreign currencies were exchanged at medieval fairs. Thus early bankers were really only brokers, arranging deals between persons wishing to buy or sell foreign currencies. It was not until the seventeenth century that the gold-smiths developed as financial intermediaries, the primary activity which characterises present-day banks.

Until the 1950s international banking was really no different in form than the high-street banking discussed above. Large international corporations maintained sterling deposits at banks in London, Deutsche Mark deposits in Frankfurt, Swiss franc deposits in Zurich and so forth. Similarly, such large corporations might also borrow sterling funds from banks located in London. The banks themselves need not have been owned by British bankers. They might have been branches of New York banks aiming to provide a full range of services to those customers carrying out a substantial amount of international business. However, by and large, the business carried out by British-based banks was denominated in sterling.

However, during the 1960s and 1970s substantial changes took place. British-based banks increasingly began to accept deposits denominated in foreign currencies, mainly dollars, but other currencies as well. The extent of this fantastic growth can be seen by referring back to Table 8.1. Between 1971 and the third quarter of 1981 the foreign currency deposits at British banks increased from about £17,650 million to £226,148 million.

In addition loans denominated in foreign currencies increased by correspondingly large amounts. An entirely new dimension was added to the activities of banks, the development of what has come to be called the 'euro-currency system'. It is distinguished by the practice of banks in one country accepting deposits denominated in the currency of another country. These are frequently referred to as 'euro-currency deposits'. About 70 per cent of these deposits are denominated in dollars and, not surprisingly, they are called 'euro-dollar deposits'.

On a world-wide basis the gross size of the euro-currency system at the end of 1980 was just about $1,500,000,000,000. But why should this practice have grown to such a phenomenal size. A complete, detailed answer is really beyond the scope of this chapter. However, experts are generally in agreement that there are two fundamental reasons:

1. The existence of national banking restrictions which rendered growth of the euro-currency system more profitable. For example, in 1957 the Bank of England introduced a policy which limited the amount of sterling which British banks could lend to foreigners. These banks then began to loan dollars in an effort to keep their traditional customers. Then in the mid-1960s the central bank of the USA, the Federal Reserve System, initiated a restrictive monetary policy which encouraged US banks to expand their activities in London and other international financial centres.

2. The growth of the euro-currency system has enabled banks to provide a wider range of services to their customers. For example, suppose that you are the treasurer of a large British corporation which does a substantial amount of business in the USA. During some periods of time you may wish to hold funds denominated in dollars for the purpose of carrying out specific transactions. In the USA, until recently, interest was not payable on deposits of less than thirty days' maturity. However, this restriction does not apply in Britain. If your company already has a good working relationship with a British bank there is already a good case for maintaining dollar balances with that institution. Periodically, your company may wish to borrow dollars, say, to expand a marketing network in the USA. It may very well be the case that you will get better terms from a British bank which has a good appreciation of you and your corporation than a US bank which does not.

Finally, there is the technical consideration of time. Generally, there is a five-hour time difference between London and New York (an eight-hour difference exists between London and San Francisco). It is thus much more convenient for your company to maintain its dollar balances at a London bank. At the best, US banks will be opening up for business just as your day is coming to an end.

In these respects the growth of the euro-currency system may be thought to enable a more efficient utilisation of financial resources on an international basis. If the availability of funds is restricted for whatever reason at home, international markets may be tapped. And in many instances the terms available may be more favourable than those obtainable from domestic sources.

However, there is another way in which the euro-currency system enables funds to be utilised to their fullest extent. As we shall see, its operations are, in principle, no different from those of a building society. Consider the scenario depicted in Table 8.3. Suppose a large international corporation, *A* (it could be US or European) moves its dollar funds from its US bank to a London bank. The latter now has additional funds which it can lend say to the British corporation, *B*. The latter, in turn, may use the borrowed dollars to import goods from the USA. Upon delivery of goods, the US exporter deposits the proceeds of his sales back in the US banking system. The result is a picture that is only slightly different from that presented earlier in connection with our analysis of building society activity.

**Table 8.3**

Balance-sheet of American commercial bank

| Liabilities | Assets |
|---|---|
| Deposit of international corporation *A* − $100 | |
| Deposit of exporter *C* + $100 | |

Balance-sheet of British commercial bank

| Liabilities | Assets |
|---|---|
| Euro-dollar deposit of international corporation *A* + $100 | Loan to British corporation *B* + $100 |

British corporation *B* imports goods from US exporter *C*.

---

For one thing, there is no change in the total asset and liability position of the US banking system; simply a change in the ownership of a $100 deposit from *A* to *C*. However, in the process, an additional euro-dollar deposit and loan have been created. In the example depicted in Table 8.3 this has led to an increase in British imports, which, by definition, represent an increase in US exports. On a global basis economic activity is at a higher level than it otherwise would have been. Clearly this form of international banking has led to a more efficient utilisation of financial resources.

A more detailed picture of the types of actors which take part in this system can be obtained by referring to Table 8.4. There we see that there are basically three categories of borrowers and lenders to the system: non-banks (e.g. corporations), banks and central banks. Some comments about each are in order. Just about 20 per cent of deposits and loans are of the form which we have just discussed in our balance-sheet example.

Half of the activity or 735 billion dollars consists of euro-banks each lending to each other. At first thought, this may appear to be a rather curious thing to happen. Why should banks want to lend to each other? There are basically two good reasons. First, at any particular time one international bank may be short of funds whereas another bank may have an excess of funds and is keen on making a short-term loan. The euro-currency system provides facilities for such short-term clearing. Second, such interbank lending may take on a longer-term character. If one bank does not have customers who desire to borrow whereas another does, the first bank may simply lend to the other on a regular basis. It is not uncommon for deposits of a very short-term nature (less than three months' maturity) to support fairly long-term loans (e.g. seven years in term). Again, this form of activity may be viewed as generating a more efficient utilisation of resources.

**Table 8.4**    *Euro-currency system size (end of 1980, billions of dollars)*

|  | Liabilities | Assets |
|---|---|---|
| Non-banks | 325 | 400 |
| Central banks | 150 | } 290 |
| Banks outside the system | 280 |  |
| Banks within the system | 760 | 760 |
| Conversion of euro-funds into domestic currencies | – | 65 |
| Gross size | 1515 | 1515 |

Finally, it is important to note that a rapidly growing source of funds to international banks has been the deposits of central banks and other official monetary institutions. These have grown from about 15 billion dollars in 1971 to 190 billion dollars in 1980. This vast increase has largely come about because of the large overall balance-of-payments surpluses that the oil-producing and other primary-product countries have enjoyed for most of the 1970s. It is also a reflection of the fact that banks operating in the euro-currency system provide the central banks with higher yields and other facilities that they presumably could not obtain elsewhere.

The rapid growth of international banking has taken place over recent years against a background of relatively restrictive monetary policies by the major industrial countries. What has happened is as follows. When any economy is pressed for funds, it attempts to use them more efficiently. This is exactly what has been happening over the past decade. Inflationary expectations have led businesses in many countries to spend now in order to avoid higher prices in the future. Then when the restrictive policies began to bite, companies had to turn to banks for another reason: to keep afloat. With the influx of funds, from whatever source, international banks have been in a strong position to meet the requirements of potential borrowers. Indeed, some bankers have told me privately that they have too much money. The result has been a situation where more risky ventures have been entered into than would otherwise have been the case. The increased loans to the Third World and Eastern bloc (particularly in 1979) are documented in Table 8.5. While one might argue that such financial assistance was in the spirit of detente and in the cause of economic development, there is little doubt that they were bound to be more risky than loans to major corporations from the industrial countries. No doubt greater awareness of the problems involved have caused banks to cut back on new undertakings to these two groups of countries as several of their members have been unable to meet scheduled repayment dates. As a result the loans have had to be renegotiated.

Of course, the borrowers are not entirely at fault, if indeed they are at fault at all. Perhaps their main error was to expect that business conditions would be buoyant. Instead, as the world-wide recession gathered steam they were caught between the two blades of a scissors. On the one hand, demand for the products of the

**Table 8.5**    *Euro-currency bank loans
(as announced each period), millions of pounds*

| Year | Industrial countries | Developing countries | Eastern bloc |
|---|---|---|---|
| 1975 | 7 231 | 11 098 | 2 597 |
| 1976 | 11 254 | 15 017 | 2 503 |
| 1977 | 17 205 | 20 976 | 3 394 |
| 1978 | 28 952 | 37 290 | 3 767 |
| 1979 | 27 248 | 47 964 | 7 325 |
| 1980 | 39 100 | 35 054 | 2 809 |
| Jan–Sep 1981 | 69 581 | 31 828 | 1 301 |

Third-World and Eastern-bloc countries has fallen. On the other hand, as restrictive monetary policies have begun to bite interest charges to these borrowers have gone up; in some cases they have doubled from around 10 per cent to over 20 per cent. As a result falling sales and higher costs have made it increasingly difficult for borrowers to meet their commitments. These are difficulties which have had to be faced by many corporations in the industrial world as well. Generally speaking, however, such enterprises will be able to withstand temporary pressures since they will be able to fall back on their own resources. Most Third-World and Eastern-bloc borrowers are stretched to the limit.

The difficulties which have just been described are fully appreciated by the central bankers of most leading industrial countries. Their reaction has been of two sorts. First, increased emphasis has been placed on systematic prudential supervision of bank portfolios. Banks have been encouraged to examine closely their overall exposure to any one country or corporation. In addition, more data are now published and this should enable individual banks to appreciate their own position relative to the operation of the international economy.

Second, while there exists no formal international lender-of-last-resort the central banks have taken steps to identify where the responsibility lies should any difficulties arise. The basic principle is that the country of ownership of an international bank is responsible. Thus if the branch of a British bank operating in Frankfurt should find itself unable to meet its commitments, under the above principle, the Deutsche Bundesbank (the German central bank) would not be obliged to act as a lender-of-last-resort. In the first instance the head office in London would be responsible for meeting the obligations of its branch. If this should prove to be difficult, then the Bank of England would presumably intervene.

However, there is one issue about which the world's monetary authorities are less aware. Previous chapters have related the difficulties which the Conservative government has had in controlling the money supply, one of their main policy instruments in their battle against inflation. One thing that has not been appreciated is the interdependence of national and international financial markets. As many countries have introduced restrictive monetary policies, financial institutions have expanded activities which have tended to counteract those policies. While international banking activities have enabled funds to be used more efficiently, this greater efficiency has tended to act as an offset to the anti-inflation drive. In other words, the operation of the international economy is much more complex than many politicians *and* economists have appreciated.

This conclusion has an important bearing on issues raised in previous chapters. You will recall that, in Chapter 1, Chris Hawkins discussed the component parts of the Quantity Theory of Money in some detail:

$$M \times V = P \times T$$

means that the quantity of money (**M**) *times* its velocity or rate of turnover (**V**) *equals* the total value of transactions undertaken; that is, price (**P**) *times* quantity (**T**). Many people consider that **V**, the velocity of circulation of money, is relatively constant. However, on the basis of our previous analysis it should be clear that, as consumers and businesses move funds from banks to other financial institutions such as the building societies and international banks, they enable a given money stock to be utilised more efficiently: a higher level of expenditure can be supported. In other words, the velocity of circulation increases. This possibility can prove to be particularly difficult if it occurs at a time when the monetary authorities are attempting to reduce spending by reducing **M**, the money stock. If **V** increases simultaneously, this policy will be offset. This is one of the various serious problems facing monetary management in today's world of sophisticated financial transactions. Alas, there is no widely acceptable means for dealing with this dilemma. We are led back to the conclusion of previous chapters that the world is a highly complex place and that we require considerably more information than is currently available in order to more clearly specify viable policy alternatives.

## INTRODUCTION TO CHAPTER 9

In economic terms the decade of the 1970s has been a momentous one in the history of Britain. In chronological order, four events stand out:

1. Abandonment of the old Bretton Woods international monetary system, based on fixed exchange rates.
2. Full membership of the European Economic Community.
3. The discovery and exploitation of North Sea oil and gas.
4. The adoption of a monetarist strategy with the aim of reducing inflation and generating full employment.

Each of these events has represented a significant change in the old order and consequently has necessitated that businesses, households and financial institutions make substantial, often costly, adjustments. Indeed, so complex are the issues involved that it has been difficult to distinguish the effects of one event from another. Nevertheless, this has not deterred many commentators from seeking to explain recent history in terms of a single cause. In the next chapter Barry McCormick argues that such an approach is bound to be over-simplistic when it comes to analysing the effects that North Sea oil is having on the British economy. In the first part of his discussion he argues that the appreciation of the pound in 1980 was due to a combination of the effects of North Sea oil and Chancellor Howe's tight monetary policy.

In the second part McCormick considers the alternative uses of North Sea oil revenues and draws some strong conclusions: he is doubtful that the much vaunted policy of lending the oil revenues to the manufacturing sector will increase manufacturing sector investment by anywhere near as much as is usually assumed; he regards the government policy of using oil revenues to reduce the public sector borrowing requirement as a backdoor method of allowing oil resources to provide a consumption boom for the present generation, and concludes that the government is bequeathing a considerable problem to the next generation by not providing 'a reliable instrument to stabilise sterling as oil runs out'. It is suggested that private investment overseas does not provide a suitable instrument to stabilise sterling and that a fund of long-term overseas assets should be accumulated by the Bank of England and be gradually repatriated so as to coincide with the running down of oil revenues. In this way the fund will both act as a means for stabilising the value of sterling and help transfer to our children a share of North Sea wealth.

The implication of the title of this chapter – from which the title for the book is drawn – is that current policies towards North Sea oil will have a significant impact on future generations and that we should aim to achieve a policy towards North Sea oil that creates a consensus between, as well as within, generations.

C.H. and G.M.

# 9   North Sea Oil: What Will Our Children Think?

*by Barry McCormick*

Only a few years ago there was widespread hope, and even well-informed expectation, that the enormous oil discoveries in British waters would lead to an economic boom in the early 1980s and a lasting increase in per capita income. During 1978 and 1979 the national debate to settle how we should enjoy the largesse slowly gained momentum, only to subside into concern about our sharpest post-war depression: the new-found self-sufficiency in oil has not led to a golden era, and, as a consequence, has resulted in disenchantment and confusion.

My purpose in this chapter is to examine (a) the two leading views of the macro-economic effects of North Sea oil, together with (b) the complementary policy proposals for utilising the oil revenues. Given the extent of writing on this topic it would be foolhardy in the space of a single chapter to do more than highlight what appear to be the key issues and problems raised by the two schools of thought. In dissecting the policies that have been advanced I shall consider in particular the implications for future generations, about which there is surprisingly little study. I shall attempt to show that in choosing between policies to use oil revenues we are also implicitly choosing the extent to which later generations will benefit. In other words, our children will probably look at our policies and infer the extent to which we wished them to share the North Sea treasure. The analysis suggests that the current policy mix is weighted towards consumption by the present generation, and that these policies will make unnecessarily difficult the transition from an economy with a high level of oil exports.

While a study of these issues may help rekindle a debate concerning the choices that remain open towards oil revenues, not all would regard focusing on a separate treatment for North Sea tax revenues as an entirely good thing. Part of my objective is to suggest that we should attempt to achieve a consensus view of how to use oil revenues before disenchantment gives way to bitterness; for otherwise the effects on the political economy of Britain later this century may not be insignificant.

In the next section of the chapter I shall describe two different views of how oil affects the British economy and the criticisms that might be made of these views. In the second half of this chapter the implications of these policies for government policy towards the use of oil revenues are discussed.

### Economists and the macroeconomics of North Sea oil

To begin with it is worth being clear that the oil sector is sufficiently large, and has grown with a rapidity that it is not at all unreasonable to suppose that it might create significant macroeconomic opportunities, changes and problems. Oil production increased steadily from the beginning of 1976 and is expected to reach a peak production in the mid-1980s at which time the Treasury estimate output will equal about $5\frac{1}{2}$ per cent of GDP. Government revenues lag behind the output and balance-of-payments effects of North Sea oil, rising from £2.2 billion in 1979/80 to a government estimate of £6 billion (1980 prices) in 1984, which should be maintained for a period of about five years (see Figure 9.1). At this point oil revenues will constitute about 8 per cent of government revenues and therefore just cover the wage bill for either the National Health Service or the entire school system. The balance-of-payments effects of North Sea oil by 1984 may comprise of the order of 16 per cent of the total exports of goods and services. Current estimates of future production are highly tentative and suggest that there exists a total of between twenty and thirty years of output at 1981–2 levels of production depending on the success of ongoing exploration, and the nature of various government taxation policies that are currently under review.

Let us now consider the two alternative analyses that have been used to assess the effects of oil production. In particular we shall be concerned with the elements of each model that are critical for policy making rather than to offer an extensive critique of its suitability.

**Figure 9.1**

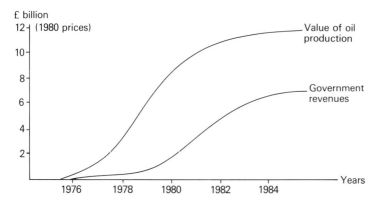

Sources: *UK Balance of Payments* (1980); *Economic Progress Report*
urces: (March 1981).

### The balance-of-payments 'constraint' approach

By far the most prevalent and influential idea prior to 1980 concerning the macroeconomic effects of North Sea oil, both in Treasury
and academic circles, was that the new sector's earnings would
remove a 'balance-of-payments constraint' and enable the economy
to grow more rapidly. Its advocates would explain this view as
follows: In the long run Britain must ensure that exports equal
imports; because imports increase with national income, whereas
exports are largely unaffected, then associated with a given level of
exports there will be a maximum level of national income that can
be sustained. Unless exports are increased the government cannot
intervene to increase national income – thereby reducing the level
of involuntary unemployment that has persistently occurred in the
economy in modern times – without causing a balance-of-payments
deficit and, perhaps, a sterling crisis. Ironic as it may currently
appear to some, North Sea oil export earnings were widely viewed
as the means of getting the economy back to full employment,
provided the government adopted expansionary policies.

To sum up: this early 'orthodox view' combines the incontestable
observation that oil production generates net export earnings, with
a diagnosis that the British economy of 1978–9 experienced involun-

tary unemployment that expansionary monetary–fiscal policy could and should reduce, once oil earnings began to filter through.

What criticisms of this approach can be advanced? The most usual criticism questions how far employment and output, as opposed to imports, would actually increase if the government were to expand the economy as suggested. Many economists would wish to stress that the ultimate source of persistent involuntary unemployment in these studies are non-competitive aspects of the labour market, such as trade unions with inflexible real wage demands. These economists would argue that firms will hire workers to the point where the product produced by an extra worker is equal to the real wage. Thus if trade unions fix the real wage, then employment can only increase if there is an increase in productivity.

This is described in Figure 9.2 where the height of *mm* describes the extra output produced by an additional worker; *mm* is downward-sloping because the higher is employment the less can be produced by the additional worker for given levels of the capital stock and technology. Since the technological conditions that determine the productivity of a given number of men change only slowly over time, the extent to which employment can rise following an increase in government expenditure or a reduction in taxes, financed by oil revenues, is extremely limited; and instead this policy would be likely to leave employment unchanged, but imports increased by the value of the increase in government expenditure or the cut in taxes. To sum up: by overlooking the labour market imperfections that are basic to the theory, this approach may substantially overstate the extent to which an increase in demand can lead to an increase in employment rather than to an increase in imports. There is not so much a 'balance-of-payments constraint' as a 'real wage constraint', which limits employment. It should be added that some members of the Keynesian school would accept this criticism, but point out that, by using oil revenues to increase investment in the manufacturing sector, they aim to increase productivity and shift *mm* to the right. We shall consider this use of oil revenues more fully later, but it should be noted that investment in the manufacturing sector may not necessarily uniformly increase productivity, shifting *mm* to the right. Instead it may, for example, twist *mm* clockwise so as to increase productivity for a few (skilled workers?), but making many others less productive (unskilled?).

**Figure 9.2**

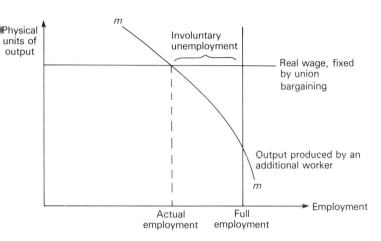

A second criticism of the balance-of-payments constraint approach also arises from the operation of the labour market, and as recent history has unfolded this factor may have carried more political weight than the previous criticism: is it realistic to assume that union real wage demands and settlements are uninfluenced by substantial additions to national wealth, and to government revenue? In the course of 1979 and 1980, following the trades union rejection of the 'Callaghan 5 per cent incomes policy', total British unemployment rose very sharply from 1.4 to 2.4 million, by far a post-war 'high', employment fell by 1.5 million to 23.5 million, and output per head in the non-oil sector of the economy fell by slightly more than 2 per cent. Simultaneously, however, average real earnings advanced by 4 per cent – public-sector workers being particularly favoured. This not insignificant increase in real earnings, despite both massive unemployment and redundancies, suggests the possibility that unions not only fix the real wage, but also dynamically adjust their real wage target in the light of windfall gains to national wealth. If the advent of oil production and its effects on national wealth – signalled by an appreciation of sterling – did raise average union real wage demands, then this severely undermines the view that oil revenues could have made possible a higher level of employment, as the balance-of-payments constraint school would have wished.

A third criticism of the constraints school is that its advocates failed to adequately develop a cogent financial strategy. The amount by which it was envisaged that aggregate demand should be expanded by the government, to absorb North Sea oil output and avoid both an appreciation of the pound and a concomitant contraction of the manufacturing sector, was possibly very large. Geoffrey Maynard ventured the following calculation. Assuming there is a balance-of-payments constraint then 'given a marginal ratio of imports to final expenditure of about 0.25, an oil-induced improvement in the balance of payments of £8.5 billion could enable final expenditure on goods and services to be increased by around £34 billion (all in 1977 prices)'. 'Comments on the Use and Management of North Sea Oil', in R.E. Caves (ed.) *Britain's Economic Performance* (Washington, D.C.: Brookings Institute, 1980) p.370.

At this higher level of final expenditure the extra value of imports just equals the additional value of oil exports, and non-oil domestic GDP is conjectured to increase by about 16 per cent. Setting aside the significant question of whether this much slack existed in the economy, unless consumers autonomously increased expenditure on the basis of an expected increase in wealth (and not all would consider this likely), we must assume that the government would have needed to increase expenditure considerably in excess of oil revenues to achieve this target. Thus, particularly in the early years of oil production while government revenues are low, a very substantial increase in the required level of public sector borrowing may have been required. One need not take the extreme view that increases in the money supply would, in Britain in 1979/80, have led to a proportionate increase in the price level to hesitate before endorsing, *a priori,* such a potentially enormous programme of funding and expansion without first checking the amounts needed; and if a Chancellor had sought to proceed as the 'constraints school' would have wished one must assume that this group's failure to analyse the financing strategy would have considerably increased his difficulties in securing support.

## Concluding remarks on the early orthodoxy

It is tempting to take the view that the balance-of-payments constraint approach is a misleading description of what its proponents assume because the 'real wage constraint' that is at the heart of the analysis is pushed into the background, thereby overstating the extent to which the planned government-led expansion would have increased employment and brought about a golden era for the economy. Nevertheless it is important to remember that the basic policy intuition of this approach is to expand aggregate demand as oil production occurs, and it may well be that this intuition was both correct and important – albeit perhaps in a milder form than was imagined. Had the expansionary case been more coherently articulated it might have withstood the intellectual revolution that befell the Treasury in the middle of 1979.

The Conservative government has decided that the effects of oil revenues on the exchange rate should not be offset by expansionary monetary policy, but rather that the effects on sterling of (a) increasing oil production, and (b) the increase in real oil prices in the middle of 1979, should coincide with a *tightening* of monetary policy. Thus the 'monetarist experiment' has not only denied us an insight into how the British economy would have responded to rapid money financed expansion on the back of escalating oil export earnings, but has also created a considerable puzzle as to how far the appreciation of sterling and the consequent contraction of the British economy during this period were due to the oil sector, and how far due to the tightening of British monetary policy. We shall argue below that this question should also be focal to thinking about how to use oil revenues. This brings our argument to work of *Forsyth and Kay* (FK), whose views concerning the effects of oil on the economy and the policies the government should adopt appear broadly in line with those of the present government. These views constitute the second economic framework, aspects of which we will now assess.

### Forsyth and Kay (FK) and how oil changes the economy

The analysis offered by FK may be separated into three interrelated sections which deal, in turn, with (1) how oil affects the economy, (2) how the economic gains to Britain may be calculated, and (3) how economic policy towards oil revenues should be formulated. (P.J. Forsyth and J. Kay 'The Economic Implications of North Sea Oil Revenues', *Fiscal Studies* (July 1980). Their study of (1) is marked by three contrasting features with the balance-of-payments constraint approach. First, FK distinguish between internationally traded goods and other goods, in order to describe a structural change in British production that they regard as central to the analysis. Second, they assume constant employment. Third, they do not assume the government expands demand to increase imports and offset the balance-of-payments effects of oil. The basis of their description of how oil affects the economy is that the balance-of-payments effects of oil revenues have caused a substantial appreciation of sterling by no less than 20–25 per cent, and restructuring of production in the economy. This is because the extra demand created by oil income is not entirely spent on internationally 'traded' goods, and thus the supply of foreign exchange created by oil sales is not entirely offset by a compensating increase in the demand for foreign exchange. For this reason the manufacturing sector must inevitably contract in order to permit resources to be drawn into the production of 'non-traded' goods, such as housing, for which there is an increased demand, and are only produced in domestic economy.

**Figure 9.3**

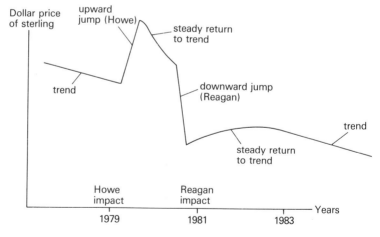

This view has the special distinction of being under siege from both Keynesians and international monetary economists, although for quite different reasons. The monetary economists doubt whether North Sea oil revenues are capable of driving up sterling by 20–25 per cent. Keynesians writing on this question may accept FK's diagnosis that oil is substantially changing the exchange rate, thereby reducing the size of the manufacturing sector, but instead sharply criticise the oil gain/loss calculation, the constant employment assumption and the economic policies advocated by FK. It appears appropriate therefore to first discuss the criticism of FK's analysis by the monetary economists, Professors *Miller, Niehans and Williamson* (hereafter referred to as MNW), that is basic to both the FK policy position and later discussion of government policy towards oil income (see M. Miller, 'Oil-funded Investment is the Only Way to Invigorate Industry', *The Guardian,* 18 August 1980; J. Niehans, *The Appreciation of Sterling,* 1980; and J. Williamson's letter to *The Guardian,* July 1980). While a decisive assessment of how far oil has altered the exchange rate must await econometric analysis and further data, reasonable preliminary points can be made on the basis of a 'back of the envelope' calculation.

## The appreciation of sterling: was it caused by oil or monetary policy?

The separate influence of oil revenues on the British exchange rate has become, and is likely to remain, a controversial central issue in the economic history of the 1970s. The chief argument made by those who doubt that the oil sector is capable of changing the value of sterling by more than about 10 per cent is that the British government's policy of being committed to reducing inflation, underlined by the sharply declining target rates of monetary growth specified in Chancellor Howe's medium-term financial strategy, has caused financial investors to revise their views concerning sterling. Thus it has been recently claimed: 'The principal cause of the recent sterling appreciation was the abrupt halt in monetary expansion in Spring 1979 . . . North Sea oil was not a major factor' (Niehans, 'The Appreciation of Sterling – Causes, Effects, Policies', *SSRC Money Study Group Discussion Paper* (1980). ) In particular Professors MNW have argued that Chancellor Howe's policy has led investors to anticipate higher rates of interest in Britain relative to those in the other chief money centres, until the new lower target rate of growth of the British money supply is reached. These higher interest yields from investing in sterling will result in capital inflows, and a substantially higher value of sterling in a short period of time. In the years following, until the money-supply target is reached, this interest-rate advantage from investing in sterling assets is assumed to just be offset by an equal proportionate annual *decline* in the relative value of sterling. To sum up, the introduction of the Conservative government's monetary strategy, which incorporates high British interest rates relative to other major currencies, is conjectured to lead to a quick jump upwards in the value of the pound, followed by a steady depreciation.

This is illustrated in Figure 9.2, where for illustrative purposes, the dollar price of sterling is drawn with a long-run declining value. The tightening of monetary policy is conjectured to first cause a sharp increase in the price of sterling, and then a gradual return to the trend.

Professors MNW accept that oil production may have increased the value of sterling but by nothing like the 20–25 per cent suggested by FK: *'The scope for real appreciation provided by the oil bonanza is well under 10%'* (Williamson, letter to the *Guardian*, July 1980). My concern here is to calculate the trend change in the real effective exchange rate since the beginning of 1979, after extracting the effects of British monetary policy under Chancellor Howe. Although the argument is statistically 'rough and ready' it does illustrate the orders of magnitude involved.

The monetary economists chief point is that, since mid-1979, movements in the Effective Exchange Rate (EER) – which is just an average exchange rate over our trading partners – have been significantly influenced by the special monetary policy of Britain. Thus, they would argue, it is not possible to draw conclusions concerning the exchange-rate effects of oil by examining the underlying trend in the EER. Fortunately, since Professors MNW contributed to this problem in 1980, there has been another and internationally highly important change in monetary policy – namely the US high-interest-rate strategy that was aided by the election and balanced budget policies of President Reagan – and this helps uncover the separate role of oil on the value of sterling. In the first half of 1981 US interest rates reached their highest levels, relative to British rates, in recent history, and therefore it does not appear unreasonable to maintain that by mid-1981 this extinguished any expectation that British interest rates would remain permanently higher, relative to US rates, than had been the case prior to Chancellor Howe. This tightening of US monetary policy makes it possible to estimate the underlying trend in the $/£ exchange rate since we may reasonably conjecture that by mid-1981 it would no longer reflect a 'Howe premium', as it possibly did during 1980. Instead by mid-1981 it may even have reflected a 'Reagan premium' with the dollar being temporarily high against sterling. Thus if we calculate the appreciation of the pound against *the dollar* between the beginning of 1979 and the middle of 1981 – prior to the introduction of Conservative policies and after the Reagan effect was properly established – we shall not overstate the underlying trend in favour of sterling, and may even understate it. This trend $/£ rate may then be used to determine the change in the EER that would have occurred in the absence of tight British monetary policy.

In Figure 9.4 the uncovered interest-rate differential between British and US Treasury Bills is charted along with the effective sterling exchange rate and the $/£ exchange rate. In the period from the beginning of 1973 until the end of 1976 the interest-rate differential moved steadily towards higher British Bill rates. At the same time the EER trended downwards – largely because of relatively high rates of inflation in Britain. Since the beginning of 1977 sterling has steadily appreciated both on average against our trading partners and against the dollar.

**Figure 9.4**

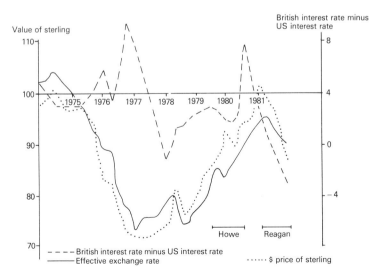

**Monetary policy counts mightily, but oil counts too**

Considering now the first year of the Conservative government, marked 'Howe' on Figure 9.4, we find that both interest differentials and exchange rates moved in favour of Britain, as Professors MNW would expect. As relative interest rates rose in the USA during the second half of 1980 the pound fell heavily. To estimate the underlying trend from the beginning of 1979 we first calculate the average index value of the $/£ exchange rate in the year preceding the Conservative election 1978:III–1979:II, which was 83.7. Suppose now we compare this with the recordings in the first half of 1981, and in an attempt to avoid criticism that the appreciation is being overstated by British monetary contraction, we shall concentrate on the second quarter of 1981 when the index stood at its lowest point to date of 86.9. Comparing these two figures implies that a sterling appreciation of 3.8 per cent occurred between the beginning of 1979 and 1981:II. During this same period US prices rose by almost exactly 10 per cent less than British prices, so that in real terms the pound appreciated by 13–14 per cent.

Our method has been to focus on the $/£ rate since we could most readily defend the view that our trend estimate of this exchange rate is not 'polluted' by recent tight British monetary policy. How far is this figure representative of the pound's appreciation against currencies other than $US if the effects of special British monetary policies were to be separated out? In the absence of good reasons, other than monetary policy, as to why in this short period the appreciation of the pound relative to the dollar should differ from the pound's appreciation against other currencies, we will simply adopt the slightly wider band of 12–15 per cent as a reasonable range for the pound's real effective appreciation from beginning 1979 to mid-1981 had British monetary policies not been tightened relative to our trading partners. This suggests that if only a small amount of the substantial real appreciation of sterling that occurred between 1976:IV and 1978:IV was a consequence of the development of the oil sector, the estimate suggested by FK that oil had caused an appreciation of at least 20–25 per cent would appear entirely feasible.

To sum up, an interim assessment suggests that there is an underlying trend increase in the value of sterling, after making a reasonable allowance for recent changes in monetary policy, that is consistent with the FK position. Nevertheless it is also clear from Figure 9.3 that the greater part of the appreciation of sterling during 1980 should be put down to the tight British monetary policy, as Professors MNW would claim. Monetary policy counts a lot in determining the exchange rate, but oil appears to count too.

Although it appears that the FK analysis of the exchange rate can be reasonably defended, it is less clear that their calculations of the benefit to the economy are immune from Keynesian criticisms of the constant employment assumption. If, for example, the sterling appreciation due to oil was responsible for one-quarter of the extra million becoming unemployed during 1979 and 1980, this reduces the net government sector benefit by about £1 billion per annum, which is about 25 per cent of current government tax income from oil. This omission tends to overstate the net benefit to the Exchequer of oil production, at least during the initial period of oil production; and if the economy were to become lodged in a high unemployment equilibrium, this cost of additional unemployment could well persist for a long portion of the life of the oil sector. However we will pass on from this point, not because it does not deserve to be part of a comprehensive assessment of the FK analysis, but rather because revising the oil gain/loss calculation will not substantially influence our discussion of how to use oil revenues. This is not to dodge the problem of oil-induced unemployment: **if involuntary unemployment persists after optimal policies towards oil revenues have been adopted, then the problem should be dealt with using preferred micro/macroeconomic policies.**

This preliminary exercise suggests (a) that the broadside of criticisms from Professors MNW do not upset the FK claim that oil may cause a real appreciation of sterling by 20–25 per cent, and (b) that economic policies that are most persuasive if there is a reasonable probability that oil production has caused a substantial real appreciation of sterling – say, 15 per cent or more – should be given serious attention.

**Choosing a government policy towards North Sea oil revenues**

The two basic views of how oil affects the economy are associated with two alternative strategies of how to use oil revenues. Many economists in the balance-of-payments-constraint school of thought wish to use the oil revenues to create a fund that will lend to the manufacturing sector and encourage investment. In this they are supported by the trade unions and the Labour party. The policy advocated by FK, which to an extent is shared by the Conservative government, involves reducing the Government Borrowing Requirement and encouraging private overseas investment. **The suitability of these two policies, it is suggested, rests on strong assumptions about either the determinants of manufacturing investment, or individual savings behaviour and the importance of labour-market rigidities.**

Initially I shall explore the coherence of each of these two established arguments within the basic assumptions of its advocates, and then contrast the implications – especially those for later generations – with a third government strategy.

(a) *The trade unions* and the Labour party in a number of statements have suggested that oil revenues should be largely used to finance investment in the manufacturing sector, as described in the last government's White Paper, *The Challenge of North Sea Oil* (1979). In the most thoughtfully specified version of this argument, Terry Barker has proposed that an investment fund be set up to: 'lend to suitable projects, reducing the interest rate to the extent required to spend *all* its allocation. This interest rate would probably be negative to begin with, amounting to a cash incentive to bring forward schemes. The criteria for the projects funded would be very tightly defined, and the investors would be accountable for their use of the funds.' And in addition: 'A worthwhile supplement would be investment for energy conservations, particularly house and office insulation, more telecommunications and more social infrastructure such as railway investment and a channel tunnel' ('What Should We Do With the Oil Money?', *The Guardian* (18 August 1980).

Let us consider first the basic programme of investment in the manufacturing sector, which allowing for other minor investments, and the envisaged level of North Sea revenues, can be assumed to amount to a fund of £3–5 billion per annum (in 1980 prices). There has been a great deal written in favour of such a project, illustrating the need to rejuvenate manufacturing; I shall attempt to balance these arguments with some criticisms.

First, because the planned annual lending of the fund is large rela-

:ive to the level of British investment, it should be emphasised that the fund will probably earn a negative real rate of return so that the real value of the accumulated capital in the oil fund will eventually, and perhaps rapidly, diminish. Thus later generations will not be able to offer a similar subsidy to manufacturing. While the significance of this is minimised if the oil fund substantially increases the stock of capital in a desirable way, the two following criticisms suggest that this may not in fact occur. (This first criticism may also be met by the objection that because of current high unemployment levels, the return to society on these investments may well be positive even though to the private firm the rate is negative. The problem here is that although this rebuttal *may* hold, there is no ready way to checking its validity in each case.)

Second, the manufacturing sector investment fund strategy has been criticised by FK because it involves concentrating oil wealth into fixed, largely immobile, capital at a time when various important relative prices (particularly those of oil and sterling) are changing in ways that are hard to predict. Thus these investments may turn out to suffer from a lack of flexibility in comparison with financial investments in overseas assets.

Third, there is a basic objection to the manufacturing investment fund strategy which has apparently gone without discussion: even though the fund may lend £4 billion or so each year it is highly unlikely that investment will rise by as much as this. Further, no economist could place hand on heart and make a confident estimate of by how much investment would increase. The following short exercise, summarised in Figure 9.5, is designed to show how the oil fund would influence investment and why the outcome is uncertain. The curve describing the annual demand for investment funds by the manufacturing sector is drawn downward-sloping on Figure 9.5, since firms will invest more at lower interest rates. The curve describing the supply of capital to manufacturing is upward-sloping, since higher rates of return to investors will attract capital into the sector. In the absence of an oil fund the supply of capital curve is *SS*, and the equilibrium level of investment is around £7 billion. If the government creates an oil fund for manufacturing it supplies additional capital to the sector, which causes *SS* to shift horizontally to the right by £4 billion. This reduces the rate of interest charged to borrowers and makes additional investment projects viable. However, the level of investment will increase by only £*x* billion, where *x* is *less* than 4. The value of $x$ is close to zero if investment, *either* does not increase as interest rates fall, *or* the private supply of capital to the manufacturing sector is highly sensitive to interest changes. Why? Because the fund causes total manufacturing investment to increase only if lower interest rates cause more investment, *and* the private supply of capital to the manufacturing sector is not deflected elsewhere by the lower rates of return in this sector. The extent to which either of these two considerations apply is not very well understood.

**Figure 9.5**

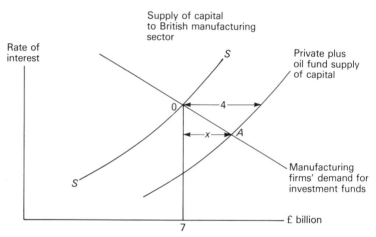

Ironically, it is economists of the balance-of-payments-constraint and oil-fund school of thought who have historically been most keen to stress that investment may not be very sensitive to the rate of interest (when discussing the usefulness of monetary policy in Keynesian macro-models). But most economists would wish to remain open-minded about the extent to which an oil fund will push private capital out of domestic manufacturing investment and into, for example, (a) corporate overseas investment, (b) corporate savings in, say, government bonds, (c) personal consumption. The amount of funds displaced, $£(4-x)$ billion, can only be roughly guessed by economists and any government mounting a programme of this sort should be made aware of this inherent uncertainty.

Those economists who wish to use oil revenues to support the British manufacturing sector may nevertheless point out that if the government wishes to increase manufacturing sector investment, then the oil fund at least achieves this ($x$ must be positive even though less than 4) and it might be claimed that this policy does so with more certainty and thus gives more definite assistance to our 'industrial base' than other policies towards oil revenues. Even this claim, however, is incorrect because different policies towards oil revenues have sharply different exchange-rate effects and thus different effects on the firms' *demand* for investment funds (and employment).

To demonstrate this central point the oil fund strategy is compared with the following policy: the government estimates the present discounted value of its tax earnings from oil – say, around £100 billion (1980 prices) – and calculates the amount that could be paid out if real wealth were left intact – say £2 billion per annum. Each year the government would inject £2 billion into the economy, and any oil revenue in excess of this would be used to accumulate a government-owned portfolio of overseas assets. It is quite possible, for two reasons, that this second strategy will generate more investment in the manufacturing sector during the period of oil production than by using oil revenues to increase the supply of funds to manufacturing.

First, note that the consequence of both of these strategies is for oil production to increase the value of sterling and to reduce the ability of the manufacturing sector to compete. This in turn can be expected to reduce investment in manufacturing. However, the strategy in which the government accumulates overseas assets is likely to cause sterling to appreciate by *less* than if the revenues are used to create an oil fund; thus the asset-accumulation strategy may reduce investment by less than the oil fund strategy. This is reflected on Figure 9.6, where $D_F D_F$ is the demand for investment funds under an oil fund strategy and is drawn to the left of $D_P D_P$, the demand for investment funds under a government overseas portfolio strategy. Because sterling will appreciate relative to its pre-oil level under either strategy, both of these curves lie to the left of the pre-oil demand for investment funds curve, $D_0 D_0$. The equilibrium level of investment with an oil fund, $I_F$, is where the supply of capital under an oil fund, $S_1 S_1$, and $D_F D_F$ intersect; under an overseas investment strategy the equilibrium level of investment, $I_P$, is where $D_P D_P$ intersects with $S_0 S_0$, the original supply of capital curve. **The critical point is this: without more information we cannot be sure**

**whether $I_F$ is greater or less than $I_P$.** The oil fund strategy may result in a lower level of manufacturing investment than a policy of purchasing overseas assets because it depresses the demand for investment more than an overseas investment strategy.

**Figure 9.6**

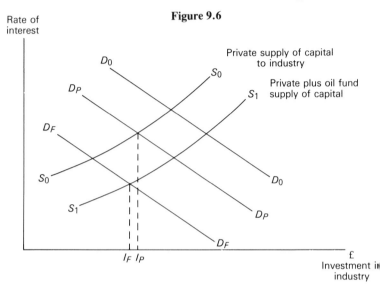

There is a second reason why investment may be less under an oil fund than if the government accumulates foreign assets. The idea that added uncertainty concerning the demand for output reduces investment has a long history. The oil-fund strategy allows the balance-of-payments effects of oil to impinge themselves on the economy without correction, so that the value of sterling will initially rise and then fall as oil is depleted. In contrast the alternative strategy of absorbing only £2 billion per annum creates an immediate small rise in the value of sterling, *which is held for ever.* It is reasonable to suppose that investors will view with concern the prospect of continuous devaluation, and inflationary pressures, that will accompany the oil-fund approach once the balance-of-payments effects of oil reach a peak, and that to allow the oil revenue windfall to impose a long-term cyclical influence on the economy will be damaging to long-term investment. The effect of the fall of oil prices in February 1982 on Chancellor Howe's Budget provides ample warning of the problems that will be faced by future Chancellors as the oil runs out.

We might characterise the oil-fund policy as a government-led 'dash for growth' that is made possible by a real temporary windfall and not, unlike previous occasions, a monetary expansion. It *could* change the nature of the British manufacturing sector, make possible the creation of more productive working environments and provide a platform for a new industrial revolution in Britain. Alternatively, this policy may create little extra domestic investment and, without micro-economic industrial reform earn such a low rate of return that virtually nothing would remain in the oil fund for the next generation. We now turn to describe a different use of oil revenues.

(b) *The Conservative government* has made strikingly few statements concerning oil revenues – preferring that the substantial part of this income is unobtrusively used to reduce the Public Sector Borrowing Requirement (PSBR). In this regard they have economic champions at hand:

> A policy which uses a major part of North Sea oil revenues to reduce the PSBR, and so puts the cash flows received into the hands of financial institutions, is likely both to encourage the use of a large proportion of these cash flows for portfolio investment and to facilitate their transfer overseas.
>
> We are sceptical of the government's ability to outguess the foreign exchange market as to the appropriate long-term level of the oil premium, and would prefer to see foreign assets acquired by the private sector rather than by large-scale official intervention in currency markets. (Forsyth and Kay (1980) p. 23.)

A basic feature of this policy, in comparison to the oil fund, is that North Sea wealth is passed directly to the private sector: in so far as taxes are cut this transfer of wealth is perceived immediately by households; in so far as a reduced PSBR means fewer government bonds need be issued, then future taxes to finance debt repayments are reduced, which conveys current oil tax income gradually over time to households. In contrast with an oil fund the government retains ownership of the accumulated oil tax income and lends it, as seen fit, to the private sector. Although one may imagine ways in which an oil fund makes households feel immediately better off, these are presumably small in magnitude when compared with the consequences of lower taxes.

Two criticisms of the government's policy are now discussed in turn:

(1) **The popular concern, when oil was first discovered, was that it should not be used to finance a 'consumption bonanza', but rather put the British economy on a healthier footing; is this policy likely to lead to a 'consumption bonanza', with little benefit to the next generation?**

(2) **This policy does not attempt to 'manage' the effects of oil on the exchange rate. Might this not be costly and, despite this government's efforts to reduce inflation, leave the economy vulnerable to a substantial depreciation of sterling and strong inflationary pressures when oil production runs down and the recent appreciation is largely undone? In other words, how far is the government laying the foundation for a lasting period of low inflation, as it claims, and how far is it bequeathing substantial stabilisation problems to the next generation by ignoring the effects of oil on the exchange rate?**

(1)  *Will North Sea wealth be consumed or saved?* First we might ask whether the value of tax revenues from the North Sea is sufficiently large to worry about whether an appropriate amount is saved. One way of assessing this is to utilise the earlier assumption that North Sea tax revenues will enable the government to convey to households in the order of £100 billion (1980 prices in present discounted terms) over the next twenty-five years. This compares with a valuation of British capital stock in plant, machinery, vehicles, dwellings, etc., described in the national income and expenditure statistics of about £600 billion (1979 figures), about half of which is in private ownership. Thus it appears that the value of tax income from the oil sector does comprise a significant fraction of British capital and it is worth seriously considering whether it will be rapidly consumed or not. (Using FK's projections the present value of North Sea wealth may well exceed £100 billion, and thus the issue of bequests to the next generation from this wealth becomes more significant.)

A great deal of North Sea wealth will materialise in the form of higher real wages, pensions and social security net of tax, spread fairly evenly across all households. Thus this windfall wealth will be distributed quite unlike the existing private-sector wealth stock, which is owned by a relatively small number of households. Because it seems reasonable that the proportion of family wealth bequeathed to later generations (i.e. family wealth not consumed) will be greater among the wealthy than among the less wealthy, the fraction of North Sea wealth bequested may well be small relative to the fraction of bequests from other wealth: perhaps the special economic characteristic of North Sea wealth from the point of view of aggregate savings and capital accumulation is not that it constitutes our children's 'heritage' any more than the machines and buildings this present generation was also lucky enough to inherit, but rather that it will not be distributed to traditional wealth-holders – for the perfectly good reasons of fairness – and the recipient households may be less disposed to increase bequests. This may occur for highly understandable reasons, such as low real rates of return in the capital market which undermine the willingness to save; a household in rental accommodation may find it particularly difficult to invest in an asset yielding a positive real rate of return.

### Does it matter if the oil wealth is consumed?

If, as I would expect on the basis of the government's policy, little is added to the stock of British capital as a consequence of North Sea oil exploitation, and the current generation enjoy a consumption 'bonanza', should the government intervene to prevent this? It could intervene directly by either (a) accumulating public-sector capital in hospitals, roads, schools, etc., or (b) purchasing foreign assets. Alternatively it could intervene indirectly by creating loans to producers – as, for example, in the case of a manufacturing sector oil fund – attempting to induce the private sector to increase its total purchases of foreign assets or investment goods with subsidies or loan capital supplied by the government. As we have seen, the oil fund policy does not necessarily achieve the objective of increasing investment by an amount equal to the loans by the fund, but by increasing the total willingness of society (public and private sectors) to hold assets, this indirect form of government intervention is likely to leave the capital stock greater than under a policy of reducing the PSBR. (Allowing the *private* sector to purchase overseas assets, by itself, may well not alter the total British capital stock in the long run; only its location.)

Perhaps the best argument against government intervention to increase bequests is the following: since technological progress will most probably bring about an increase in output per head for later generations, then if the present generation consumes the oil wealth, consumption between generations will have been made more equal.

In other words, why should this generation save to raise the incomes of later generations who will be richer anyway? This argument is more plausible if productivity growth is large relative to the oil benefits: in Britain the 5–10 per cent gain to national income accruing from oil will take in the order of 3–5 years to make up. This is described in Figure 9.7, where the 'blip' in the solid line describes the oil benefits. Clearly if oil benefits were very large, and the dotted line were more appropriate, then a policy of current consumption would be an intolerable blow to the next generation.

**Figure 9.7**

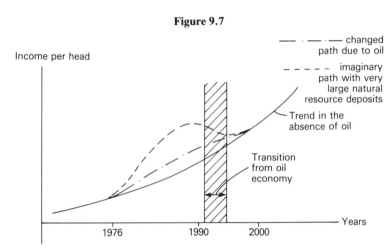

This view that present consumption of oil wealth is acceptable may be countered with the argument that the utility of each generation is influenced by its income relative to that in other countries; and a policy which worsens income discrepancies between economies which otherwise share a great deal in common, is likely to reduce utility a great deal. Since future British residents are already likely to be poorer than those in Western Europe, it would appear harder to argue that future British residents should be denied part of the North Sea spoils.

It might be thought that our children would be more prepared to embrace the idea that the oil wealth is rapidly consumed provided

(a) real incomes are only slightly moderated as oil runs out, and
(b) the macroeconomic stabilisation problems that will accompany the sterling devaluation as oil production runs down – possibly a 25 per cent depreciation – are only slight.

Before turning to the choice of an actual policy to increase
ational savings and capital accumulation it is helpful to turn now to
iscuss the second problem listed above, namely the *stabilisation*
roblems associated with oil production that are created because
ritain is a trading nation with other countries.

(2) *Will there be macroeconomic stabilisation problems as oil runs
ut?* The presence of rigidities in the labour market (and perhaps
1 other markets) suggest that sharp changes in the exchange rate
re not readily accommodated, and not untypically result in a long-
rawn-out and socially costly adjustment of the sort we are current-
' experiencing. Many economists term the unemployment that
:sults as 'structural', and it is assumed that it will dissipate gradual-
' as the economy returns to a new equilibrium with only frictional
nemployment. Others are concerned that there exist many
ossible equilibria, some of which may be highly undesirable –
volving large-scale involuntary unemployment – and that by
lowing North Sea oil to rapidly reduce the size of the manufactur-
ig sector we may possibly finish up in such an unsatisfactory
quilibrium. Unless a fairly simple view of how an economy works is
ken on faith, there may be genuine concern that government
itervention to moderate the rate of appreciation during 1976–82
ould have substantially increased social welfare. Similarly, it may
e supposed that a large part of this appreciation will be undone in a
ecade or so, creating powerful inflationary pressures.

These problems of stabilising the price level will coincide with the
naded zone on Figure 9.7 which describes the reverse transition
om an 'oil' to 'manufacturing' economy, when real incomes in
ritain will rise less rapidly or perhaps fall. Since the control of
iflation is likely to involve depressing output and employment at a
me when foreign income is declining, it appears highly likely that
1e transition will possibly create a substantial 'economic crisis'.

By encouraging private direct investment overseas it may be
rgued that the government has to a certain extent reduced the
pward pressure on sterling and provided a source of overseas
1come to replace oil production. But how far can we expect private
ecisions concerning overseas investment to be close to that which is
est for society? The crucial element that appears likely to drive a
'edge between the incentives of private investors and a social opti-
1um are the social costs of unemployment and inflation. The
overnment will wish to allow for these substantial costs when

determining the optimal level of capital flows to smooth exchange rate fluctuations. There cannot, therefore, be any reasonable presumption that relying on private direct investment overseas will optimally modify the value of sterling either during its appreciation or when the balance-of-payments effects are declining.

The most natural way that the government might intervene to ease the crisis is by accumulating reserves, perhaps in the form of US bonds that could be repatriated in a planned way as oil production runs down. The government may also attempt to ensure that the level of investment overseas reflects the national interest by imposing an optimal tax on foreign capital earnings, and by carefully controlling this tax rate it is possible that the government is able to optimally control net private capital flows overseas. Thus, in principle, it may be possible for the government to both pass on the windfall to the private sector, and still optimally influence the level of investment overseas and the exchange rate. However, in practice such deft control of the tax/subsidy on overseas earnings is impossible to envisage, even if it could be shown to be feasible in principle.

In summary there are grounds for doubting that private direct investment will result in optimal capital flows to mitigate either the unemployment consequent upon a sharp rise in the value of sterling or the tendency towards inflation that will accompany falls in sterling as oil production runs down. Although the income from private direct investment will reduce the total amount by which sterling will depreciate in the transition, it cannot be assumed that British pension-fund managers will reflect the needs of the economy as opposed to their investors, and repatriate funds in a way that sensibly smoothes the depreciation of sterling; certainly it appears likely that a pre-announced policy of steadily repatriating government-owned foreign assets is likely to have a more favourable stabilising effect.

For the government to be able to improve matters by smoothing the cycle in the EER it is not necessary to 'outguess' the foreign exchange market as FK suggest. The government need only use the estimates of the balance-of-payments effects of oil production, and decide to offset a certain fraction by accumulating foreign assets. Merely by openly trading in the foreign-exchange market, the pound would rapidly find a new lower level. Although the government cannot fix sterling at unrealistic levels in this way, it is quite

ossible to influence the value of sterling by an appropriate amount.
t is now too late to avoid the force of the oil appreciation, but a
olicy of gradual foreign-asset accumulation by the British govern-
ent would, if the asset disposal rate later this century were pre-
nnounced, greatly modify the impending sterling depreciation. At
e same time this portfolio of assets would represent a trust for
ture generations that could sustain real incomes during the transi-
on from an 'Oil economy'.

**oncluding comments: towards a consensus**

was proposed at the outset that if North Sea oil is not to become a
urce of bitterness there is a need for a national consensus and
nderstanding as to how our oil wealth is being used. It has been
rgued that both the 'oil fund' strategy and the government's
rategy, although different, are likely to result in outcomes which
ave not been made clear. My purpose here has been to illustrate
e nature of some of the effects of these policies, particularly for
e accumulation of capital; **and to caution that both the policies that
ave been discussed appear particularly vulnerable to the criticism
at they fail to provide a reliable means to stabilise sterling and real
comes as oil runs out.** Rather than use oil revenues towards one
articular activity, it appears more sensible to undertake a coherent
ortfolio of investments. My concern is that under present policies
) the exchange-rate appreciation of 1976–81 will be largely (but
ot totally) reversed later this century, with possibly grave implica-
ons, and that (b) the welfare of the young may not, on balance, be
fficiently protected. **These points suggest that perhaps £1–1½
illion (1980 prices) per annum – about 20% of the peak oil revenues
should be used to allow the Bank of England to accumulate foreign
ng-term assets that can eventually be disposed of in a planned way.**
or those who consider investing in the order of £30 billion overseas
'risky' it should be recalled that both British assets overseas, and
verseas investment in Britain, exceeded £200 billion in 1980.
urther, to help reduce this generation's overseas indebtedness,
ere should no longer be any Treasury financial encouragement for
ublic corporations or local authorities to borrow from overseas –
ver £8 billion of overseas liabilities have been incurred under the
xchange cover scheme.

Part of the remaining oil revenues could be used to develop high return public projects which would accumulate public-sector capital and create private-sector jobs and investment by increasing demand: a rejuvenation of our school and apprenticeship system would channel funds to the young and enable the diverse objective of the present generation to coalesce around the aim of providing the unborn with both a more challenging start and an increased investment in human capital. One might do worse than recall the famous words of Alfred Marshall: 'The most valuable of all capital that invested in human beings.' Finally, the government could also explore: (a) the possibility of reducing various taxes which particularly distort the market mechanism, and (b) the present national policies for both investment in high technology/scientific research designed to provide spin-off benefits for a wide variety of industries and the communication of these advances to the commercial sector. There are very strong economic reasons for believing that government intervention in these areas is socially desirable, and I am impressed with the observations of my science colleagues that present policies are not what they might be.

Questions concerning capital accumulation out of North Sea oil have been largely disregarded in the confusion that has accompanied the problem of separating out the effects of oil production and monetary policy on the exchange rate and unemployment. The confusion was probably made much more severe by the unfortunate decision to introduce significantly tighter monetary targets at a time when the doubling of the world price of oil in 1979 was delivering an additional boost to the value of sterling. The twin shocks of tighter monetary targets and higher oil prices reinforced each other to create a rapid appreciation and the sharpest crisis for UK manufacturing industry since the war; we have not therefore made a great success of becoming an 'oil economy' and must hope that our policies towards both capital accumulation out of the oil surplus and the transition from being an 'oil economy', will be more thoughtfully constructed.

## INTRODUCTION TO CHAPTER 10

Great Britain joined the European Economic Community – the EEC or 'Common Market' – on 1 July 1973, almost fifteen years after its foundation. The debate leading up to this momentous event in British history found opinion deeply divided. On the one hand, there were those who argued against membership of the EEC by calling attention to the loss of national sovereignty that would be involved. This, however, was a minority view.

The major debate regarding entry concentrated on the claims and counterclaims regarding the economic benefits and costs of membership. The eventual majority view stressed the importance of joining and claimed that whatever problems and weaknesses beset the EEC could be changed for the better by Britain's membership.

Although it is only rarely emphasised today, the forefathers of the EEC strongly believed that such an institution was necessary in order to bring a permanent end to the hostilities which had characterised Europe for much of the first half of this century. Such an aim is easier to announce than to achieve. Indeed, to many observers at the end of the Second World War, European 'unification' would have appeared to be as difficult to achieve as the equivalent 'unification' of the Middle East appears today.

The trick employed to turn hope into reality was quite subtle. It was believed that if countries could be induced to co-operate in the economic sphere by the promise of mutual benefits this would lead them into a degree of interdependence which would almost force them into political co-operation.

This plan has certainly worked in at least some areas. There are no tariffs on trade between member countries; there is some co-ordination of industrial and agricultural policy and certainly the EEC provides a forum for political debate and exchange regarding the major world issues of the day. However even a casual reading of European news would indicate that all is not well within the EEC. The continuing wrangles over the size of Britain's financial contribution, the existence of wine 'lakes' and butter mountains, the boycotts of various agricultural products are but a few examples of the state of dissatisfaction regarding current EEC policy.

In the next chapter Alan Hamlin describes why and how funds are redistributed among the members of the EEC in the way they are, and how member countries might view their own national interests. He then proceeds to examine the basic issues which would be involved in reforming the constitution of the EEC. He develops the theme that a constitution such as the EEC's Treaty of Rome may be viewed as a set of rules for games in which participants co-operate and those in which they are in conflict. The Conservative party and Labour party views are analysed against this background and the cases for and against British withdrawal are discussed.

C.H. and G.M.

# 10   The EEC:
# A Framework for
# Evaluation

*by Alan Hamlin*

## Introduction

A popular image of the EEC is of a large group of politicians and Eurocrats' careering between Brussels, Strasbourg and Luxembourg engaged in long and detailed discussions ranging from the reform of the EEC budget to the standardisation of the definition of a sausage. The outcomes of these various summits, committees and round-table discussions are normally portrayed as being indecisive in the cases of major issues, and in the cases of the more ordinary issues are contained in an enormous mountain of multilingual paperwork which few people read and even fewer understand.

In contrast to this somewhat cynical view of the EEC we have the various images of the EEC put forward by the parties to British political debate. Here all sides agree that the EEC is of major – even central – importance to Britain; there is also widespread agreement that the EEC as currently constituted is not perfect, so that all parties see a need for reform. However, thereafter opinions diverge dramatically. For some the EEC is an economic millstone around the country's neck so that the appropriate reform is one of immediate and unilateral withdrawal; for others the EEC is a vital lifeline guaranteeing peace and economic harmony in a developing Europe so that such reform as is necessary is seen as rearranging the details of policy to fit the changing circumstances of the various member states.

A third group regard the EEC as a constitutional evil that undermines the authority of the British government so that withdrawal is seen as the only means of reasserting Britain's claim to national sovereignty. Another group see the EEC in its present form as a

failed attempt at international economic co-operation, but argue fo
basic constitutional reform rather than for the complete abandon
ment of the experiment.

In this chapter I shall attempt to set out a framework within which
we can compare these alternative positions on Britain's future in (o
out of) Europe. Such a framework requires two distinct approaches
first we shall view the present situation within the EEC and it:
member states so as to assess the nature and significance of the
impacts of current EEC policies on those member states. Thereafte:
we shall be concerned to characterise the workings of the EEC by
examining the broad nature of its constitution; this will lead us on to
consider various possible constitutional reforms and the appro
priate means of comparing such reforms.

Finally we shall return to the British political debate in order to
apply our discussions to the range of issues sketched above.

## The current situation of Europe

### The member states

The first step is to provide some general background information on
the relative economic positions of the member states – for thi
purpose I shall examine just the nine established members owing to
a lack of comparable data on the newly elected member, Greece
There are any number of ways of comparing the nine nations. I shall
limit attention to just two. Table 10.1 gives comparisons of GDP pe
capita in each of the nations for two selected years and under two
alternative methods of calculation. In columns 1 and 2 we take
market exchange rates as being the means of translating data in the
various currencies to a common base and report GDP per capita fo
each nation as an index where the average for the EEC as a whole i
taken as 100.

### Standard of living

However, market exchange rates are influenced by a wide variety of
economic and political forces and so may not be the most approp-

**Table 10.1** *Per capita GDP of EEC member states (EEC = 100)*

|  |  | At market exchange rates | | At purchasing-power parity | |
| --- | --- | --- | --- | --- | --- |
|  |  | 1975 | 1979 | 1975 | 1979 |
| Belgium | (B) | 120 | 124 | 109 | 108 |
| Denmark | (D) | 142 | 138 | 119 | 115 |
| France | (F) | 123 | 116 | 113 | 112 |
| Germany | (G) | 130 | 135 | 116 | 118 |
| Ireland | (Ir) | 50 | 49 | 61 | 60 |
| Italy | (It) | 60 | 62 | 73 | 76 |
| Luxembourg | (L) | 123 | 125 | 117 | 109 |
| Netherlands | (N) | 116 | 117 | 108 | 103 |
| Britain | (Br) | 78 | 76 | 94 | 93 |

Source: D. Strasser (1981) *The Finances of Europe,* Commission of the European Communities.

riate means of comparing national data if our intention is to interpret our index as a measure of the average standard of living. In columns 3 and 4 we therefore adopt an alternative procedure, utilising the concept of a **purchasing power parity exchange rate so that these indices reflect the ability of an average citizen of each nation to purchase a standard bundle of goods and services.**

Two points arise immediately from Table 10.1. First, that the absolute dispersion of countries around the EEC average varies greatly with the method of calculation; thus one should take great care in interpreting such statements as, 'average living standards in Germany are X per cent higher than in Britain.'

**League tables of prosperity**

Second, it is clear that the ranking of nations – their league table positions – vary noticeably both between years and methods of calculation. Again, then, hard-and-fast statements of 'league positions' are unlikely to be very reliable.

Despite these warnings it seems clear that we can at least divide our league table into three divisions. A first division, made up of Denmark and Germany, which enjoys a standard of living – on either measure – very markedly above the European average; a second division, made up of France, Belgium, Luxembourg and the Netherlands, all of which are consistently placed just above the average; and finally a third division, comprising Britain, Italy and Ireland, which all lie below the European par figure.

The adoption of this three-tier classification should not be taken to imply that countries within the same division are more or less equivalent in terms of standards of living. In particular it should be noted that Britain is very clearly the third-division leader and that the gap in living standards between Britain and Ireland – both members of our third division – is in fact larger than the gap between Britain and the first-division nations.

A final point on these simple measures of relative living standards is simply that the national averages presented tell us nothing about the distribution of living standards within the various countries. The general question of distribution and re-distribution is one which we shall return to.

**Relative size of economies**

Turning now to column 1 of Table 10.2, which shows a measure of the relative sizes of the nine economies by recording each nation's GNP as a percentage of the total communities GNP. This information requires little comment beyond emphasising the tremendous variations in size with the largest economy (Germany) being some 134 times the size of the smallest (Luxembourg), and the four largest member states constituting over 85 per cent of the total. It should also be noted that there is no substantial relationship between the size of an economy as measured here and the average living standards within that economy as previously discussed; both large and small economies are represented in each of our three divisions of the prosperity league.

**The impact of the EEC budget**

The *direct* effects of the EEC on the member states are brought about by the operation of the EEC budget and the remainder of

**Table 10.2**  *Shares of member states in Community, GNP, budget contributions and budget payments 1980 (estimates)*

|  | % of GNP | Gross budget contribution £m | Gross budget contribution % | Gross receipts £m | Gross receipts % | Net receipts £m |
|---|---|---|---|---|---|---|
| B | 4.64 | 527.6 | 6.17 | 818.4 | 9.57 | 290.8 |
| D | 2.84 | 202.7 | 2.37 | 443.3 | 5.19 | 240.6 |
| F | 24.36 | 1 620.7 | 18.96 | 1 646.1 | 19.26 | 25.4 |
| G | 30.92 | 2 548.2 | 29.81 | 1 856.3 | 21.71 | − 691.9 |
| Ir | 0.67 | 76.9 | 0.90 | 388.1 | 4.54 | 311.2 |
| It | 13.94 | 1 017.4 | 11.90 | 1 484.9 | 17.37 | 467.5 |
| L | 0.23 | 10 | 0.12 | 187.9 | 2.20 | 177.9 |
| N | 6.36 | 742.1 | 8.68 | 964.1 | 11.28 | 222 |
| Br | 16.04 | 1 803 | 21.09 | 759.5 | 8.88 | −1 043.5 |
| EEC | 100 | 8 548.6 | 100 | 8 548.6 | 100 | 0 |

Sources: column 1 from *European Community Commission Background Report* ISEC/B41/79; remainder calculated from *Background Report* ISEC/B15/80.

Table 10.2 summarises these effects for the year 1980. Taking the gross contribution to the budget first, and comparing columns 1 and 3, we note that the contributions made by each nation do not correspond to their relative size with any degree of precision. For four countries (Belgium, Ireland, Netherlands and Britain) the share of budget contributions exceeds the share of that country in total Community GNP and it should be noted that these countries were not identified as those with high standards of living. Indeed in the cases of Britain and Ireland we have nations lying in the third division contributing more than proportionally to the EEC budget, while the first division nations both contribute rather less than proportionally.

In fact the means of calculating each member's contribution is largely based, first, on the collection of the common EEC import tariffs, and, second, on the yield of the member's own VAT system. **Thus it is the structure of each nation's imports and tax system that largely determines its contribution to the EEC and not any consideration of the nation's ability to pay.**

Similar comments hold true in respect of the gross receipts from the EEC budget summarised in column 4 and 5 of Table 10.2. Here three countries receive less than proportional benefits (France, Germany and Britain) and these include one country from each of our standard-of-living divisions.

By adopting this measuring-rod of proportionality I am not suggesting that each nation should contribute and benefit purely in proportion to its size. If this were the case each country would simply receive back its own contribution. I am simply pointing out that **such redistribution as does occur as a direct result of the EEC budget is not systematically related either to relative size or relative prosperity of the member states.**

The final column of Table 10.2 then identifies the pattern of redistribution explicitly. Whilst Italy and Ireland, which were the two nations at the foot of our third division, are each in receipt of a substantial net budgetary flow; and Germany, a first-division nation, faces a substantial net contribution; it is also the case that the other first-division nation (Denmark) receives a net income whilst Britain – of the third division – makes the largest net payment.

Table 10.3 presents data on the pattern of EEC budget expenditures by policy area and the most obvious point here concerns the massive preponderance of expenditures on agriculture and fisheries made mostly under the auspices of the Common Agricultural Policy (CAP); certainly it is this aspect of expenditure policy that largely determines the redistributive impact of the overall EEC expenditure package. So that **just as it is the pattern of imports and taxation that principally determines each nation's payments to the EEC so it is the pattern and level of agricultural production that principally determines each nation's receipts.**

We may also use the data of Table 10.2 to calculate the overall scale of importance to Britain of the EEC budget. Total British GNP in 1980 measured at market prices was some £222,960 millions; in relation to this figure our gross contribution to the EEC budget was some 0.81 per cent whilst our gross receipts amounted to 0.34 per cent of GNP, so that the net contribution made corresponds to slightly less than one-half of 1 per cent of GNP. This is not to deny that in absolute terms a large amount of money is involved, but it does place the EEC budget in the proper perspective of the overall national accounts.

**Table 10.3**  *EEC budget expenditures by sectors 1977 and 1981 (estimates)*

|  | 1977 | 1981 | |
|---|---|---|---|
|  | % of budget | £m | % of budget |
| Agriculture and fisheries policy | 67.38 | 6 721.6 | 66.10 |
| Social policy | 0.82 | 365.0 | 3.59 |
| Regional policy | 3.99 | 1 057.2 | 10.40 |
| Manpower policy | 6.62 | | |
| International relations | 6.80 | 537.3 | 5.28 |
| Research | 1.90 | 141.3 | 1.39 |
| Industry policy | 0.70 | 6.3 | 0.06 |
| Energy policy | 0.80 | 18.3 | 0.18 |
| Administration and reserves | 4.68 | 334.9 | 3.29 |
| Reimbursements to members | 5.85 | 801.2 | 7.88 |
| Other | 0.46 | 186.6 | 1.83 |
| Total | 100 | 10 169.7 | 100 |

Sources: column 1 from the *Report of the Study Group in the Role of Public Finance in European Integration* (Chairman: D. MacDougall), 2 vols Commission of the European Communities, Brussels, 1977), remainder calculated from *Bulletin of the European Communities,* no. 5, vol. 14 (1981).

The various data discussed provide a reasonable view of the present state of the European economies and the impacts on those economies of the EEC budget; however, they do not tell the whole story. In order to complete the picture we need to consider the *indirect* effects of the EEC.

**The non-budgetary impact of the EEC**

**The cost of agricultural imports**

The operation of the CAP has effects over and above those measured in the budget; by raising agricultural prices above world market levels it acts to the advantage of agricultural producers and the disadvantage of consumers. At the national level this implies extra income for those countries that are net agricultural exporters

(Denmark, France, ireland and the Netherlands) at the expense of the net importing nations (Belgium, Luxembourg, Italy and Britain). In the case of Britain, it has been estimated that this indirect cost of the EEC was approximately £130 millions in 1980.

### Pattern of international trade effects

This estimate is based on the assumption that the general pattern of international trade would be unaffected by withdrawal from the EEC, and this must be regarded as a dubious assumption. The pattern of tariffs imposed by the EEC would be unlikely to be repro-duced exactly by any individual country that withdrew from the Community and thus we would expect the prices of internationally traded goods to change as a result of withdrawal. Of course some prices might rise while others fell, and it is extremely difficult to evaluate this indirect effect of membership of the EEC in monetary terms. However, difficulty in estimating the magnitude of the effect is not the same as saying that the effect is unimportant.

### Internal redistribution

The operation of the EEC's policies clearly involves redistribution between groups of persons – we have already noted the redistribu-tion from the consumers of agricultural produce to the producers and similar redistributions arise as the result of EEC regional, social and manpower policies. So far we have only noted these redistribu-tions in so far as they involve transfers between countries; however, it is clear that even if a country was in perfect balance with the EEC there would still be a degree of *internal* redistribution caused by the operation of EEC policies. Of course such internal redistribution may be perceived as either a benefit or a cost, depending upon the political judgements of the society in question, but in either case these benefits/costs should properly be attributed to membership of the EEC.

### Regulatory effects

The Community budget only reflects those areas of policy which involve direct expenditure. In addition the EEC engages in many types of non-financial policy. For example, the European legislation on common standards for many industrial products has important effects on both the producers and consumers of a wide range of goods and services. In order to assess the impact of such regulatory intervention we would need to embark on a major study of the costs and benefits of compliance to European regulations as borne by the citizens of each member state. Such a task has, to my knowledge, not been undertaken at the official level, and is certainly far beyond our present scope. But, again, our current inability to quantify this indirect effect of EEC membership should not blind us to its potential importance.

**Foreign direct investment**

The final indirect effect of membership of the EEC to be mentioned relates to the decisions of overseas (non-European as well as European) firms to invest in productive assets within Britain. It is a commonplace to read that some multinational corporation has set up a European production unit so as to gain access to the EEC market from inside the tariff wall, and we may expect that the particular member state in which the corporation locates its plant will reap some benefits in terms of income and employment generation, payments of domestic taxes, balance-of-trade effects, etc. Since the firm has been set up by reason of the nation's membership of the EEC, these benefits must be counted as flowing from that membership. Subsequent withdrawal from the EEC would both reduce direct foreign investment in the future and jeopardise those benefits deriving from earlier investment.

**The story so far**

I have suggested a number of indirect effects of the EEC on its member states – the reader can no doubt think of others – which make it clear that we cannot reasonably assess the value of the EEC, or any changes in its policy, purely by reference to a simple calculation of budgetary transfers. Rather the operation of the EEC budget forms just a single, albeit the most visible, thread in a relatively complex web of interrelations between the various member states.

Of course, pro- and anti-marketeers alike can be expected to concentrate attention on those effects of the EEC which lend support for their case whilst simultaneously playing down or ignoring effects with the opposite impact. The above discussion should make it clear that there is no simple calculation which unambiguously supports either view. Just as at the time of the original referendum on EEC membership, the expected benefits and costs of continued membership depend crucially on the assumptions made and the political judgements used; all we have been able to offer is a framework within which the claims of the rival camps can be meaningfully compared.

Even here, however, we have taken a very restrictive view of the EEC. We have essentially viewed the present impact of EEC policies and used some conception of the 'national interest' to judge between the alternative positions of continued membership and withdrawal. We have therefore ignored all questions concerned with the possibility of future reform of the EEC in terms of its basic mode of operation – its constitution; and equally we have simply assumed that it is the 'national interests' of the member states which are the proper measuring-rods of the EEC's value. It is to these more fundamental questions that we turn now.

**Constitutions and reform**

In analysing questions of policy choice economists normally assume a given constitutional framework and a given objective. The value of this approach being that it provides the analyst with both a means of identifying feasible policy options (i.e. those policies which are constitutionally viable) and a yardstick by which to measure and compare the expected effects of those feasible policies. The analysis of the previous section was of this type.

However, much of the current EEC debate centres on possible changes in the constitutional framework itself, so that this mode of analysis will be inappropriate except as a first step. It is this constitutional aspect of the EEC 'problem' which renders discussion both more complex and of potentially greater significance.

In order to simplify our discussion as far as possible without losing its essential character I shall first attempt to characterise the nature of constitutions and their reform before going on to apply this perspective to the case of the EEC.

## Constitutions as rules of a game

We may think of a constitution by analogy with the rules of a game. A constitution specifies the players and their basic goals or objectives and, furthermore, gives details of the process by which the players interact in reaching a conclusion or result of the game. If we think of our own parliamentary 'game', the constitution tells us the players – the members of parliament – by specifying the process of election to be used, it tells us the way in which the subject-matter of the game will be derived by laying down rules for the setting of the parliamentary agenda, and finally it details the process of debate and voting which will produce the outcomes of the game – policies.

This simple analogy will be of considerable use, not least because it makes clear the possibility that purely constitutional reform – changes in the rules of the game – will in general be expected to produce changes in both the behaviour of the players and in the games outcome.

## Competitive and co-operative games

We may extend this analogy by distinguishing between two broad classes of games. The major characteristic of a *competitive* game is that the outcome or result typically involves some players 'winning' while others 'lose' (although a 'draw' is possible), thus the various players of the game see themselves essentially as rivals. A *co-operative* game, on the other hand, is one in which the joint actions of the players can lead to outcomes where all players 'win' simultaneously. Here players view themselves as partners or members of a team.

In the former class of games each player's interest is separately identified and are such as to be in conflict with each other, whilst in co-operative games the players share a common interest. Note, however, that in each case it is each player's own self-interest which is the basic motivating force of the game; the difference lies simply in the degree to which these interests diverge.

Having made this distinction it is important to note that in some cases the status of a game is a matter of choice. That is, a game which appears to be competitive under some particular set of rules or constitution may be converted into a co-operative game by an appropriate reform of the rules. A simple example will be sufficient to illustrate this point; let the subject-matter of the game – the 'issue' – be the possibility of redistributing income from one region (the South) to another (the North) within the same country. We also assume that the rules of the game are such that each region sends a representative, or team of representatives, to a committee in which the issue is discussed and voted upon. In this setting the game appears to be a classic example of a competitive game with the North and the South attempting to improve or preserve their respective positions at the expense of the aspirations of the other side. In short, any solution to this game could be viewed as being *imposed* by one side (the winner) on the other (the loser).

However, if we reform the constitution so as to specify the basic motivation in terms of the national interest rather than the separately defined regional interests, and select our players to represent such national concerns, the character of the game changes dramatically. No longer are the committee members rivals fighting for mutually opposed objectives and the possibility of co-operation arises. In short, it is now possible to imagine a decision involving some real amount of redistribution being *unanimously* agreed by the committee members.

### The constitution of the EEC

The central point around which the decision-making processes of the EEC revolve is the Council of Ministers, and it is in this body that the general nature of the EEC 'game' is most clear. The Council is made up of representatives of the ruling governments of each of the member states; it is therefore clear that the 'players' in our EEC game are in every real sense the national governments themselves. Thus, the basic motivations underlying the game are the various national interests as seen by the respective governments.

This is not to deny that appeals to the wider 'European View' are common in the rhetoric of EEC debates, but simply to point out that this rhetoric is not matched by the actual practice of bargaining between member states in the Council of Ministers and elsewhere.

### A compendium of games

Once we are clear as to the identity of the players and their motivation we may note that the policy areas defined as being within the current constitutional framework include both competitive and co-operative issues. For example, we might expect the pursuit of free trade to be in the common interest of all member states whilst the redistribution of resources brought about by the CAP carries the clear hallmark of a competitive game.

In this way we see that the EEC is not a single game but is rather a compendium of games, some competitive and some co-operative, linked together by the same group of players. Like a compendium of games, the EEC comes as a boxed set or package deal – if you play in one game you must, under the current constitution, play in them all.

## The strategy of withdrawal

Armed with this view of the current EEC constitution we may now review our earlier analysis of the strategy of withdrawal. Seen from the perspective of the nation considering withdrawal, this strategy is only a credible, practical policy if the 'losses' in the competitive games within the compendium outweigh the 'gains' made in the co-operative games – this is simply to restate our view that *all* costs and benefits of EEC membership must be taken into account.

However, a credible *threat* of withdrawal is also a strategy which may be expected to influence the other players. In respect of the *competitive* games the potential withdrawal of a losing player will obviously reduce the gains which the other players can expect to make in the future in exactly the same way that the withdrawal of a consistent loser from a poker game will reduce the expected winnings (or increase the expected losses) of the remaining players.

Additionally by withdrawing from the *co-operative* games further costs would be imposed on the remaining players, for example by restricting the area over which free trade is possible.

In this way one would expect the remaining players to react to a credible threat of withdrawal by attempting to reduce the losses of the threatening player in the competitive games to the point where they were fully compensated for by the gains from the co-operative games. By this means the threat of withdrawal would become incredible since it would no longer be in the nation's own self-interest and so the remaining players avoid the various losses which would be imposed on them by an actual withdrawal.

This view of the explicit or implicit use of a threat to withdraw as a bargaining counter in the attempt to reduce competitive losses to an 'acceptable' scale seems to accord well with the observed behaviour of the EEC in the context of the recent repayments made to Britain

### Constitutional reform

It is tempting to think of the threat of withdrawal in terms of the more familiar bargaining situation of wage negotiations, where the parallel threat is a threat to strike. However, there is an important difference between the two threats. A strike, if it actually occurs, is normally a temporary phenomenon leading ultimately to the resumption of work under the newly agreed conditions whereas withdrawal from the EEC, if actually carried out, is an act which we might reasonably expect to be irreversible. Thus withdrawal not only implies withdrawal from the current compendium of games – with the associated costs and benefits discussed above – but also the withdrawal from all future compendia which might be brought about by a process of constitutional reform; and indeed withdrawal from the ability to take part in the process which generates such constitutional reform.

The final part of our framework then requires some discussion of alternative constitutions and the processes which might bring them into existence.

Clearly there are very many possible alternative constitutions and it would be a hopeless task to attempt to describe or analyse them all; instead I shall simply discuss two possibilities from the available range so as to illustrate the appropriate mode of thought. The first alternative implies an EEC rather reduced in importance from its present position, whilst the second implies greater scope for EEC activities.

### A European co-operative alliance

Under this alternative we start from the presumption that it is the individually identified national interests that are to be the basic motivating forces in our reformed game, but we depart from the status quo by breaking the links which tie the various games in our compendium together. Thus each nation now has the authority to opt out of any particular game – we might term it 'the power of partial withdrawal'. Under this rubric, concentration upon the co-operative games might be expected to follow since any attempt to play a competitive game will simply result in the losers (or those who expect to lose) refusing to play.

Because of the shift in emphasis from competitive to co-operative games, produced by this reform of the rules, we would expect much less redistribution of resources between countries and a more urgent search for genuine opportunities for European co-operation. Threats of total withdrawal would no longer be credible strategies and the 'political' benefits claimed of the present EEC – the claim concerning its role in maintaining peace in Europe, for example – would seem to be preserved intact.

## A European federation

The second alternative also revolves around the possibility of shifting emphasis from competitive to co-operative games, but by a very different process of reform.

The basic change here concerns the players and their motivation, and takes the rhetoric regarding the importance of taking a broad European view at face value, so that the present nationalist players would be replaced by players whose prime motivation was some conception of the general European interest.

This fundamental reform of the rules of the game would have the effect of transforming some policy areas which are currently competitive into co-operative games by a process identical to that discussed in the case of the North/South example earlier. Of course there would still be competitive games, but they would no longer be competitive between nations since, by assumption, national interests are no longer an appropriate measuring-rod. Such competitive games as remain would therefore be seen to be based on alternative beliefs about the true nature of the European interest.

It is clear that a European federation of this type would differ sharply in terms of policy outcomes from both the present EEC and the European co-operative alliance outlined earlier; however noting that they differ is not the same as being able to decide which is to be preferred. The crucial problem is therefore to establish a means of comparison or choice between alternative specifications of possible European constitutions.

Since the constitutions differ from each other largely in terms of the underlying objectives which motivate them, it is clearly inappropriate to attempt to evaluate them by a process of direct comparison – which objective would you use as the measuring-rod for such comparison? It is rather as though you are asked whether a particular set of playing-cards is a 'good' hand or not without being told which game is to be played.

### Choice of constitution

Given this difficulty in attempting to directly compare various constitutions or games, the alternative is simply to ask people to choose between the options and thereby reveal their preference. The problem here is which people to ask and how to interpret their replies.

At one extreme we could simply entrust matters of constitutional reform to the presently constituted Council of Ministers, but this would clearly amount to prejudging the issue since the constitutional decision would be made by exactly the process of bargaining between entrenched nationalistic positions that produces the present policy outcomes, which in turn motivate the search for more appropriate constitutions – this would be rather akin to asking the defendant in a court case to act also as judge.

Alternatively we could resort to a general referendum as being an essentially democratic means of deciding on the appropriate constitutional reform, but this also raises problems. Let us imagine that, say, 60 per cent of all Europeans voted in favour of a fully federal constitution – is this to be taken as a sufficient reason for adopting such a constitution? Would your answer to this question change if you were given the additional information that all these 60 per cent were in fact German, French and Italian, and that all other Europeans were opposed to federalism?

These points focus attention on an aspect of the EEC problem which receives little public attention; namely, by what process should we identify the constitution which is desired and which should therefore form the long-run target for European reform. This problem – which amounts to asking how we should decide which game to play – is clearly a complex one and I make no apology for the fact that I have not, in this chapter, provided an answer. The purpose here has been the more limited one of detailing the sorts of consideration that should underlie any answer to this and other related questions so as to stimulate a re-examination of the various proposals put forward by British and other European politicians from a new and possibly more critical standpoint. In short, while we recognise that answering the questions thrown up by this discussion is by no means easy, recognising that they are relevant questions to ask is an important first step.

## The British debate revisited

How then do the positions taken up by the major British political groupings relate to our discussion of the potential costs and benefits of the EEC seen either as the policies resulting from the present compendium of games or as the opportunity for constitutional reform of these games? I shall examine, briefly, the two major policy positions before attempting an evaluation of the debate.

### The Labour party anti-marketeer's view

Under this view, withdrawal from the EEC is seen as one essential element in a broader 'alternative strategy' for the British economy. Taken by itself, withdrawal is argued to have three major effects: first, the direct effect of a gain to Britain of the net budgetary payments currently made; the second gain to Britain results from reducing food prices artificially supported by the CAP. In our terms these two gains are brought about by the withdrawal from competitive games that we are currently losing. The third effect is a loss to Britain caused by the withdrawal of free access to European markets for our exporters. This, then, is the cost of withdrawal from the co-operative game.

It is then argued that this third effect can be overcome and indeed transformed into a benefit by appropriate use of other policies that are only available to Britain if we leave the EEC.

In outline this argument is that by simultaneously devaluing the pound and imposing selective tariffs on manufactured imports we can achieve a 'one-sided devaluation' that both makes our exports more competitive overseas (thereby overcoming the newly imposed EEC tariffs) and reduces imports of manufactured goods. This, it is argued, would lead to increased domestic demand for British-produced manufactured goods, which would in turn imply increases in output and employment. The extra output could be produced at falling average costs as existing excess capacity could be utilised and this would improve still further the competitiveness of British manufacturers in export markets.

Thus withdrawal is seen both as a benefit in its own right and – more importantly – a necessary prerequisite for the adoption of a policy of domestic demand management via active use of exchange rate and tariff policies.

## The Conservative party pro-marketeer's view

Under this view it is claimed, largely by assertion rather than argument, that the *indirect* (i.e. non-budgetary) impacts of the EEC are of benefit to Britain; particularly important here seem to be the direct foreign investment argument and the tariff-free export argument. On the other hand, it is recognised that the direct, budgetary impact of the EEC imposes a cost on Britain and that this cost is in some sense 'unfair'. Thus it is argued that while the EEC represents a net benefit the position could be further improved by detailed reform of the budgetary process and the CAP: such reform is claimed to be attainable within the present constitution.

The Conservative pro-marketeer would refute the analysis of the Labour anti-marketeer in two distinct ways; first, by arguing that the present costs and benefits of membership have been wrongly evaluated, and, second, by arguing that the form of demand-management policy which lies at the heart of the 'alternative strategy' would lead not to increased output, employment and competitiveness, but rather to further inflation with consequent loss of competitiveness, output and employment.

## An evaluation of the debate

This brief and necessarily sketchy description of the major debating positions identifies the nature of the debate as consisting of two principal elements. First, the evaluation of current costs and benefits of membership. We have already said that pro- and anti-marketeers alike tend to present incomplete pictures of the present position and it is to be hoped that the discussion of the direct and indirect effects of membership above will provide a framework within which the rival claims can be evaluated.

The second aspect of the present debate is simply the controversy between the 'Keynesian' or demand-management school of thought and the 'monetarist' or supply-side school being played out under the guise of an EEC debate. While the two debates are interconnected – since all economic policy issues are interconnected – they are by no means identical. It would be possible to invoke demand-management policies in a Britain within the EEC just as it would be possible to invoke monetarist policies in a post-EEC Britain. If sensible decisions are to be made it is necessary to clearly distinguish between alternatives rather than to blur important issues together.

In two respects, however, the two views of the EEC problem are similar. Both sides of the debate are clearly presenting their cases in terms of purely *national* interests, and both sides seem to view the present EEC constitution as a fixture and therefore ignore the possibility of long-term constitutional reform.

Thus the present policy debate is an essentially short-term analysis of what is an essentially long-term problem. The same point could be made, with the advantage of hindsight, of the original debate in respect of entry into the EEC; no one would now claim that this entry has been an unqualified success and yet fundamentally similar arguments are now being used to justify the choice of current EEC policy that may (in the case of withdrawal) prove irreversible.

It would seem from our earlier discussion that both Labour anti-marketeers and Conservative pro-marketeers could best meet their long-term objectives by some appropriate constitutional reform of the EEC rather than by simply withdrawing or attempting to fine-tune present budgetary arrangements. Despite this, there seems to be little public or political debate aimed at identifying the desired constitution or at assessing the possibilities of achieving major constitutional reform. We are, perhaps, so involved in playing the game that we find it difficult to stand back and ask if we are playing the right game.

# Index